The Corning Museum of Glass
Catalog Series

AMERICAN AND EUROPEAN PRESSED GLASS

in The Corning Museum of Glass

JANE SHADEL SPILLMAN

The Corning Museum of Glass
Corning, New York
1981

Cover: Desk set in three pieces;
probably Boston & Sandwich Glass
Company, Sandwich, Massachusetts,
ca. 1825-1830. *Catalog no. 54.*

Printed in U.S.A.
Standard Book Number 0-87290-103-3
Library of Congress Catalog Card Number 81-69639

Photography: Nicholas L. Williams and Raymond F. Errett
Art Direction: Anthony Russell, Inc.
Design: Peg Patterson
Typography: Lettra Graphics, Inc.
Printing: Murray Printing, Inc.

For Lowell Innes and Don Spillman
who have constantly encouraged me.

Table of Contents

Foreword

In May of 1976, the twenty-fifth anniversary of the opening of The Corning Museum of Glass, the Board of Trustees approved the recommendation that a series of illustrated catalogs of everything in the collections be published. As these have grown, so have the Museum's scholarly contributions toward understanding the art, history, and technology of glass. The first volume in the series was *Pre-Roman and Early Roman Glass in The Corning Museum of Glass*; this volume, the second in the series, covers all of the pressed glass in the Museum's collection, both American and non-American.

In terms of the American contribution to the history of glass, there is no achievement more important than the development of the mechanical press. Usually viewed as an industrial phenomenon, the press has also had a profound aesthetic impact. Although it greatly speeded up the manufacturing process—eventually making glass so cheap that large sets could be built by regular attendance at the movies, where it was given away free—it also provided a new way to form glass. Previously, blowing and cutting were responsible for shape as well as decoration. Pieces blown in a mold were relatively "soft" and thin walled. With the press, hot glass could be jammed into a mold forcing it to take both a *precise* shape and the *sharp* imprint of whatever decoration was incised in the mold. This catalog contains one of the great bodies of evidence on the evolution of this new technology—this new decorative medium.

Written by Jane Shadel Spillman in whose care the collection has flourished over the past fifteen years, this book records 1,536 pieces pressed between 1825 and 1940. Her predecessors-in-responsibility were the directors, particularly Paul N. Perrot (assistant director 1955 to 1961, director 1961-1972). But of the greatest help was the scholar-dealer

James Rose (1899-1975) and his friend and client, the collector Louise Esterly. During the early 1950's they patiently educated us in the complexities of the highly specialized world of lacy pressed glass; the result was a major exhibition and catalog in 1954.

The collection's first American pressed glass objects were acquired in 1950 from George S. McKearin and cataloged by his daughter Helen. From 1958 through 1963, Mrs. Esterly gave much of her lacy glass to the Museum, and in 1968 the remainder of her outstanding collection, much of it colored, was acquired by purchase. Mr. and Mrs. Harry A. Snyder of Canandaigua, New York, added many pieces of lacy glass, especially miniatures, from 1967 to 1972; Mrs. Leon Bard bequeathed her collection of cup plates to the Museum in 1965; Preston R. Bassett gave a collection of lamps in 1972; Mrs. Ruth I. Roth presented a collection of late nineteenth-century butter dishes in 1974. Other generous donors are noted in the individual catalog entries.

There is no intent here to provide the definitive history of pressing—that has been written before, most notably by Helen McKearin and James Rose. Rather, it is our hope that both scholars and collectors will find this catalog of interest in identifying pressed glass patterns and manufacturers from the invention of mechanical pressing to the development of modern machine production, prelude to the technical and aesthetic evolution now underway of this relatively new medium.

Thomas S. Buechner, President
The Corning Museum of Glass

Acknowledgments

This catalog would not have been possible without the help of many people on the Museum staff. I especially want to thank Jane Lanahan, who typed and retyped the manuscript; Priscilla Price, Registrar, whose careful records document the collection; her assistant, J. C. Lapp; Nick Williams and Raymond Errett, Museum photographers, and Charleen Edwards, who edited the manuscript.

Lowell Innes, Helen McKearin, William Elsholz, Miriam Mucha, Kenneth Wilson, and the late James Rose and Caleb Ewing all shared their knowledge of pressed glass and their collections with me. Hugh Wakefield and Barbara Morris have been helpful in identifying some of the objects in the English section. I am most grateful to all of them.

Finally, I would like to thank Louis C. Jones and Frank Spinney who set my feet on this path sixteen years ago in Cooperstown and my family — for their patience.

List of References Cited

All of the works below are cited frequently in the text by the abbreviations listed here. Full references are given for periodical articles cited.

Belknap
Belknap, E.M. *Milk Glass*. New York: Crown Publishers, Inc. 1949.

Innes, Early Glass
Innes, Lowell. *Early Glass of the Pittsburgh District, 1797-1900*. Pittsburgh; Carnegie Institute Museum of Art, 1949.

Innes, Pittsburgh Glass
Innes, Lowell. *Pittsburgh Glass, 1797-1891: A History and Guide for Collectors*. Boston: Houghton Mifflin Co., 1976.

Kamm, Books I-VIII
Kamm, Minnie Watson. *Pattern Glass, Pitchers, Books I-VIII*. Grosse Pointe, Michigan: author, 1940-1954.

Klamkin
Klamkin, Marian. *The Collectors Guide to Depression Glass*, New York, Hawthorn Books, 1973.

Launay, Hautin 1840
Launay, Hautin 1842
Collection des Dessins Représentant Exactement les Cristaux, compris dans le tarif général de Launay, Hautin & Cie. seul dépôt des manufactures de Baccarat, St. Louis, Choisy et Bercy, Paris, 1840; *Usages principaux pour services de table des divers numéros de carafes goblets et verres*. Paris, probably 1842.

Lattimore
Lattimore, Colin R. *English 19th-Century Press-Moulded Glass*, London, Barrie & Jenkins, 1979.

Lee, E.A.P.G.
Lee, Ruth Webb. *Early American Pressed Glass*. Northboro, Massachusetts: author, 1960.

Lee, Sandwich Glass
Lee, Ruth Webb. *Sandwich Glass* (rev. ed.). Northboro, Massachusetts: author, 1966.

Lee, Victorian Glass
Lee, Ruth Webb. *Victorian Glass Specialties of the Nineteenth Century.* 4th ed. Northboro, Massachusetts: author, 1944.

Lee and Rose
Lee, Ruth Webb, and Rose, James H. *American Glass Cup Plates*. Northboro, Massachusetts: R. W. Lee, 1948.

Lindsey, Books I, II
Lindsey, Bessie M. *Lore of Our Land Pictured in Glass, Books I, II*. Forsyth, Illinois: author, 1948, 1950.

McKearin, American Glass
McKearin, George S. and Helen. *American Glass*. New York: Crown Publishers, Inc., 1948.

Metz, Books I, II
Metz, Alice Hulett. *Early American Pattern Glass, Book 1*; *Much More Early American Pattern Glass, Book 2*. Chicago: author, 1958, 1965.

Morris
Morris, Barbara. *Victorian Table Glass and Ornaments*. London: Barrie & Jenkins, 1978.

Neal
Neal, Logan W. and Dorothy B. *Pressed Glass Salt Dishes of the* Lacy Period 1825-1850. Philadelphia: authors, 1962.

Revi
Revi, Albert C. *American Pressed Glass and Figure Bottles*. New York: Thomas Nelson & Sons, 1964.

Rose
Rose, James H. *The Story of American Pressed Glass of the Lacy Period, 1825-1850*. Corning, New York: The Corning Museum of Glass, 1954.

Russell
Russell, Loris. *A Heritage of Light*. Toronto: University of Toronto Press, 1968.

S.H.S.
Sandwich Historical Society. *Glass Exhibited in the Sandwich Glass Museum*, 1969.

Val St. Lambert 1832
Collection des Dessins Représentant Exactement les Cristaux de la Manufacture du Val St. Lambert. Liège, 1832.

Wakefield
Wakefield, Hugh. *Nineteenth Century British Glass*. London: Faber and Faber, Ltd., 1961.

Warren
Warren, Phelps. *Irish Glass*. London: Faber and Faber, Ltd., 1971.

Watkins, Cambridge Glass
Watkins, Lura W. *Cambridge Glass 1818 to 1888: The Story of the New England Glass Company*. Boston: Marshall Jones Company, 1930.

Watkins, Pressed Glass
Watkins, Lura W. "Pressed Glass of the New England Glass Company—An Early Catalogue at The Corning Museum." *Journal of Glass Studies*, 12, 1970.

Wilson
Wilson, Kenneth M. *New England Glass and Glassmaking*. New York: Thomas Y. Crowell Company, 1972.

Introduction

Pressing Technology

Fig. 1   Astarte figure, mold-pressed.
Near East, late 16th to mid 13th
century B.C. L.8.2 cm. (55.1.64).

The revolution in industrial methods brought about in the United States in glassmaking in the early 19th century was as innovative and drastic in its results as was the invention of the blowpipe in Roman days. The development in America of the pressing of glass by the use of machines was to bring the industrial revolution to a traditional hand craft and to affect cultural tastes both in America and overseas from that time forth in this area of the decorative arts.

The pressing of glass into molds was not in itself a new technique for its ancestry can be traced back to the earliest of times. One of the first known examples, dating from between the 16th to mid-13th century B.C., is the one piece mold-pressed figure of the Near Eastern goddess Astarte (Fig. 1).

Thousands of years later than the Astarte pendant, glass pressing became a common practice in Europe. Around 1780 small hand presses, probably in the form of large pliers with a design cut in the faces of the jaws, were used to make decanter stoppers and bases for lamps, goblets, compotes, salts, and other small articles. These bases usually were very simple, often square, perhaps with a concave rosette or fluted design on the bottom and, like the Astarte pendant, they were finished by cutting. As early as 1740 chandelier pendants were being pressed by a similar tool in Bohemia. Deming Jarves, whose *Reminiscences of Glass Making* was published in 1865, commented that "Fifty years back [1815] the writer imported from Holland salts made by being pressed in metallic molds, and from England glass candlesticks, table centre-bowls, plain, with pressed square feet, and rudely made, somewhat after the present mode of moulding glass."[1] Both pressed stoppers and bases for blown objects were being made in America early in the 19th century, probably by Thomas Cains in South Boston and by the New England Glass Company in Cambridge.[2]

There seems to be no question that the process of pressing molten glass into metal molds by machine instead of by hand was perfected in the United States between 1820 and 1825, but the identity of the person or company remains an intriguing puzzle. All early patents were destroyed in the Patent Office fire of 1836, and the information recorded thereafter is little more than a list of dates, titles, and occasional descriptive material. The first patent which *may* be related to pressing was granted to John P.

Bakewell[3] of Pittsburgh Flint Glass Manufactory on September 9, 1825, for an "improvement in making furniture knob" (see nos. 35,36 in this catalog). The fact that the patent was issued for an "improvement" may indicate that it was not the first such patent recorded. A year later, on November 4, 1826, Enoch Robinson, a Boston mechanic, and Henry Whitney of The New England Glass Company received a patent for glass knobs for doors.[4] John Robinson of Pittsburgh was given a patent on October 6, 1827, for "Pressed Glass Door Knobs,"[5] and Phineas C. Dummer and his associates of Jersey City, New Jersey, were granted two patents in 1827 for improvements in the molds for glass pressing.[6] One of these was for a "cover-plate," which may be the all-important "cap ring." The problem of overfilled and underfilled molds was partly overcome by the cap ring, a separate part of the mold which controlled the flow of glass to the rim and insured a uniform thickness at the edge of plates and other flat pieces. Mechanical pressing was becoming an important part of the glass manufacturing process.

The innovations continued to be recorded by the Patent Office as Deming Jarves of the Boston & Sandwich Company obtained patents in 1828, 1829, and 1830 for improvements in the pressing process and for knobs with a glass screw shank; his 1830 patent covered the pressing of a handled piece in one operation.[7] That and John M'Gann's patent of 1830 for "Pressed Hollow Glassware" are the first indication that shapes other than flat plates and bowls or solid knobs were being made by mechanical pressing.[8]

If advertising is regarded as an accurate mirror of the times, the word *prest* first appeared in advertisements dating from 1819,[9] but probably mold-blown rather than machine-pressed glass was being described. The earliest use of the phrase *pressed glass* in an advertisement dates from September 19, 1822, and occurs in the *Boston Commercial Gazette*: "On hand, a good assortment of cut, flint, pressed and plain Glass Ware."[10] This description also may refer to mold-blown glass or perhaps to objects with hand-pressed parts mentioned above. Whether the pressing of complete objects began in 1822 or 1825, the process spread rapidly.

James Boardman, an English traveler to the United States, obviously realized the importance of pressed glass exhibited at the Fair of the American Institute of the City of

New York in 1829. "The most novel article was the pressed glass which was far superior, both in design and execution, to anything of the kind I have ever seen either in London or elsewhere. The merit of its invention is due to the Americans and it is likely to prove one of great national importance."[11] His enthusiasm, notable from one not influenced by nationalistic and patriotic impulses, was evidence of the adoption and improvement of the process. By the 1830's, factories in Pittsburgh, New England, and probably Philadelphia must have been producing machine-pressed glass.

What exactly was this invention credited to Americans and of such national importance? How did the press work? Mold pressing in its simplest form involved two men at a machine. One cut a measured hot gather of glass from the punty rod and dropped it into a metal mold heated to an exact temperature. The other immediately depressed a lever to lower a metal plunger and force the glass into the pattern of the mold. Apsley Pellatt, who included a detailed illustration (Fig. 2) in his 1849 *Curiosities of Glass-Making*, has described the process and its attendant problems:

Pressing is a mechanical operation. . . . It may be thus described: a die being prepared, secured by the ring and handle, A, metal is gathered and dropped into, B, and the matrix, or plunger, C, operated upon by the lever, &c. D, pressed the metal into the required form of the article. If an overplus of metal be gathered, it thickens the article throughout; but if too little, it fails to fill up the mould, and is spoiled. This is a rapid mode of reproduction, but great practice is required to gather the exact quantity of metal. The chief condition of success, in getting a polished surface on pressed Glass, depends upon the moulds being kept at a regular temperature, a little short of red heat. The effect is not so good as pillar-moulding, nor does it anneal so well; but it is much less expensive. The interior plungers and the outer die will adhere to the Glass if too hot; and if not at proper temperature, will fail in producing a clear transparent surface.

If the finished glass object was to be uniform in thickness, the plunger had to be lowered precisely into the middle of the mold. When the mass had solidified, the mold was opened, and the object was removed. If the glass had chilled too quickly, wrinkles appeared on the surface. To conceal such blemishes, the moldmaker, who became more important than the blower between 1825 and 1830, designed ornate styles, sometimes imitating expensive cut glass patterns (see nos. 59,65,69).

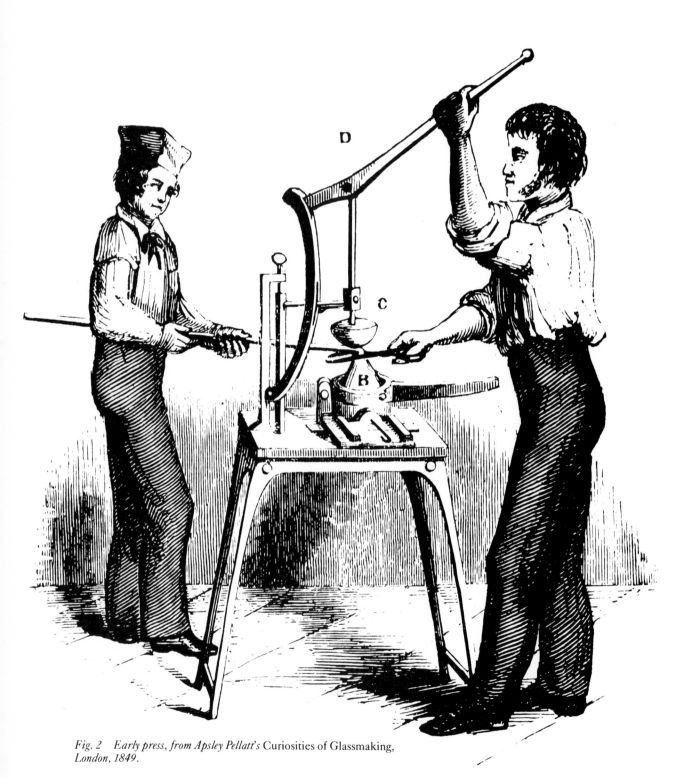

Fig. 2   Early press, from Apsley Pellatt's Curiosities of Glassmaking,
London, 1849.

By 1830, geometric patterns were succeeded by lacy designs completely covered by tiny background dots or stipples to reflect light and camouflage surface defects. Just as the blowpipe had revolutionized glassmaking in the Roman Empire, so did mechanical pressing stimulate glass manufacturers of the 1800's. The advantages were obvious. Costs were lowered because brass or iron molds could be used again and again, and little or no hand finishing was necessary; the men operating the presses could be hired for less money than those who blew glass. Production accelerated, design and quality were standardized, and glassware could be sold more cheaply in an expanding market. The following description of tumbler manufacture comes from Hunt's *Merchant's Magazine and Commercial Review* [XV (October, 1846), 418] and emphasizes the advantages of this process.

"In the first place, the workmen have a brass mould, consisting of a solid mass, about as large over as a half-peck measure, containing a hollow in it exactly of the form of the tumbler to be made, with a follower of brass of the same form, but so much smaller as to fit the inside of the tumbler. When the two parts of the mould are put together, the space between them is the exact thickness of the vessel required. In the process of manufacturing, three men and two boys are required. . . . [When the tumbler is done] He then turns his mould bottom up, with a little blow, and the tumbler drops red hot upon the stone table. One of the boys, with an iron rod having a little melted glass on its end, presses it on the bottom of the tumbler and it slightly adheres. He then holds it in the mouth of a glowing furnace, turning it rapidly, till it is almost in a melted state, when the third man takes it, and whirling the rod and tumbler on a sort of arm of a chair, he holds a smooth iron tool against the edge of the tumbler, till all the roughness is removed from its edges, when a boy takes the rod from him, and, by a slight stroke on the end of it, drops the tumbler, and places it in a hot oven to cool gradually. These five hands will make a beautiful tumbler in about forty seconds, or about one hundred in an hour."

The refinement of the mold was a most important contribution of the American glass industry. Even outdated molds were sold or traded to other companies, an indication of their cost and continuing value.[12] Large factories had their own mold shops, and the head of the shop may have designed some of the pieces. Hiram Dillaway, head moldmaker at the Boston & Sandwich Glass Company, is supposed to have designed many patterns.[13]

The new ornate style of glassware was extremely popular. Serving pieces of various styles were made most frequently, but cup plates and salts were among the individual items made. Surprisingly, drinking vessels scarcely occur at all in this early period, perhaps because manufacturers had difficulty controlling the thinness and smoothness of the edge of any object and rough, thick-rimmed glasses were not pleasant to drink from. Many decorative motifs were inspired by architectural elements (acanthus leaves, Gothic arches), by natural forms (shells, flowers, beehives, leaves), and frequently by historical events or personages (Henry Clay, Washington, William Henry Harrison, the Bunker Hill Monument). The design features most objects share are the general use of stippling and scalloped edges, but even those are not universal.

By the mid-1830's, manufacturers changed pressed glass production methods in other ways. The desirable surface gloss found on blown and cut glass was restored by fire-polishing, reheating glass after it came from the press in order to remove tool or mold marks. Since fire-polishing blurred the details of a lacy pattern, the expensive stippled molds were replaced by simpler designs. Making complex objects by combining parts from several simpler molds reduced the cost of the molds. By the 1850's factories produced complete place settings and services of "pattern glass," including large serving pieces of a variety of types and drinking vessels in a range of sizes.

If the glass manufacturers were appealing to a public fond of the brilliance of cut glass, much of that brilliance was due to the high lead content of the formula first developed by George Ravenscroft in England about 1674 and refined from that date until about the middle of the 18th century. Each factory had its own formula, but most of them used varying amounts of lead, and the glass was usually advertised as "flint" to indicate that it had some lead content. The lead content, however, was not the same as that of cut glass in the period, and pieces pressed of what appears to be bottle glass occasionally appear. Such glasses may have been trial runs by a factory experimenting with pressing methods. Nevertheless, most pressed glass of the 1825-1864 period has at least some lead content. In 1864, William Leighton of Hobbs, Brockunier and Company in Wheeling, perfected a formula for a clear soda-lime glass which could be pressed. Lime glass was much less expensive than lead glass and almost as brilliant; due to its different viscosity, thinner glasses could be made and therefore pattern glass of the 1870's became more intricate. Most of the Midwestern factories switched to the cheaper formula and some in the East must have done so as well. During the same period, the patenting of pressed glass designs became traditional.

Most Eastern factories used wood until mid-century when the discovery of natural gas in western Pennsylvania in 1859 led to a switch from coal or wood. Perhaps because of these two technical developments, the center of the table glass industry shifted westward as new factories were built near the gas fields. The use of steam to power the presses was also introduced in 1864[14] although it did not become common until the 1870's.

In an attempt to develop an ever-larger market, manufacturers made greater use of color in table settings in the latter part of the 19th century and again introduced pressed imitations of the more expensive cut glass patterns and art glass. Some of these styles, such as the Opalescent Hobnail or Dewdrop produced at Hobbs, Brockunier in Wheeling, West Virginia, and the golden agate glass now called "Holly Amber" produced by the Indiana Tumbler and Goblet Company in Greentown, Indiana, are considered art glasses in their own right.

Around the turn of the century, "Carnival" glass, a pressed iridescent glass in imitation of the Art Nouveau wares made by Louis Comfort Tiffany and his competitors, was also quite popular. The iridescence was the result of a spray applied while the piece was hot. Such ware was marketed as "iridescent glass" from about 1905 until 1930 in elaborate patterns and a wide range of base colors and iridescent surfaces. Most Carnival glass was made by four companies in the Ohio River basin—the Harry Northwood Glass Company of Wheeling, West Virginia; the Fenton Art Glass Company of Williamstown, West Virginia; the Imperial Glass Company of Bellaire, Ohio; and the Millersburg Glass Company of Millersburg, Ohio. Its greatest popularity was from 1905 to 1920, but it was still offered in Sears, Roebuck and Company catalogs as late as 1927.

Another development to be considered in the pressing of glass was also an American innovation: glass melted in tanks and fed directly to the pressing machine to emerge as fully-formed tableware. This automatic process was first developed to speed the production of containers. Semi-automatic blowing machinery was in use in the 1890's, and by 1903 Michael Owens of Toledo had invented the first fully automatic blowing machine; glass went from tank to forming to annealing without being shaped by human hands. The process soon was adapted to pressing and in 1916 Corning Glass Works used this type of machinery to make its Pyrex® line of baking ware. Other companies soon followed, and colored glass tableware was made nearly as cheaply as bottles and preserving jars. By 1929, a columnist in *Better Homes and Gardens* suggested that "Whatever it is, serve it in glass,"[15] and the popular colored glasswares could be had in such pieces as dinner plates and soup bowls as well as the more traditional serving pieces and drinking vessels. From the first patent for machine pressing in 1825 to the use of fully automatic machinery in 1915 was only ninety years, but the social implications were enormous. Just as the blowpipe had made glassware a non-luxury item in the Roman Empire, so the invention of mechanical pressing provided glassware for everyone, regardless of income or social status. It was America's major contribution to the history of glassmaking.

Footnotes

1 Jarves, Deming, *Reminiscences of Glass Manufacture*, 1865, p. 93.
2 *Wilson*, p. 226.
3 *American Glass*, p. 334.
4 *Cambridge Glass*, pp. 85, 86.
5 *American Glass*, p. 334.
6, 7, 8 *Ibid.*
9 *Cambridge Glass*, p. 87.
10 *Ibid.*, p. 88.
11 Boardman, James. *America and the Americans*, London, 1830.
12 Sheeler, John. "Factors Affecting Attributions: The Burlington Glass Company," *Material History Bulletin 6*, (National Museum of Man), 1978, p. 31.
13 Crane, Priscilla C. "The Boston & Sandwich Glass Company," *Antiques*, April 1925, p. 187.
14 *Revi*, p. 4.
15 *Klamkin*, p. 41.

The objects in this volume have been grouped by type, date, and decoration; related objects will be found together. The asterisked objects are *not illustrated* in black and white as in most cases they are identical to objects pictured. The dagger (†) identifies objects illustrated in color. The catalog includes all pressed glass acquired by The Corning Museum of Glass before January 1981, except for that in the collection of 2,400 drinking glasses bequeathed to the Museum by Jerome Strauss in 1979.

Assessing the relative rarity of specific pieces is difficult; many private collectors are unknown to me, and it is impossible to be certain whether the same or different objects have been published in the past. Where data has been gathered by authorities such as James Rose and the Neals, I have included their determination without comment. In descending order, the scale is *unique* (one known), *extremely rare* (two to ten known), *very rare*, (ten to thirty known). — JSS

1 Salt
England
ca. 1720
H. 3.3 cm; L. 6.8 cm; W. 5.4

80.2.26

Colorless lead glass. Rectangular
shape with cut corners.
Comments: This is the earliest
hand-pressed piece in the Corning collection.

2 Goblet
England or Ireland
ca. 1790-1810
H. 12.3 cm; D.(rim) 8.8 cm

50.2.77

Colorless lead glass; pressed and
blown; cup-shaped bowl with
engraved festoons and tassels;
attached by a wafer to a pressed
"lemon-squeezer" base, square,
fluted underneath.

3 Pair of goblets
England
ca. 1790-1810
H. 13.8 cm; D.(rim) 9 cm

51.2.203A,B

Colorless lead glass; pressed and
blown; ovoid bowl engraved
with a coat of arms and motto
"GOD IS OUR FRIEND"; with
English rose and Scotch thistle
and monogram "REP" on
reverse; attached by a wafer to a
pressed "lemon-squeezer" base,
square, fluted underneath.

4 Goblet
England or Ireland
ca. 1790-1810
H. 13.3 cm; D.(rim) 8 cm

51.2.227

Colorless lead glass; pressed and blown; conical bowl engraved with festoons, swags, and cut flutes; attached by a wafer to a pressed "lemon-squeezer" base, square, fluted underneath.

5 Goblet
England or Ireland
ca. 1790-1810
H. 13.3 cm; D.(rim) 8 cm

50.2.78

Colorless lead glass; pressed and blown; ovoid bowl with band of cut ovals around top; cut flutes at base; attached by a wafer to a pressed, square "lemon-squeezer" base; polished on bottom.
Parallels: Warren, pl. 70C.

6 Goblet
England or Ireland
ca. 1790-1810
H. 13.5 cm; D.(rim) 8.8 cm

66.2.1

Colorless lead glass; pressed and blown; conical bowl with pattern-molded vertical flutes around lower half; attached by a wafer to a pressed, square "lemon-squeezer" base.
Gift of Mrs. Jason Westerfield

7 Salt
Ireland
ca. 1790-1810
H. 8.1 cm; L. 8.5 cm

64.2.16

Colorless lead glass; pressed and blown; oval bowl cut with fan design on ends and diamonds and swags around sides; attached by a wafer to a short stem and pressed diamond-shaped base fluted underneath.
Gift of Mrs. Jason Westerfield

8 Pair of salts
Ireland
ca. 1790-1810
H. 7 cm; L.(rim) 8.8 cm

50.2.51 A,B

Colorless lead glass; pressed and blown; oval bowl; cut in blazes and swags; attached by a wafer to a short stem; oval base fluted underneath.
Published: Warren, pl. 78C.

9 Salt
Ireland
ca. 1790-1810
H. 8.5 cm; L.(rim) 8.3 cm

50.2.122

Colorless lead glass; pressed and blown; oval bowl; cut in blazes and swags; attached by a wafer to a short stem; diamond-shaped base fluted underneath.

10 Salt
England or Ireland
ca. 1820-1840
H. 7.3 cm; L. 7.6 cm;
W. 4.9 cm

78.2.11

Colorless lead glass; blown, cut and pressed; rectangular bowl with diamond pattern cut on sides; diamond-shaped hand-pressed base with rosette underneath.
Ex coll: Mr. and Mrs. George Lookup

11   Pair of candlesticks
England or Ireland
ca. 1800-1810
H. 21.3 cm

50.2.85 A,B

Colorless lead glass; pressed and blown; cylindrical blown socket with cut rim; attached by a wafer to an urn-shaped shaft with diamond-cut decoration; attached by another merese to a pressed "lemon-squeezer" base, square and fluted underneath. *Published:* (B) Fitzpatrick, Paul J. "Waterford Glass Houses," *Antiques Journal*, June, 1977, p. 32; *Warren*, pl. 35A.

12   Pair of candlesticks
England or Ireland
ca. 1790-1810
H. 26.3 cm;
D.(foot) 9 cm square

51.2.221 A,B

Grayish lead glass; pressed and blown; cylindrical sockets with cut vertical panels; attached by a wafer to urn-shaped standards also with cut vertical panels; attached by a wafer to a pressed "lemon-squeezer" base, square and fluted underneath. *Parallels: Warren*, pl. 35A.

13   Candelabrum
England, possibly Falcon Glass Works, London
ca. 1796-1810
H. 61.9 cm

51.2.226

Colorless lead glass, metal mounts; blown, pattern-molded and pressed; vertical central shaft attached by a wafer to a blown urn-shaped section with diamond cutting; attached by a wafer to a pressed "lemon-squeezer" base, square and fluted underneath; attached with metal color are two C-scroll arms, each holding one cut candle socket with dependent prisms; "LAFOUNT PATENT" is stamped on central metal mounting.

14 Footed bowl
Ireland
ca. 1790-1810
H.(ends) 21.3 cm;
L.(bowl) 38.5 cm

50.2.41

Colorless lead glass; pressed and blown; oval bowl with flat diamond cutting and scalloped rim; attached by a wafer to a pressed fluted oval base.
Ex coll: Lord Parmoor, Freith, Buckinghamshire, England.
Published: Antiques Magazine, 57 no. 3, March, 1950, advertisement, p. 176.
Parallels: Warren, pl. 39A.

15 Footed bowl
Ireland
ca. 1790-1810
H. 11.5 cm; D.(rim) 16.8 cm

50.2.96

Colorless lead glass; pressed and blown; oval bowl with turned-over rim and flat diamond cutting; attached by a wafer to a pressed hollow oval base.
Parallels: Warren, pl. 81C.

16 Footed bowl
Ireland
ca. 1790-1810
H. 15.8 cm; D.(rim) 21.8 cm

51.2.168

Grayish lead glass; pressed and blown; hemispherical bowl cut with narrow band of ovals and sheaves around top; applied with a wafer to a pressed "lemon-squeezer" base, square, fluted underneath.

17 Footed bowl
Ireland
ca. 1790-1810
H. (ends) 14.8 cm;
L. (bowl) 21.8 cm

51.2.216

Grayish lead glass; free-blown and cut oval bowl with scalloped rim and cut decoration of blazes and deep swags; attached by a wafer to a pressed "lemon-squeezer" base, square, fluted underneath.

18   Footed bowl
England or Ireland
ca. 1790-1810
H. 21 cm; L.(bowl) 26 cm

60.2.62

Colorless lead glass; pressed, cut and blown; oval bowl with scalloped rim and flat diamond cutting; attached by a wafer to a cylindrical solid stem and a pressed square base with fluted design underneath; polished on bottom.
Gift of Mrs. William Esty
Parallels: Warren, pls. 41B, 41C.

19   Footed bowl
ca. 1800-1820
England or Ireland
H. 20.8 cm; D. 26 cm

60.2.65

Colorless lead glass; pressed, cut and blown; bowl with turned-over rim and diamond cutting; attached by a wafer to a heavy straight stem ending in a pressed square base with fluted design underneath.
Gift of Mrs. William Esty
Parallels: Warren, pls. 41B, 41C.

20   Footed bowl
England or Ireland
ca. 1790-1810
H. 20.3 cm; D. 21.5 cm

65.2.4

Colorless lead glass, pressed and mold-blown; spherical bowl with diamond pattern; attached by a wafer to an inverted baluster shape stem and a pressed square base with fluted design underneath.
Ex coll: Lura Woodside Watkins
Parallels: Warren, pl. 41D.

21   Covered bowl
England or Ireland
ca. 1790-1810
H.(with cover) 17 cm; W.(base) 6.5 cm

60.2.24a

Colorless lead glass; pressed and mold-blown; deep bowl with turned-over rim and twelve-diamond pattern; attached by a wafer to a pressed square base with fluted design underneath; matching dome lid blown in a ten-diamond mold.
Parallels: Warren, pl. 69D (a).

22 Lamp
New England, probably
Thomas Cains' South Boston or
Phoenix Glass Works
ca. 1813-1830
H. 20.5 cm; D. 7.7 cm

72.4.29

Colorless lead glass; spherical
blown font with horizontal air-
trap around sides; attached by a
wafer to hollow inverted
baluster-shape stem containing
Spanish silver coin with hole;
on one side is inscribed "DEI
GRATIA [illegible] CAROLUS
III," an illegible inscription
with the date "1782" on the
other; stem attached by wafer
to pressed square base with
fluted design underneath.
Gift of Preston R. Bassett
Comments: Coin dates from the
reign of Charles III (1759-1788).
Published: Bassett, Preston R.
"The Evolution of the American
Glass Lamp," *The Rushlight* 33,
no. 1, Feb. 1967, p. 1468, fig. 10.
Parallels: Wilson, pp. 224-226.

23 Lamp
New England; probably
Thomas Cains' South Boston or
Phoenix Glass Works
ca. 1813-1830
H. 28.3 cm; D.(base) 9.6 cm

72.4.27

Colorless lead glass; spherical
blown font with a horizontal air
trap; attached by broad circular
disk to hollow blown stem; attached by wafer to square
pressed hollow base with fluted
design underneath.
Gift of Preston R. Bassett
Published: The Toledo Museum
of Art. *New England Glass Company, 1818-1888*, 1963, no. 189,
p. 57, p. 73.
Bassett, Preston R. "The
Evolution of the American
Glass Lamp," *The Rushlight* 33,
no. 1, Feb. 1967, p. 1467, fig. 6.
Parallels: Wilson, p. 224-226.

24 Lamp
New England, probably
Thomas Cains' South Boston or
Phoenix Glass Works
ca. 1813-1830
H. 23.8 cm; D.(base) 12 cm

68.4.52

Colorless lead glass; spherical
blown font with horizontal air-
trap; attached by wafer to a
blown stem; attached to a
square pressed base with fluted
design underneath.
Published: Wilson, Fig. 182, left,
p. 225.

25 Lamp
New England, possibly Thomas
Cains' South Boston or Phoenix
Glass Works
ca. 1813-1830
H. 26.9 cm; D.(base) 8.5 cm

70.4.82

Colorless lead glass with a blown
globular font with horizontal air-
trap; attached by a wafer to a
pressed mushroom stopper
below which is a baluster-shape
hollow stem; attached by a
wafer to a square pressed base
with fluted design underneath.
Ex coll: Dr. Edward A.
Rushford
Parallels: Wilson, Fig. 184,
p. 226.

26 Lamp
New England
ca. 1813-1830
H. 25.1 cm; D. 8.4 cm

72.4.32

Slightly grayish lead glass;
spherical mold-blown font with
panels around lower half; attached to blown hollow baluster
form shaft; decorated with spiral
trail running most of length;
applied by wafer to square
pressed base with fluted design
underneath.
Gift of Preston R. Bassett
Parallels: Wilson, Figs. 185, 186.

27 Lamp
New England, probably
Thomas Cains' South Boston or
Phoenix Glass Works
ca. 1813-1830
H. 25.2 cm; D.(base) 8.5 cm

72.4.33

Colorless lead glass; spherical
blown font with horizontal air
trap; attached by a broad flat
collar to blown inverted baluster
stem with chain decoration; attached by a wafer to square
pressed base with fluted design
underneath.
Gift of Preston R. Bassett
Published: Bassett, Preston R.
"The Evolution of the American
Glass Lamp," *The Rushlight* 33,
no. 1, Feb. 1967, p. 1467, Fig. 8.
Parallels: Wilson, Figs. 183, 190.

28 Lamp
New England
ca. 1813-1830
H. 24.6 cm; D. 8.1 cm

72.4.42

Colorless lead glass and opaque white glass; blown spherical opaque white font attached by a wafer to hollow, three-knopped blown colorless stem; attached by a wafer to pressed square base with fluted design underneath.
Gift of Preston R. Bassett
Parallels: Wilson, pp. 224-226.

29 Lamp
New England
ca. 1813-1830
H. 27.8 cm; D.(base) 9.2 cm

72.4.28

Colorless lead glass; spherical blown font attached by two wafers to a blown stem; attached by two wafers to a square pressed base with fluted design underneath.
Gift of Preston R. Bassett
Published: Bassett, Preston R. "The Evolution of the American Glass Lamp," *The Rushlight* 33, no. 1, Feb. 1967, p. 1467, Fig. 7.

30 Candlestick
New England or Midwest
ca. 1813-1830
H. 21.8 cm; base, 8 cm square

50.4.240

Colorless lead glass with a free-blown socket and baluster shaft; attached to a square pressed base with fluted design underneath.
Ex coll: George S. McKearin

Early Machine Pressing

Since the earliest known pressed glass patents refer to furniture knobs, it is likely that these were produced before the manufacture of hollow vessels. In the absence of specific evidence, we can only guess which patterns were the first to appear on early pressed wares. We assume that the designs were geometric. Certainly by 1830, a full range of stippled "lacy" patterns was available, judging from the Curling creamer (no. 136), the Providence salt (no. 742), and the Ritchie pane (no. 311), all of which may be dated between 1829 and 1834.

As early as 1902, a drawing of what purported to be the first pressed glass vessel was published. The drawing was taken from Thomas Gaffield's notebook and showed a tumbler supposed to have been manufactured by Deming Jarves at Sandwich in 1827. Examples of this tumbler were known by 1954 when one was exhibited at The Corning Museum of Glass. However, the few tumblers which have appeared in this

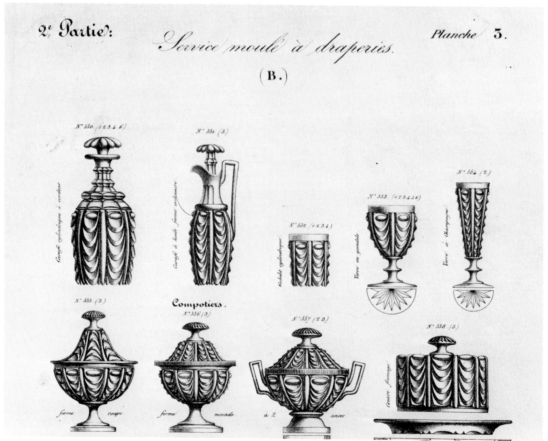

Fig. 3   Mold-blown tumbler and other wares from a catalog of Launay, Hautin et Cie, Paris, 1840.

pattern so far are mold-blown rather than pressed and the pattern itself is shown in a French glass-seller's catalog of 1840 (Fig. 3). It seems most likely, therefore, that the scale tumblers are French (Fig. 4).

We assume that lacy patterns were popular for fifteen to twenty years before changing tastes and new technology rendered them old-fashioned. Nevertheless, some stippled patterns were produced as late as the 1870's when a few still appear in the manufacturers' catalogs of the period. Among the best known producers of early pressed glass were the New England Glass Company in Cambridge, Massachusetts, and the Boston & Sandwich Glass Company in Sandwich, but we now realize that as much pressed glass was produced in the Midwest, in some of the same patterns, as in the New England factories.

Attributions of the earliest pressed patterns are difficult to make because so few pieces were marked, and no American catalogs of that period are known to exist. The Sandwich factory marked its molds for several types of boat salts (nos. 652-656); the New England Glass Company for a salt and a lamp (nos. 696-699; 788); and the Providence Flint Glass Works for a salt (nos. 742, 743). Bakewell marked his molds for a window pane and furniture knobs (nos. 171, 35, 36); the Fort Pitt Glass Works for a creamer, a cup plate, and a pane (nos. 136, 451, 452); the Stourbridge Flint Glass Works for a boat salt and a plate (nos. 648, 649, 138); and the Union Glass Works for a cup plate dated 1836 (no. 431). J. & C. Ritchie of Wheeling, West Virginia, marked the mold for a pane (no. 311) and

Fig. 4   Mold-blown champagne glass, lamp, and tumbler in the scale pattern. French, ca. 1840-1860 (60.3.54. 72.3.188, 60.3.53).

the Jersey Glass Company for a salt (no. 685). These examples are a mere handful compared to the thousands of different items produced, and only a few specimens from each mold are known at present. The Dummer factory in Jersey City, the Brooklyn Flint Glass Company, the American Flint Glass Works in Boston, and probably a factory in Philadelphia, all produced pressed glass without marking it. Thus, positive attributions are often impossible.

An account book of the Sandwich factory for the 1820's and 1830's is in the library of the Edison Institute at the Greenfield Village and Henry Ford Museum. It lists lamps, toy decanters, hats, tumblers, and patent salts, but all of these may be blown, rather than pressed. Invoices of the New England Glass Company for that period are at the Maryland Historical Society, but no specific patterns can be identified on the basis of either of these written descriptions. Attributions can sometimes be made on the similarity of objects to other marked objects, but the possibility of one factory copying another must always be considered.

In the 1930's, quantities of pressed glass fragments were discovered at the dump under a Sandwich factory building erected in 1849. The fragments were thought to be representative of the factory's production before 1849 and were studied extensively by Helen McKearin, Ruth Webb Lee, Dr. and Mrs. Charles Green, and Albert C. Marble, noted collectors and authors on American glass. They carefully matched the fragments (subsequently given to the Massachusetts Institute of Technology and now at the Smithsonian Institution) to pieces in their respective collections. It was evident that this dump of fragments contained not only pieces made at the Sandwich factory, but also included pieces brought there for study or as cullet. Most factories advertised for broken glass (cullet) which was added to the glass batch to help the melting process. Some fragments found at the Sandwich site are clearly European; hence the evidence presented by the fragments must be treated with caution. The patterns which are illustrated reflect both European and American derivation.

31 Furniture knob
Probably New England
ca. 1829-1840
H. 4 cm; D. 5.8 cm

61.4.157

Colorless lead glass; mushroom
shape with floral design top;
metal screw.
Ex coll: Helen McKearin
Parallels: Lee, Sandwich Glass,
pl. 18, center; *McKearin, American Glass,* pl. 130, no. 2; *Rose,*
no. 25.

*32 Another

61.4.158

Opalescent.
Ex coll: Helen McKearin

33 Furniture knob
Probably New England
ca. 1829-1840
H. 4 cm; D. 5.3 cm

61.4.156

Opaque blue glass; mushroom
shape with diamond pattern on
top and metal screw.
Ex coll: Helen McKearin

*34 A pair

68.4.393 A,B

Opaque blue.
Ex coll: Louise S. Esterly

35 Furniture knob
Pittsburgh, Pennsylvania,
Bakewell, Page & Bakewell
ca. 1825-1835
H. 3.8 cm; D. 4.6 cm

68.4.382

Colorless lead glass; mushroom
shape with bull's-eyes and diamonds on top; square base with
"BAKEWELL'S P. . . ."
Ex coll: Louise S. Esterly
Comments: These were presumably made under John P.
Bakewell's patent of September
9, 1825 "for a method of pressing glass knobs."
Parallels: McKearin, Helen.
"The Case of the Pressed Glass
Knobs," *Antiques,* 60, no. 2,
Aug. 1951, Fig. 1, p. 118; *Rose,*
nos. 10-15.

*36 Another
H. 4.3 cm; D. 5.4 cm

68.4.394

Blue.
Ex coll: Louise Esterly

37 Furniture knob
Probably New England Glass
Company, Cambridge, Mas-
sachusetts
ca. 1827-1840
H. 2.5 cm; D. 3.5 cm

61.4.159

Opalescent glass; mushroom
shape; rosette design on top
surface.
Ex coll: Helen McKearin
Comments: This presumably was
made under Henry Whitney
and Enoch Robinson's patent of
Nov. 4, 1826, for "an improvement in the manufacture of
glass knobs."
*Parallels: McKearin, American
Glass,* pl. 130, no. 7; McKearin,
Helen, "The Case of the
Pressed Glass Knobs," *Antiques,*
60, no. 2, Aug. 1951, Figs. 3, 4
pp. 119-120.

*38 A pair
H. 2.6 cm; D. 3.8 cm

68.4.392 A, B

Opaque light blue.
Ex coll: Louise Esterly

*39 Set
H. 2 cm; D. 2.5 cm

68.4.645 A-H

Four transparent blue, and four
opalescent.
Ex coll: Louise Esterly

*40 Another
L. 4.4 cm; D. 6.1 cm

80.4.79

Colorless.
Bequest of Donald F. Clark

41 Set of small knobs
United States, New England
ca. 1840-1850
L. 1.2 cm; D. 1.5 cm

68.4.645 I-N

Opalescent glass; capstan shape
with concentric circles on top
and metal screw through.
Ex coll: Louise S. Esterly
Comments: These knobs are so
tiny it is difficult to know what
they might have been used for.

42 Furniture knob
Probably New England
ca. 1829-1840
H. 3.2 cm D. 3.9 cm.

80.4.80

Colorless lead glass; mushroom
shape with scroll design on top.
Bequest of Donald F. Clark

43 Pair of furniture knobs
Probably Midwest
ca. 1840-1860
H. 7.1 cm; D. 5.1 cm

63.4.78 A, B

"Vaseline" glass; waisted
octagonal shape; rayed design
on top.
Gift of Louise S. Esterly

44 Furniture knob
Probably Boston & Sandwich
Glass Company, Sandwich,
Massachusetts
ca. 1829-1840
H. 4.8 cm; D. 4.5 cm

70.4.83

Colorless lead glass; mushroom
shape, rosette design on top;
glass screw shank on bottom
with "PATENT."
Comments: This presumably is
the knob patented by Deming
Jarves, June 11, 1829.
Published: Wilson, Fig. 216, p.
258.
*Parallels: McKearin, American
Glass*, pl. 30, no. 3;
McKearin, Helen. "The Case
of the Pressed Glass Knobs,"
Antiques, 60, no. 2, Aug. 1951,
p. 119, Fig. 2; *Rose*, no. 24.

*45 Another
L. 6.8 cm

80.4.32

Opaque white

*46 Set of knobs
(as above)
D. 6.4 cm, H. 6.7 cm

80.4.78 A-D

Bequest of Donald F. Clark

*47 Another
D. 4.2 cm, H. 5.5 cm.

80.4.81

No inscription.
Bequest of Donald F. Clark

48 Knob
Probably New England
ca. 1830-1840
H. 3.9 cm. D. 5.2 cm

80.4.82

Colorless glass with diamond
pattern on top and around
sides; hole for metal shank in
center, shank missing.
Bequest of Donald F. Clark

†49 **Bowl**
Probably Cambridge, Massachusetts, New England Glass
Company
ca. 1830
H. 3.3 cm; D. 16.5 cm

50.4.191

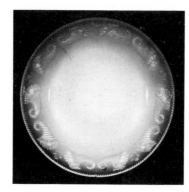

Fiery opalescent glass; design
on inner surface of pair of cornucopias filled with fruit and
flowers; fine concentric rings on
inner and outer surface.
Ex coll: George S. McKearin
*Published: McKearin, American
Glass*, pl. 141, no. 2.
Parallels: Lee, Sandwich Glass,
pl. 108, lower right; *Rose*, no. 79.

†*50 **Another**

68.4.148

Ex coll: Louise S. Esterly

†51 **Plate**
Probably Cambridge, Massachusetts, New England Glass
Company
ca. 1830
D. 14.9 cm

68.4.627

Pale opaque blue glass; circular
with pairs of cornucopias around
sides and fine concentric rings in
base.
Ex colls: Louise S. Esterly;
George S. McKearin
Comments: See bowls above.
Published: Rose, no. 77.

†*52 **Another**

68.4.239

Opaque white.
Ex colls: Louise S. Esterly,
George S. McKearin

53 **Tea plate**
New England
ca. 1830
D. 15 cm

68.4.185

Opalescent white glass; circular,
ring of oak leaves on outer edge
enclosing ring of acorns; base
with three concentric circles of
beading.
Ex coll: Louise S. Esterly
Parallels: Lee, Sandwich Glass,
pl. 108, lower left.

†54 **Desk Set**
Probably Boston & Sandwich
Glass Company, Sandwich,
Massachusetts
ca. 1830
(a) L. 18.5 cm;
H. (overall) 7.4 cm;
(b & c) H. 5 cm

68.4.532 a,b,c

Light blue opaque glass; rectangular tray with four feet; two wells to hold inkwell and sand shaker; slot for pen; flowers in relief on base; inkwell and sand shaker are globular, mold-blown bottles with pewter tops.
Ex colls: Louise S. Esterly; Mrs. Harlan Miller
Comments: Extremely rare; only six of these are known: two in The Metropolitan Museum of Art from the Green collection in light and dark blue, one in the William Elsholz collection in light blue, and two in the Caleb Ewing collection in green and light blue. One large light blue fragment of this design was found at the Sandwich factory site.
Parallels: Green, Charles W. "Little-Known Sandwich," *Antiques*, 28, no. 2, Aug. 1940, Fig. 2, p. 69; *Rose*, no. 72.

---

55 **Bowl**
New England
ca. 1830
H. 3.5 cm; D. 20.4 cm

68.4.399

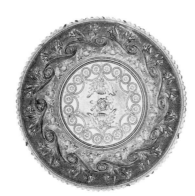

Colorless lead glass; circular; sides with scrolls, leaves, and thistles; base encircled by loops of cable.
Ex coll: Louise S. Esterly
Parallels: Lee, Sandwich Glass, pl. 94, upper right.

---

56 **Butter strainer**
New England
ca. 1830
D. 10.5 cm

68.4.545

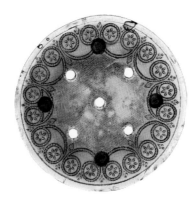

Opalescent glass; flat circular disk with a design of a cable looping around flowers around edge and concentric circles in center; five scattered holes in design for drainage.
Ex coll: Louise S. Esterly
Comments: See pieces above for related designs. Although several of these strainers are known, few have remained with their original holders.

57 Plate
New England
ca. 1830-1835
D. 14.2 cm

68.4.192

Opalescent, nearly opaque
white glass; circular with alternating pine trees and shields
around sides; geometric ornament in center.
Ex colls: Louise S. Esterly;
George S. McKearin
Comments: Very rare in color.
Parallels: Keefe, John. "American Lacy and Pressed Glass in
The Toledo Museum of Art,"
Antiques, 100, no. 1, July 1971, p.
104; *Lee, Sandwich Glass*, pl.
104, pl. 108; *McKearin, American
Glass*, pl. 143, no. 4; *Rose*, nos.
59, 65.

58 Compote
New England
ca. 1830-1835
H. 9.6 cm; D. 13.9 cm

59.4.66

Colorless lead glass; pressed and
blown; circular with alternating
pine trees and shields around
sides; geometric ornament in
center; applied stem and circular
base.
Gift of Louise S. Esterly

59 Bowl
New England
ca. 1830-1840
H. 4.6 cm; L. 20.5 cm

69.4.16

Colorless lead glass; oval with
flambeaux around sides; scroll
pattern in oval base.

60 Plate
New England, or possibly
Philadelphia area
ca. 1830's-1840's
D. 15.5 cm;

59.4.90

Colorless lead glass; circular; rim
of flambeaux, pattern repeated
in base around a circle of cross-
hatching.
Gift of Louise S. Esterly
Parallel: Lee, Sandwich Glass, pl.
110, lower left.

61 Bowl
New England
ca. 1830-1840
H. 3.8 cm; L. 18.1 cm

63.4.57

Colorless lead glass; oval; diamond pattern around sides,
wheat sheaf in each end; star
and wheat sheaf in center.
Gift of Louise S. Esterly

62 Bowl
New England
ca. 1830-1835
H. 5 cm; L. 23.8 cm

68.4.182

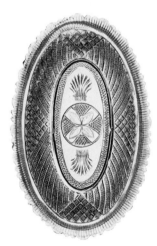

Colorless glass; oval shape
parallel rows of small diamonds
around the sides, interrupted by
four wedges of strawberry diamonds; oval base with a quatrefoil and wheat sheaf design.
Ex coll: Louise S. Esterly
Comments: Extremely rare.
Parallels: Rose, no. 60, pl. 5
(similar bowl); Rose, J. H.
"Unrecorded Rarities in Lacy
Glass," *Antiques*, 65, no. 3,
March, 1954 p. 225.

63 Bowl
New England area, or possibly
England
ca. 1830-1835
H. 4.4 cm; L. 17.6 cm

68.4.412

Colorless lead glass; oval, waffle
pattern on sides with diamonds
and stars; crosshatched pattern
filling oval base.
Ex coll: Louise S. Esterly
Comments: Very rare
Published: Rose, no. 61.

64 Plate
New England
ca. 1830-1835
D. 14.8 cm

50.4.412

Colorless lead glass; circular,
fans in rim, star and fans in cen-
ter.
Ex coll: George S. McKearin
*Parallels: McKearin, American
Glass,* pl. 131, no. 2.

65 Plate
New England
ca. 1830-1835
D. 15.2 cm

58.4.72

Colorless lead glass; circular,
arched rim with fan; plain sides;
waffled center.
Gift of Louise S. Esterly
*Parallels: Ayer, Rose, "Six Inch
Glass Tea Plates," Antiques,* 20,
no. 1, July 1931, p. 35, Figs.
3-10; *Lee, Sandwich Glass,* pl. 64;
McKearin, American Glass, pls.
131-137, 151-155; *Rose,* nos. 41,
42, pl. I.

66 Bowl
New England, or possibly
England
ca. 1830-1835
H. 4.2 cm; D. 25.5 cm

60.4.810

Colorless lead glass; circular,
with fans alternating with swags
in shoulder; waffle pattern in
center.
Gift of Louise S. Esterly
Comments: An oval piece in the
same pattern was in the Corning
Lacy show in 1954.
Parallels: Rose, no. 64, pl. 5.

67 Bowl
New England, or possibly
Europe
ca. 1830-1835, or ca. 1860
H. 3.8 cm; D. 18.4 cm

63.4.66

Colorless non-lead glass; octagonal, with horizontally ribbed sides; ribbing radiating from center to cover base.
Gift of Louise S. Esterly
Comments: It is difficult to say whether this piece is very early or very late; it is non-lacy in character and does not relate to any other designs.

68 Bowl
Probably Cambridge, Massachusetts, New England Glass Company
ca. 1827-1835
H. 4.7 cm; D. 14.7 cm

70.4.81

Colorless lead glass; circular, sides of eight panels of strawberry diamonds separated by vertical ribs; eight-point star base.
Ex coll: Lura Woodside Watkins
Comments: This is closely similar to No. 47 in the 1954 Corning Lacy Show and now in the Elsholz collection.
Parallels: Rose, pl. 25, no. 47.

69 Bowl
New England
H. 5 cm; D. 22.9 cm
ca. 1835

68.4.193

Colorless glass; circular; large cross across bowl, surrounded by strawberry diamonds and swirls. Center of cross is flower surrounded by strawberry diamonds.
Ex colls: Louise S. Esterly; Dr. W. Stanley Curtis
Parallels: Kerr, Anna B. "A Midwestern Collection of Glass," *Antiques*, 45, no. 4, April 1944, p. 186, Fig. 8, center left. (This may be Mrs. Esterly's bowl, but it was then in Dr. Grace Doane's collection.)
McKearin, American Glass, pls. 132, no. 2, and 149, no. 1.

70 Bowl
New England
ca. 1835
H. 3.2 cm; D. 15.4 cm

63.4.65

Colorless lead glass with a cross design across bowl and a rope rim.
Gift of Louise S. Esterly
Parallels: McKearin, American Glass, pl. 149, a larger size; *Rose*, no. 55.

71 Plate
New England
ca. 1830-1840
D. 15.7 cm

68.4.447

Colorless lead glass; edge of alternating scallops and points formed by diamonds and fans on sides; circular base has a sunburst pattern filled with elongated diamonds.
Ex coll: Louise S. Esterly

72 Plate
New England
ca. 1830-1835
D. 30.6 cm

68.4.115

Colorless lead glass; circular; scalloped edge; center with large equal armed cross filled with diamonds.
Ex coll: Louise S. Esterly
Comments: One of four recorded examples.
Published: Rose, no. 67, pl. VI. Rose, James H. "Unrecorded Rarities in Lacy Glass," *Antiques,* 65, no. 3. March, 1954, p. 226.
Parallels: Kerr, Anna B. "A Midwestern Collection of Glass," *Antiques,* 45, no. 4, April 1944, p. 184, Fig. 3, no. 2.

73 Plate
Midwest
ca. 1830-1835
D. 14 cm

68.4.389

Colorless lead glass; octagonal with bull's-eye rim; sides and center filled with strawberry diamonds.
Ex coll: Louise S. Esterly
Comments: Unique as far as known.
Published: Rose, no. 357, pl. XVI; Rose, James H. "Unrecorded Rarities in Lacy Glass," *Antiques,* 65, no. 3, March 1954, p. 227.

74 Bowl
New England
ca. 1830
H. 10.7 cm; D. 23.1 cm

78.4.44

Colorless lead glass; circular;
swirled feathers around sides;
diamond pattern in base.
Gift of Blanche Robinson
Parallels: Rose, no. 53, frontispiece and cover.

75 Bowl
Probably New England, possibly United States
ca. 1835-1850
H. 2.6 cm; L. 15.5 cm

68.4.411

Colorless lead glass with scalloped rim and a pattern of scrolls
on a finely ribbed background
around sides and base.
Ex coll: Louise S. Esterly
Published: Rose, no. 201, pl. XII.

†76 **Covered sugar bowl**
New England, probably Providence, Rhode Island
Providence Flint Glass Works
ca. 1830-1833
H.(with cover) 15.2 cm;
D.(rim) 12.5 cm

68.4.168 a,b

Fiery opalescent glass; cylindrical shape with galleried rim; design on body of three baskets of flowers above a double-headed eagle, alternating with three acanthus leaves; conical lid, stippled, with six vertical acanthus leaves; mushroom-shaped knob.
Ex colls: Louise S. Esterly; Paul Carson
Comments: The attribution of this sugar bowl to Providence is based on its obvious similarity to the marked "Providence" salts, nos. 742, 743.
Published: Rose, no. 163.
Parallels: Lee, Sandwich Glass, pls. 154, 156; *McKearin, American Glass*, pl. 163.

*77 **Another**

68.4.547

Colorless.
Ex coll: Louise S. Esterly

78 **Tray**
Probably New England area
ca. 1835-1845
H. 1.8 cm; L. 16.5 cm

60.4.800

Colorless lead glass; rectangular; scroll design around sides; paired acanthus leaves at each end; scrolls in center.
Gift of Louise S. Esterly
Comments: The pattern of a pressed glass pane by the firm of Curling and Robertson in Pittsburgh was copied from this. Fragments of this pattern were found at the Sandwich factory site.
Parallels: Lee, Sandwich Glass, pl. 160; *McKearin, American Glass*, pl. 156, no. 2; *Rose*, no. 216.

79 **Sugar bowl**
New England
ca. 1830-1840
H.(with cover) 14.5 cm; D.(rim) 12.2 cm

61.4.102

Colorless lead glass; octagonal shape; galleried rim; stippled design of shields, diamonds, and acanthus leaves; scalloped foot; domed cover with acanthus leaves and diamonds; open knob.
Gift of Louise S. Esterly
Comments: See following for matching creamer.
Parallels: Lee, Sandwich Glass, pl. 154; *Rose*, no. 208.

80 Creamer
New England
ca. 1830-1840
H. 11.1 cm; D. (base) 6.5 cm

61.4.103

Colorless lead glass; handle pressed in one piece with body; stippled design of shields and diamonds around sides; scalloped foot.
Gift of Louise S. Esterly
Comments: see sugar bowl, preceding.
Parallels: Keyes, H.E. "Museum Examples of Sandwich Glass," *Antiques*, 34, no. 1, July 1938, pp. 20-22; *Lee, Sandwich Glass*, pl. 157; *McKearin, American Glass*, pl. 163, no.6; *Rose*, nos. 207, 251.

*81 Another

68.4.169

Opalescent.
Ex colls: Louise S. Esterly; Paul Carson

82 Candlestick
New England
ca. 1830-1835
H. 14 cm; D. (base) 9.5 cm

68.4.513

Colorless lead glass; vertically ribbed and fluted socket; attached to an octagonal-shaped stippled base with acanthus leaves.
Ex coll: Louise S. Esterly
Parallels: Lee, Sandwich Glass, pl. 177, bottom center - base; *McKearin, American Glass*, pl. 192, no. 1; *Rose*, no. 87.

*83 Another
H. 12.7 cm
68.4.518

A variant.
Ex coll: Louise S. Esterly

*84 Another

68.4.519

As above.

85 Lamp
New England
ca. 1830-1840
H. 20 cm; D. (base) 9.4 cm

68.4.483

Colorless lead glass, inverted pear-shaped font blown in a mold with Horn of Plenty pattern on sides, attached to a pressed octagonal stippled base with acanthus leaves.
Ex colls: Louise Esterly; Dr. and Mrs. Charles W. Green
Comments: This combination of mold-blowing and pressing is rare.
Parallels: McKearin, American Glass, pl. 190. no. 1.

*86 Another

50.4.166

Ex coll: George S. McKearin

87 Lamp
New England
ca. 1830-1835
H. 20.2 cm; D. (base) 11 cm

68.4.546

Colorless lead glass with an inverted pear-shaped blown font, attached by three wafers to a round knop above pressed domed circular base with acanthus leaf decoration.
Ex coll: Louise S. Esterly
Parallels: McKearin, American Glass, pl. 189, no. 21.

88 Plate
New England
ca. 1830-1845
D. 15.9 cm

60.4.799

Colorless lead glass; twelve-sided, stippled; acanthus leaves around sides; four pairs of acanthus leaves in base.
Gift of Louise S. Esterly
Comments: There is an identical plate in the Duckworth collection at The Toledo Museum of Art, published as unique.
Parallels: Keefe, John W. "American Lacy and Pressed Glass in The Toledo Museum of Art," *Antiques*, 100, no. 1, July 1971, p. 106, Fig. 4; *Lee, Sandwich Glass*, pl. 103, upper left; *McKearin, American Glass*, pl. 156, no. 1.

89 Bowl
New England
ca. 1830-1840
H. 4.4 cm; D. 24 cm

68.4.243

Colorless lead glass; circular; finely stippled; rim with alternating acanthus leaves and shield medallions; base with stylized flower in center.
Ex coll: Louise S. Esterly
Comments: Very rare.
Parallels: Lee, Sandwich Glass, pl. 122; *Rose*, no. 113.

90 Bowl
New England
ca. 1835-1850
H. 4.8 cm; D. 23.8 cm

58.4.56

Colorless lead glass; circular; acanthus leaves, six-pointed stars and hexagons alternating around sides; hexagon in center of circular base.
Gift of Louise S. Esterly
Parallels: Keyes, H.E. "Museum Examples of Sandwich Glass," *Antiques*, 34, no. 1, July, 1938, pp. 20-22; *Lee, Sandwich Glass*, pl. 121; *Rose*, no. 121.

91 Plate
Midwest
ca. 1830-1840
D. 12.1 cm

68.4.405

Colorless lead glass; circular with bull's-eye rim; acanthus leaves and bull's-eyes around sides and in a circle around base.
Ex coll: Louise S. Esterly
Parallels: Lee, Sandwich Glass, pl. 107, top left; *McKearin, American Glass*, pl. 142, no. 4.

92 Plate
D. 17.5 cm

63.4.60

A variant.
Gift of Louise S. Esterly

93 Bowl
Midwest
ca. 1835-1850
H. 4.5 cm; L. 22.6 cm

68.4.440

Colorless lead glass; rectangular with bull's-eye rim; lyre in each corner; acanthus leaf clusters on sides and ends; row of table rests around base; lunette and acanthus leaf clusters in base.
Ex coll: Louise S. Esterly
Parallels: Lee, Sandwich Glass, pl. 102, upper right; *McKearin, American Glass*, pl. 146 (similar); *Rose*, no. 346.

94 Bowl
New England
ca. 1830-1845
H. 2.8 cm; D. 15.9 cm

68.4.109

Bluish-aqua glass pressed in a design of overlapping scales.
Ex colls: Louise S. Esterly; Dr. and Mrs. Charles W. Green
Comments: Many fragments of this pattern in various sizes and colors were found at the site of the Sandwich factory.
Parallels: McKearin, *American Glass*, pl. 152, no. 4, p. 359; *Lee, Sandwich Glass*, pl. 134, upper; Green, Dr. Charles W. "Little-known Sandwich," *Antiques*, 38, No. 2, Aug. 1940, Fig. 5, p. 70.

*95 Another
D. 15.9 cm

68.4.112

Cobalt blue.
Ex colls: Louise S. Esterly; Dr. and Mrs. Charles W. Green

*96 Another
D. 13.4 cm

68.4.184

Olive green.
Ex colls: Louise S. Esterly; George S. McKearin

*97 Another
D. 15.9 cm

68.4.461

Wisteria.
Ex colls: Louise S. Esterly; Dr. and Mrs. Charles W. Green

98 Compote
New England
ca. 1830-1845
H. 7.3 cm; D. (rim) 11.3 cm

68.4.530

Colorless glass; top pressed in a design of overlapping scales like pieces above; joined by a wafer to a pressed trapezoidal base.
Ex coll: Louise S. Esterly; Forrest Macmillan

99 Bowl
New England
ca. 1835-1845
H. 2.9 cm; D. 16.1 cm

60.4.802

Colorless lead glass; pressed in a design of overlapping scales with a scalloped border.
Ex coll: Louise S. Esterly
Comments: Except for the border, which is separate from the pattern, this piece is identical to those preceding.

†100 **Cake plate**
New England, probably Boston
& Sandwich Glass Company,
Sandwich, Massachusetts
ca. 1830-1850
D. 23.3 cm

68.4.493

Light blue glass; octagonal with
acanthus leaves, scrolls, and
shields in sides; beehives and
thistles in center.
Ex colls: Louise S. Esterly; Mrs.
G.H. Lloyd; Mrs. Oscar R.
Haase
Comments: Unique in this color;
many fragments of this pattern
in several colors were found at
the Sandwich factory site.
Published: Rose, no. 156; Keyes,
H.E. "Museum Examples of
Sandwich Glass," *Antiques,* 34,
no. 1, July 1938, pp. 20-22.
Parallels: Lee, Sandwich Glass,
pl. 136; *McKearin, American
Glass,* pl. 149, no. 3.

*101 **Another**

68.4.407

Colorless.
Ex coll: Louise S. Esterly.

†*102 **Another**

68.4.474

Light yellow.
Ex Coll: Louise S. Esterly

103 Tray
Probably New England
ca. 1835-1850
H. 2.8 cm; L. 25.3 cm

68.4.506

Colorless lead glass; oval shape with fleur-de-lis, pinwheels and fans in sides, and butterfly in center of base.
Ex colls: Louise S. Esterly; Dr. and Mrs. Charles W. Green
Comments: Rare in this large size.
Parallels: Keyes, H.E. "Sandwich Lacy Glass," *Antiques*, 24, no. 2, August 1933, Fig. 19, p. 61; *Lee, Sandwich Glass*, pl. 95, p. 309; *Rose*, no. 200.

*104 Another
L. 22.8 cm

68.4.509

Ex coll: Louise S. Esterly

*105 Another
L. 17.5 cm

68.4.520

Ex coll: Louise S. Esterly

*106 Another
L. 20.6 cm

68.4.522

Ex colls: Louise S. Esterly; Edward MacGowan

107 Plate
Probably New England
ca. 1835-1850
H. 2.5 cm; L. 19.7 cm

68.4.521

Colorless glass; oval shape with fleur-de-lis, leaves and fans in sides, and cartouche in center.
Ex colls: Louise S. Esterly; Dr. and Mrs. Charles W. Green
Comments: See butterfly trays, above.
Parallels: Rose, no. 204.

108 Pane
Pittsburgh, probably Pittsburgh
Flint Glass Manufactory of
Benjamin Bakewell
ca. 1835-1845
L. 17.6 cm; . 12.6 cm

50.4.208

Colorless glass; rectangular with
sunburst at each corner; rays
radiating to diamond in center
with palmettes.
Ex colls: George S. McKearin;
James H. Rose
Comments: A number of panes in
this design were found in the
panels beside the doors between
the dining room and the parlor of
the Schenley Mansion, *Picnic*, in
Pittsburgh. One is in the
Duckworth collection at The
Toledo Museum of Art.
Parallels: Innes, Pittsburgh Glass,
Fig. 303, left; Keefe, John W.
"American Lacy and Pressed
Glass in The Toledo Museum of
Art," *Antiques*, 100, no. 1, July
1971, p. 106, Fig 4; *Lee,
Sandwich Glass*, pl. 161, upper;
Rose, James H. "Lacy Glass
Window Panes," *Antiques*, 51,
no. 2, Feb. 1947. p. 120, Fig. 3.

109 Pane
Probably Boston & Sandwich
Glass Company, Sandwich,
Massachusetts
ca. 1830-1845
L. 25.5 cm; W. 20.5 cm

50.4.209

Colorless glass; rectangular with
sunbursts in corners and diamond in center.
Ex coll: George S. McKearin
Comments: Although the design
of this pane is similar to the one
from the Schenley Mansion,
preceding, numerous fragments
of the pattern were found at the
Sandwich factory site and one
pane was found in a corn shed in
Sandwich.
Parallels: Innes, Pittsburgh Glass,
Fig. 307.

110 Compote
Pittsburgh, Pennsylvania, R.B.
Curling & Sons, Fort Pitt Glass
Works
ca. 1830's
H. 11.1 cm; D. 15 cm

68.4.448

Colorless lead glass; blown and
pressed; circular rim with alternating wedge-shaped panels,
diamond-filled and plain, radiating from center of pressed top;
applied blown stem with one
knop, round flat foot; rough
pontil mark.
Ex coll: Louise S. Esterly
Comments: This compote top occurs with two different cup plate
bases, both reliably attributed to
Curling, hence this attribution.
See compote following.
Parallels: Innes, Early Glass,
p. 47; *Innes, Pittsburgh Glass,*
Fig. 232.

111 Compote
United States, Pittsburgh,
Pennsylvania, R. B. Curling &
Sons
ca. 1830-1840
H. 11.4 cm; D. (rim) 15.2 cm

80.4.42

Colorless lead glass; bowl having
alternating plain and "hairpin"
panels and a bull's-eye rim; foot
is formed from a cup plate.
Comments: Foot is cup plate
216C attributed by Lee and
Rose to Curling.
Parallels: Innes, *Pittsburgh
Glass*, p. 292, figs. 231-232, *Lee
and Rose*, no. 216C.

112 Bowl
Midwest
ca. 1835-1850
H. 1.6 cm; D. 9.4 cm

63.4.85

Nearly colorless glass with slight
yellowish tinge; scalloped edge;
diamond and scroll pattern
around sides and in base.
Gift of Louise S. Esterly

113 Bowl
Midwest
ca. 1840-1855
H. 2.7 cm; D. 14.2 cm

63.4.87

Medium green glass; circular;
rim of large and small scallops;
diamond pattern around sides;
sunburst in base.
Gift of Louise S. Esterly

114 Plate
New England
ca. 1827-1835
D. 12 cm

60.4.805

Colorless lead glass; arched rim
with fans just inside edge; pinwheel design filling center.
Gift of Louise S. Esterly

115 Sand Shaker
New England
ca. 1835-1850
H. 7 cm; D.(rim) 6.9 cm

59.4.61

Colorless lead glass; cylindrical
with concentric lines and stippling on top surface; vertical
beading around sides; fitted
with pewter shaker top.
Gift of Louise S. Esterly
Parallels: Lee, Sandwich Glass,
pl. 179, no. 2.

*116 Another**

68.4.514

Opalescent.
Ex coll: Louise S. Esterly

*117 Another**

68.4.515

Green.
Ex coll: Louise S. Esterly

*118 Another**

68.4.517.

Bluish-violet.
Ex coll: Louise S. Esterly

119 Sand shaker
New England
ca. 1835-1850
H. 7 cm; D.(rim) 6.9 cm

68.4.516

Colorless glass; cylindrical with
concentric lines on top surface,
no stippling; otherwise same as
shakers above.
Ex coll: Louise S. Esterly
Comments: See shakers above.

120 Plate
Probably Pittsburgh area
ca. 1830-1845
D. 19.3 cm

50.4.201

Colorless lead glass; octagonal
rim of bull's-eye and points;
acanthus leaves and fleur-de-lis
around sides; American eagle in
center.
Ex coll: George S. McKearin
*Published: American Antiques Col-
lector*, Dec. 1941-March 1942,
cover; *Rose*, no. 417, pl. XIX;
Innes, Pittsburgh Glass, Fig. 272.
*Parallels: McKearin, American
Glass*, pl. 142, nos. 1, 3; *Innes,
Pittsburgh Glass*, no. 273.

121 Another
D. 13 cm

50.4.198

Circular.
Ex coll: George S. McKearin
*Published: McKearin, American
Glass* pl. 142, 143; *Rose*, no. 418.

122 Another
D. 15 cm

50.4.199

Circular.
Ex coll: George S. McKearin

123 Another
D. 18 cm

50.4.200

Circular.
Ex coll: George S. McKearin
Published: Rose, no. 419.

124 Sauce dish
United States
ca. 1830-1845
H. 3.6 cm; D. 10.3 cm

50.4.203

Colorless lead glass; scalloped
rim; American eagle in base.
Ex coll: George S. McKearin

125 Bowl
New England
ca. 1830-1845
H. 2.3 cm; D. 17.5 cm

68.4.329

Colorless lead glass; octagonal
with acanthus leaves and shields
in sides and American eagle in
center.
Ex coll: Louise S. Esterly
Published: Spillman, Jane S.
*Glassmaking, America's First In-
dustry*, 1976, Cover and Frontispiece.
Parallels: Lee, Sandwich Glass,
pl. 116; *McKearin, American
Glass*, pl. 157, no. 2; *Rose*, no.
100.

†126 **Bowl**
D. 15 cm

68.4.237

A variant, alternate side panels
silver-stained yellow.
Ex coll: Louise S. Esterly

127 **Bowl**
D. 16 cm

58.4.74

A variant, colorless.
Gift of Louise S. Esterly

128 Bowl
New England
ca. 1835-1850
H. 2.8 cm; D. 13.3 cm

68.4.426

Colorless lead glass; octagonal;
two side panels with a shell, two
with a thistle, two with a rose
and two with a sunflower.
Ex coll: Louise S. Esterly
Parallels: Lee, Sandwich Glass,
pl. 86, upper right.

129 Bowl
New England
ca. 1835-1850
H. 5 cm; D. 22.2 cm

68.4.427

Colorless lead glass; octagonal;
two side panels with a thistle,
two with a rose, four with
sunflowers.
Ex colls: Louise S. Esterly; Dr.
and Mrs. Charles W. Green
Comments: See bowls above and
below.
Parallels: Keyes, H.E.
"Sandwich Lacy Glass," *Antiques,* 24, no. 2, Aug. 1933, Fig.
16, p. 68; *Lee, Sandwich Glass,*
pl. 136, lower; *McKearin, American Glass,* pl. 137.

130 Plate
New England
ca. 1835-1850
H. 4 cm; D. 18.4 cm

68.4.527

Colorless lead glass; circular; rim
divided into nine panels; three
each with thistles, a rose, and a
sunflower.
Ex coll: Louise S. Esterly
Comments: See bowls above.

131 Bowl
Midwest
ca. 1835-1850
H. 3.8 cm; L. 15.4 cm

68.4.388

Colorless lead glass; rectangular;
leaf or floral motif in each of
eight side panels; four stippled,
four with herringbone background; stars, flowers, and
scrolls deeply sculptured on
eight-sided bases.
Ex coll: Louise S. Esterly
Parallels: Lee, Sandwich Glass,
pls. 102, 103; *McKearin, American Glass,* 157, no. 4; *Rose,* nos.
416-420.

*132 Another
L. 20.5 cm

68.4.441

Ex colls: Louise S. Esterly;
Dr. and Mrs. Charles W. Green

133 Plate
Midwest
ca. 1835-1845
D. 20.2 cm

58.4.58

Colorless lead glass; circular;
three concentric circles of
geometric motif around a
starflower on a stippled background.
Gift of Louise S. Esterly

134 Pane
Midwest, Probably Pittsburgh or
Wheeling
ca. 1835-1850
L. 17.4 cm; W. 12.6 cm

68.4.541

Deep amethyst glass; rectangular with flower in center and
sunburst in each corner.
Ex coll: Louise S. Esterly
Comments: This pane was discovered in the sidelights of the
front door of a home built in
1850 in Franklin County, Indiana. It was part of a set which al-
ternated amethyst and colorless
panes. Dr. William Ashton came
from England to settle there in
1834 and is said to have acquired
the panes in the Ohio River valley before building the house.
Published: Innes, Pittsburgh Glass,
Fig. 305.
Parallels: Keyes, H.E. "Decorative Window Panes of the
1830's," *Antiques,* 30, no. 2, Feb.
1938, p. 81; Rose, James H.
"Lacy Glass Window Panes,"
Antiques, 51, no. 2, Feb. 1947, p.
120, Fig. 2.

135 Bowl
Midwest
ca. 1835-1850
H. 4.5 cm; D. 18.5 cm

61.4.107

Colorless lead glass; alternating
shells, flowers, and circles
around edge; leaves, flowers,
and lunettes in center.
Gift of Louise S. Esterly
Parallels: Lee, Sandwich Glass,
pl. 93, lower right.

†136 Pitcher
Pittsburgh, Pennsylvania, Fort
Pitt Glass Works of R.B. Curling
& Sons
ca. 1829-1832
H. 10.3 cm; D. (rim) 8.8 cm

50.4.205

Colorless lead glass; chain de-
sign above flower baskets on
body; inscription on base, "R.B.
CURLING & SONS FORT PITT."
Ex colls: George S. McKearin,
J.H. Rose
Comments: Extremely rare. This
is the first known example and
only one more has been pub-
lished, from the collection of
William J. Elsholz. The design
was probably introduced be-
tween September 1829 when
Price, Curling & Co. became
R.B. Curling & Sons, and Octo-
ber 1832 when the latter became
Curling, Higby and Curling.
See also no. 161
Published: Lee, Sandwich Glass,
pl. 159; *McKearin, American
Glass*, pl. 147, no. 4.

137 Compote
New England
ca. 1835-1850
H. 14.3 cm; D. 18.5 cm

61.4.101

Colorless lead glass with a floral
pattern in the bowl and a
tripodal base; pressed separately
and joined with a wafer.
Gift of Louise S. Esterly
Comments: Fragments of the pattern of the top were found at the
Sandwich factory site.
Parallels: Lee, Sandwich Glass,
pl. 94, upper left, pl. 146. right;
McKearin, American Glass, pl.
157, no. 3.

138 Plate
United States, Pittsburgh,
Pennsylvania, T. & J. Robin-
son's Stourbridge Flint Glass
Works
1830-1836
D. 14.5 cm

80.4.48

Colorless plate with leaf design
on rim; inscribed "T. & J.
ROBINSON/PITTSB^G." in center.
Parallels: Innes, *Pittsburgh Glass*,
Fig. 264.

139 Tea plate
Probably Midwest
ca. 1840
D. 15 cm;

68.4.183

Colorless non-lead glass; circular; stippled rim with a series of
circles or portholes; base filled
with multi-petaled flower.
Ex coll: Louise S. Esterly

140 Bowl
United States
ca. 1830-1845
H. 1.8 cm; D. 8.8 cm

68.4.235

Colorless lead glass; circular;
finely stippled background;
edged with alternating flowers
and circles; center of base with
circles surrounded by lunettes.
Ex coll: Louise S. Esterly

141 Plate
Probably New England
ca. 1830-1840
D. 14.7 cm

61.4.99

Colorless lead glass; circular,
with a row of leaves just inside
rim; design of flowers, grape
leaves, and kneeling men
around flat rim; waffled design
filling center.
Gift of Louise S. Esterly

142 Bowl
New England
ca. 1830-1845
H. 4.8 cm; L. 27.4 cm

68.4.432

Colorless lead glass; oval; sides
and ends with fans and scrolls;
center with diamond enclosing a
flower.
Ex colls: Louise S. Esterly; Dr.
and Mrs. Charles W. Green
Parallels: Lee, Sandwich Glass,
pl. 164; *McKearin, American
Glass,* pl. 139; *Rose,* no. 119.

143 Bowl
Probably New England
ca. 1835-1850
H. 4.8 cm; D. 21 cm

67.4.56

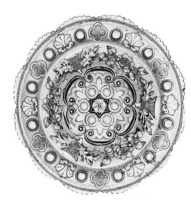

Colorless lead glass; circular
shape; stippled shells, circles,
and clubs in upper shoulder
above row of beading; lower part
of shoulder has alternating thistles and roses; center with lunettes, scrolls, and fleur-de-lis.
Gift of Mr. and Mrs. John F.
Staub
Parallels: Lee, Sandwich Glass,
pl. 93.

144 Bowl
New England
ca. 1830-1840
D. 28 cm

68.4.107

Colorless lead glass; concentric bands of decoration from rim to center; beading/zigzags/ diamond-filled circles/leafy branches and stylized flowers/ beading/fans/zigzags and diamonds/fleur-de-lis/beading; center with octafoil on stippled glass.
Ex coll: Louise S. Esterly
Comments: Very rare
Parallels: Keyes, H.E. "Sandwich Lacy Glass," *Antiques*, 24, no. 2, August, 1933, p. 61; *Lee, Sandwich Glass,* pl. 109; *Rose,* no. 107.

145 Bowl
New England
ca. 1835-1845
H. 4.8 cm; D. 23 cm

68.4.143

Colorless lead glass; sides filled with snail shells and thistles, alternating with princess feather medallions; circular base has roses and leaves.
Ex colls: Louise S. Esterly; Dr. and Mrs. Charles W. Green
Comments: Fragments of this pattern were found at the Sandwich factory site.
Published: Green, Charles W. "A Most Important Discovery at Sandwich," *Antiques*, 32, no. 2, August, 1937, p. 58, Fig. 2; Keyes, H.E. "Museum Examples of Sandwich Glass," *Antiques*, 24, no. 1, July, 1938, p. 21.
Parallels: Lee, Sandwich Glass, pl. 120; *McKearin, American Glass,* pl. 159; Rose, no. 111.

146 Plate
New England
ca. 1835-1845
D. 17.7 cm

68.4.373

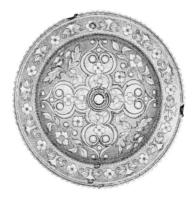

Colorless lead glass; finely stippled; flat rim has scrolls alternating with single flowers; center has scrolls alternating with floral sprays.
Ex coll: Louise S. Esterly
Parallels: Lee, Sandwich Glass, pl. 93, lower right.

147 **Bowl**
New England
ca. 1830-1840
H. 3.6 cm; D. 17.4 cm

68.4.379

Colorless lead glass; scalloped edge with ribbing; sides with cloth-like stippling around four pineapples surrounded with lunettes with scattered flowers; diamonds surrounded with four lunettes on circular base.
Ex coll: Louise S. Esterly
Parallels: Keyes, Homer E. "Museum Examples of Sandwich Glass," *Antiques,* 34, no. 1, July, 1938, pp. 20-22; *Lee, Sandwich Glass,* pl. 90, upper left; *Rose,* no. 125.

148 **Tea plate**
New England
ca. 1832
D. 15 cm

59.4.67

Colorglass glass; circular, bust of man in center with "WASH-INGTON GEORGE" above, surrounded by acorns, oak leaves, scrolls and stars.
Gift of Louise S. Esterly
Comments: Probably made around the centennial of Washington's birth, in 1832. The border is the same as that on the plates following.
Parallels: Ayers, Rose L. "Six Inch Glass Tea Plates," *Antiques,* 20, no. 1, July 1931, pp. 34-35; Dyer, Walter. "Pressed Glassware of Old Sandwich," *Antiques,* 1, no. 2, Feb. 1922, p. 60; *Lee, Sandwich Glass,* pl. 109; *McKearin, American Glass,* pl. 151; *Rose,* no. 238.

149 **Tea plate**
New England
ca. 1830
D. 15.3 cm

59.4.68

Colorless lead glass; circular; scrolls around rim; center with wreath of acorns and a star.
Gift of Louise S. Esterly
Parallels: Lee, Sandwich Glass, pl. 109, lower left; *McKearin, American Glass,* pl. 151, no. 9; *Rose,* nos. 143, 192.

*150 **Another**

68.4.189

Blue.
Ex coll: Louise S. Esterly

151 Dish
New England
ca. 1830-1845
H. 3.8 cm; L. 20.2 cm

68.4.341

Colorless lead glass; rectangular, with thistles, scrolls, leaves and crossed agricultural implements in sides; Pan playing pipes in base.
Ex colls: Louise S. Esterly; Dr. and Mrs. Charles W. Green
Parallels: Keefe, John W. "American Lacy and Pressed Glass in The Toledo Museum of Art," *Antiques*, 100, no. 1, July 1971, p. 106; Keyes, H.E. "Sandwich Lacy Glass," *Antiques*, 24, no. 2, August 1933, Fig. 15, p. 60; *Lee, Sandwich Glass*, pl. 166, top; *Rose*, no. 213.

152 Plate
Midwest
ca. 1835-1850
D. 15.3 cm

63.4.61

Grayish glass; circular; leaf design around sides and center surrounding a quatrefoil.
Gift of Louise S. Esterly

153 Plate
Midwest
ca. 1835-1850
D. 17.8 cm

63.4.70

Colorless non-lead glass; bull's-eye rim; thistles and drapery on sides; lunette around a central star in base.
Gift of Louise S. Esterly
Parallels: McKearin, *American Glass*, pl. 144, no. 1.

154 Plate
Probably Midwest
ca. 1835-1845
D. 13.3 cm

68.4.251

Light green glass; circular;
closely stippled; rim with scrolls
and flowers; center with scrolls
and flowers surrounding a quatrefoil.
Ex coll: Louise S. Esterly

155 Bowl
Midwest
ca. 1835-1845
H. 3.3 cm; D. 23.1 cm

68.4.154

Colorless lead glass with brown-
ish gray discoloration in center;
circular; bull's-eye rim; row of
stylized blossoms, zigzags,
S-scrolls, shell motifs, and bead-
ing around a central star.
Ex colls: Louise S. Esterly;
George C. Cannon
Comments: Extremely rare.
*Parallels: McKearin, American
Glass,* pl. 145; Rose, no. 379.

156 Celery vase
Probably Sandwich, Mas-
sachusetts, Boston & Sandwich
Glass Company
ca. 1830-1840
H. 17.5 cm; D. (rim) 11.9 cm

59.4.95

Colorless lead glass; stylized
leaves and lilies around sides;
applied stem; pressed foot with
leaf design on underside; pontil
mark.
Gift of Louise S. Esterly
Comments: Extremely rare. Two
more of these vases are known,
one each in the collections of
The Sandwich Historical Society and that of William J. Elsholz (Detroit); two without
bases are known—one each at
Old Sturbridge Village and in
the collection of Mr. Elsholz.
One large opaque light blue
fragment of such a vase was
found at the Sandwich factory
site, as well as some smaller
ones. All known examples of the
vase are in colorless glass, but
the fragments found are all light
blue. The stem and base of this
piece appear to be of a better
quality glass than the top, but
this is true on the other two
known. Corning's vase has been
broken and repaired in the past
with the break at the top of the
stem. However, since the foot is
like those on the other two
vases, it is presumed to be original.
Parallels: Antiques, 37, no. 3,
Feb. 1940, advertisement, p. 54;
Green, Charles W. "Little
Known Sandwich," *Antiques*, 38,
no. 2, Aug. 1940, p. 69, Fig. 1;
Lee, Sandwich Glass, pl. 68,
lower left; *McKearin, American
Glass*, pl. 163, no. 8; *Rose*, no.
57; *SHS*, pp. 14-15.

†157 **Covered casket with tray**
Midwest
ca. 1830-1840
H.(with cover) 12.7 cm; L. 20.1 cm

56.4.2

Colorless lead glass; rectangular form; casket has vertical ellipses around sides and a high scrolled rim; two-stepped cover has Gothic arches and a fan knob; rectangular tray has ellipses in center and Gothic arches around rim.
Ex coll: George S. McKearin
Comments: Extremely rare; only four of these caskets are known, all colorless. The Ewing and Elsholz collections each have one, and another is owned by a dealer. Mr. McKearin acquired tray and casket separately.
Published: Rose, no. 349, frontispiece (casket and cover only); Innes, *Pittsburgh Glass* Fig. 287; Innes, Lowell. "Lacy Hairpin in French and American Glass," *Antiques* 100, No. 2, Aug. 1971, Fig. 8, Fig. 8a (tray only).

158 **Covered casket with tray**
New England
ca. 1830-1840
H.(with cover and tray); 13.3 cm; L. 17.9 cm

68.4.437

Colorless lead glass; rectangular; galleried rim; Gothic arches, with hearts above, around sides of casket; double-domed cover with Gothic arches and pyramidal knob; tray with hearts around sides.
Ex coll: Louise S. Esterly
Comments: These caskets are extremely rare. The tray is related in design to the *Constitution* tray, see no. 309.
Published: Innes, *Pittsburgh Glass,* Fig. 278 (tray only).
Parallels: Lee, *Sandwich Glass,* pl. 168; McKearin, *American Glass,* pl. 134, no. 2; *Rose,* no. 81, cover.

159 Another
60.4.795

Identical except for cover which has Gothic arches and thistles.
Gift of Louise S. Esterly

160 Covered bowl
Probably Midwest
ca. 1835-1845
H. (with cover) 15.5 cm;
D.(rim) 12.7 cm

65.4.46

Colorless lead glass; cylindrical with Gothic arches and peacock feathers on sides; galleried rim; round foot; lid has Gothic arches and beehive knob.
Published: Howe, Katherine S. and Warren, David B. *The Gothic Revival Style in America 1830-1870*, 1976, no. 129.
Parallels: Lee, Sandwich Glass, pl. 155, lower right.

161 Creamer
New England
ca. 1830-1840
H. 10.5 cm; D. (base) 6.5 cm

68.4.167

Opalescent blue glass; cylindrical; chain decoration; beading and Gothic arches around lower part of body; round scalloped base.
Ex Coll: Louise S. Esterly
Comments: Very rare in color. Fragments of this pattern have been found at the Sandwich factory site. For a midwestern use of the same motifs, see the Curling creamer, no. 136.
Parallels: Lee, Sandwich Glass, pl. 157; *McKearin, American Glass*, pl. 163, no. 5; *Rose*, nos. 130, 164.

*162 Another
68.4.548

Colorless.
Ex coll: Louise S. Esterly

163 Tumbler
New England, or possibly
Europe
ca. 1830-1840
H. 6.4 cm; D. (rim) 6 cm

68.4.417

Colorless lead glass; cylindrical
with Gothic arches around sides.
Ex coll: Louise S. Esterly
Comments: Rare, possibly
unique. This and the mug, no.
203, are the only known drinking vessels in American lacy
glass.
Published: Innes, Pittsburgh Glass,
Fig. 296; Rose, James H. "Unrecorded Rarities in American
Glass," *Antiques,* 71, no. 2, Feb.
1957, p. 162.

164 Bowl
Midwest
ca. 1835-1845
H. 3 cm; L. 15.5 cm

68.4.445

Colorless lead glass; oval with
Gothic arches, fleur-de-lis, and
thistles in sides; fleur-de-lis in
base.
Ex coll: Louise S. Esterly
Comments: Only four known.
Parallels: Pittsburgh Glass, Fig.
270; Green, Charles W. "Little
Known Sandwich," *Antiques,* 38,
no. 2, Aug. 1940, p. 71, Fig. 10;
Rose, no. 351.

165 Bowl
Midwest
ca. 1835-1845
H. 3.8 cm; L. 17.5 cm

58.4.60

Colorless lead glass; rectangular
with bull's-eye cap ring; Gothic
arches and thistles around sides;
thistles in base.
Gift of Louise S. Esterly
Parallels: Innes, Pittsburgh Glass,
Fig. 285, *Lee, Sandwich Glass,*
pl. 102.

166 Bowl
New England, possibly Boston
& Sandwich Glass Company,
Sandwich, Massachusetts
ca. 1835-1845
H. 3.3 cm; L. 18 cm

67.4.23

Colorless lead glass; rectangular
with Gothic arches and flowers
around sides; pineapples and
arches in base.
Gift of Mr. and Mrs. Harry A.
Snyder
Comments: Fragments of this
pattern were found at the
Sandwich factory site.
Parallels: Lee, Sandwich Glass,
pl. 102, no. 4; *McKearin, American Glass,* pl. 150, no. 4; Keyes,
Homer E. "Museum Examples
of Sandwich Glass," *Antiques,*
34, no. 1, July 1938, pp. 20-22;
McKearin, Helen. "New England Glass Company Invoices,"
Antiques, 52, no. 4, Oct. 1947,
Fig. 3, p. 276.

*167 Bowl
63.4.62

A variant with rope rim.
Gift of Louise S. Esterly

168 Bowl
New England
ca. 1830-1845
H. 4.1 cm; L. 18 cm

69.4.17

Colorless lead glass; oval with
Gothic arches and sides; wreath
of flowers in base.
Comments: See also no. 308, the
"Constitution" bowl which is
slightly smaller but has an identical base design.
Parallels: Lee, Sandwich Glass,
pl. 97, upper; *McKearin, American Glass,* pl. 128; *Rose,* no. 203.

169 Compote
New England
ca. 1830-1845
H. 7.6 cm; L. 15.7 cm

68.4.531

Colorless lead glass; rectangular
top with Gothic arches and
leaves in sides; square stepped
standard pressed separately and
joined while hot.
Ex coll: Louise S. Esterly
Comments: Only two of these
were known in 1954. Fragments
matching the top design have
been found at the Sandwich factory site.
Published: Rose, no. 228.

170 Plate
Midwest
ca. 1830-1845
D. 15 cm

68.4.499

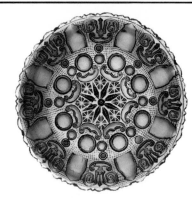

Deep amethyst glass; circular; arches and fleur-de-lis on sides; eight-pointed star with lunettes in center of base.
Ex coll: Louise S. Esterly
Comments: Extremely rare.
Parallels: Innes, Early Glass, p. 25, top left; *Rose,* no. 428.

171 Pane
Pittsburgh, Pennsylvania, Pittsburgh Flint Glass Manufactory of Benjamin Bakewell
ca. 1830-1845
H. 17.6 cm; W. 12.5 cm

56.4.10

Colorless glass; rectangular; design of Gothic arches; marked on smooth side, "BAKEWELL."
Comments: One of several found in a secretary in a house near Wheeling, West Virginia, in 1956.
Published: Howe, Katherine Susman, and Warren, David B. *The Gothic Revival Style in America, 1830-1870,* Houston, Texas: Museum of Fine Arts, 1976, p. 65, no. 123 (illus.).
Parallels: Innes, Pittsburgh Glass, Fig. 303, no. 2.

172 Compote
New England
ca. 1835-1850
H. 15 cm; D. 26.5 cm

64.4.87

Colorless lead glass; hearts and grape leaves around rim; arches around sides; chevrons in center; applied, pressed standard with a quadruple knop and scrolled circular base.
Comments: Rare. The only other known compote in this pattern is in the Elsholz collection.
Parallels: Lee, Sandwich Glass, pl. 141, left; *Rose,* no. 225; Rose, James H. "Unrecorded Rarities in American Glass," *Antiques,* 71, no. 2, Feb. 1957, p.161.

173 Covered bowl
New England
ca. 1835-1845
H. (with cover) 13.8 cm; D. (rim) 17.8 cm

68.4.485

Colorless lead glass; cylindrical; thistles, scrolls, and arches around body; nearly flat cover with open crown knob.
Ex coll: Louise S. Esterly
Comments: Extremely rare
Parallels: Lee, Sandwich Glass, pl. 155, center (different cover); *McKearin, American Glass,* pl. 134, no. 1; *Rose,* no. 99 (different cover) and no. 101.

174 Plate
Probably New England
ca. 1830-1845
H. 3 cm; D. 17.7 cm

59.4.74

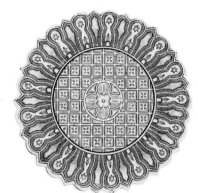

Colorless lead glass; circular
with hairpin design in sides and
grid in base.
Gift of Louise S. Esterly
Parallels: Sandwich Glass, pls.
96, 166.

175 Another
D. 20.5 cm

63.4.88

Colorless.
Gift of Louise S. Esterly

176 Oval bowl
L. 21 cm

68.4.505

Colorless.
Ex colls: Louise S. Esterly; Dr.
and Mrs. Charles W. Green

177 Bowl
New England
ca. 1830-1845
H. 2.8 cm; L. 19.8 cm

68.4.489

Colorless lead glass, square with hairpin design in sides and grid in base.
Ex colls: Louise S. Esterly; Edward MacGowan
Comments: Extremely rare.
Parallels: Rose, pl. IX.

178 Tray
New England
ca. 1830-1845
L. 23.8 cm

68.4.501

Colorless lead glass; shell-shaped with hairpins running from handle to end.
Ex coll: Louise S. Esterly
Comments: Extremely rare.
Parallels: Rose, pl. XXVIII.

179 Compote
Midwest
ca. 1830-1845
H. 8 cm; D. 19 cm

50.4.211

Colorless lead glass; pressed circular top with "princess feather" design around sides; attached by a wafer to a hollow, hairpin base.
Ex coll: George S. McKearin
Comments: See above.
Published: Innes, Pittsburgh Glass, Fig. 290.

180 Covered sugar bowl
Midwest
ca. 1830-1845
H. (with cover) 19.3 cm;
D.(rim) 11.5 cm

50.4.296

Colorless lead glass; blown in a mold with twelve panels around base of bowl; attached by a wafer to a pressed "hairpin" pattern base; domed cover with button knob sits in galleried rim.
Ex coll: George S. McKearin
Comments: The mold-blown panels in this sugar bowl are found on several other pieces in the Museum's collection and in other collections. The pressed hairpin foot has been found on candlesticks, a lamp, a covered bowl, and several compotes.
Published: McKearin, American Glass, pl. 147, no. 3; *Rose,* no. 391.
Parallels: Rose, nos. 341, 356, 382, 383, 384.

181 Pair of candlesticks
Midwest
ca. 1830-1845
H. 21 cm; D. (base) 9.5 cm

50.4.204 A, B

Colorless lead glass; blown and pressed; blown cylindrical sockets with baluster-shaped stem and pressed hairpin base.
Ex coll: George S. McKearin
Comments: See above.
Published: Innes, Pittsburgh Glass, Fig. 302; Innes, Lowell, "Lacy Hairpin in French and American Glass," *Antiques,* 100, no. 2, Aug. 1971, Fig. 7, p. 231.

182 Plate
Midwest
ca. 1830-1845
H. 2.2 cm; D. 15.3 cm

59.4.75

Colorless lead glass; circular with hairpin design in sides and radiating pattern of squares in center.
Gift of Louise S. Esterly
Published: Rose, pl. XX, no. 421; *Innes, Pittsburgh Glass,* pl. 263.

183 Compote
New England, probably Boston
& Sandwich Glass Company
ca. 1828-1835
H. 10.5 cm; D. 15.8 cm

50.4.411

Slightly grayish lead glass; bowl
pressed with hearts and sheaves
of wheat on sides and strawberry
diamonds in bottom; applied
and tooled stem and foot.
Ex coll: George S. McKearin
Comments: Fragments of this
heart design were found at the
site of the Sandwich factory; it
seems to be one of the earliest
pressed patterns.
Parallels: Lee, Sandwich Glass,
pl. 105, lower right; *McKearin,*
American Glass, pl. 151, no. 2.

184 Bowl
D. 14.6 cm

68.4.144

Deep amethyst.
Ex colls: Louise S. Esterly;
Dr. and Mrs. Charles W. Green

185 Plate
D. 18.8 cm

68.4.381

Colorless.
Ex coll: Louise S. Esterly

186 Tea plate
New England, probably Boston
& Sandwich Glass Company
ca. 1828-1835
D. 17.9 cm

68.4.188

Opalescent white glass; circular;
hearts and sheaves around rim;
strawberry diamonds in center.
Ex coll: Louise S. Esterly
Comments: Fragments of this
pattern were found at the
Sandwich factory site. It is rare
in color.
Published: Rose, no. 31.
Parallels: Lee, Sandwich Glass,
pl. 105, lower left, p. 106, upper
right; *McKearin, American Glass,*
pl. 151, no. 1.

187 **Bowl**
D. 10.1 cm

68.4.345

Colorless.
Ex coll: Louise S. Esterly

188 **Plate**
New England
ca. 1830-1840
D. 23.3 cm

58.4.75

Colorless lead glass; circular; rim
with alternating hearts and lyres;
base with strawberry diamonds
around an eight-pointed star.
Gift of Louise S. Esterly
Comments: This is another early
pattern.
Parallels: Lee, Sandwich Glass,
pl. 66, pl. 106, upper left;
McKearin, American Glass, pl.
133, no. 1.

189 **Plate**
New England
ca. 1830-1840
D. 19.8 cm

68.4.397

Colorless lead glass; circular; rim
with alternating hearts and lyres;
base with strawberry diamonds
around a four-pointed star.
Ex colls: Louise S. Esterly
Comments: See above.
Parallels: Lee, Sandwich Glass,
pl. 106, upper left.

*190 **Another**

68.4.419

A variant.
Ex coll: Louise S. Esterly

191 **Oval plate**
Midwest
ca. 1840-1850
L. 20.3 cm; W. 13.3 cm

59.4.85

Opaque white glass; oval with
hearts, pinwheels, and fans in
base.
Gift of Louise S. Esterly
Comments: The design is obviously related to that on the butterfly trays, nos. 103-107 in this
catalog.
Parallels: Rose, no. 452.

*192 **Another**

68.4.420

Colorless.
Ex coll: Louise S. Esterly

193 Bowl
Midwest
ca. 1840-1850
H. 2.5 cm; L. 20 cm

63.4.59

Colorless lead glass; oval with
lunettes and trefoils in sides;
acanthus motif at each end;
medallion in center.
Gift of Louise S. Esterly

194 Creamer
New England
ca. 1830-1845
H. 11.5 cm; D. (base) 7.1 cm

68.4.127

*195 Another

59.4.63

Opaque white glass; handle
pressed in one piece with body;
scale design around sides; two
hearts beneath spout.
Ex coll: Louise S. Esterly
Comments: Fragments of this
pattern were found at the
Sandwich site.

Colorless.
Gift of Louise S. Esterly

196 Tea plate
New England
ca. 1830-1835
D. 15 cm

68.4.151

Opalescent glass; running vine
around rim; five hearts in base.
Ex colls: Louise S. Esterly;
George S. McKearin
Comments: Fragments of this
pattern were found at the
Sandwich factory site.
Parallels: Ayer, Rose L. "Six-
Inch Tea Plates," *Antiques*, 20,
no. 1, July 1931, p. 35, Figs. 3-8;
Keefe, John W. "American Lacy
and Pressed Glass in The To-
ledo Museum of Art," *Antiques*,
100, no. 1, July 1971, p. 104; *Lee,
Sandwich Glass*, pl. 107, no. 2;
Watkins, Lura W. "Early Glass
Pressing at Cambridge and
Sandwich," *Antiques*, 28, no. 4,
October 1935, p. 151, Fig. 3.

*197 Another

63.4.68

Colorless.
Gift of Louise S. Esterly

198 **Tea plate**
Midwest, possibly Wheeling,
West Virginia
ca. 1835-1850
D. 14.6 cm

68.4.146

Green shading to amber glass;
circular with a Roman Rosette
design around the edge and
three diamond filled hearts in
center.
Ex colls: Louise S. Esterly; Mrs.
Harlan Miller
Comments: The attribution is
based on the resemblance of this
plate to two compotes illustrated
in *American Glass* (see Parallels)
as of Wheeling make.
Parallels: Ayers, Rose L. "Six-
Inch Tea Plates," *Antiques*, 20,
No. 1, July 1931, Figs. 3-7;
McKearin, American Glass, pl.
162; Keefe, John W. "American
Lacy and Pressed Glass in The
Toledo Museum of Art," *Antiques*, 100, no. 1, July 1971, p.
107, Fig. 7.

*199 **Another**

68.4.240

Cobalt blue.
Ex coll: Louise S. Esterly

*200 **Another**

68.4.401

Colorless.
Ex coll: Louise S. Esterly

201 **Another**

68.4.242

Light green with striped hearts.
Ex coll: Louise S. Esterly;
Mrs. Harlan Miller

202 Dish

Midwest, probably Wheeling,
West Virginia
ca. 1835-1850
L. 13.2 cm; W. 7.1 cm;
H. 3.8 cm

68.4.387

Colorless glass; rectangular with
hearts, circles, and strawberry
diamonds in sides.
Ex coll: Louise S. Esterly
Comments: See tea plates, above.
Published: Rose, James H.
"Unrecorded Rarities in Lacy
Glass," *Antiques*, 71, no. 2, Feb-
ruary 1957, p. 162.

203 Mug

Probably New England,
possibly Europe
ca. 1835-1850
H. 5 cm; D. (rim) 5 cm

68.4.429

Colorless lead glass; three hearts
around body; ear-shaped handle
pressed as part of mug.
Ex coll: Louise S. Esterly
Comments: This and the tumbler, no. 163, are the only known
drinking vessels in American
lacy pressed glass. Only two of
these are known.
Published: Rose, James H.
"Unrecorded Rarities in Lacy
Glass," *Antiques*, 71, no. 2,
February 1957, p. 162.

204 Plate

United States
ca. 1840-1850
D. 14.1 cm

60.4.803

Colorless lead glass with scrolls,
leaves and flowers around rim
and winged hearts in center.
Gift of Louise S. Esterly
Parallels: Lee, Sandwich Glass,
pl. 104, upper left.

205 Bowl
New England
ca. 1830-1845
H. 4.5 cm; L. 20 cm

58.4.57

Colorless lead glass; eight-lobed oval shape; leaf and scroll design in sides; oak leaves and scrolls in base.
Gift of Louise S. Esterly
Comments: Many fragments of this pattern were found at the Sandwich site.
Parallels: Lee, Sandwich Glass, p. 98, top; *McKearin, American Glass,* pl. 133, no. 2; *Rose,* no. 204.

206 Shallow plate
New England
ca. 1830-1845
H. 3.3 cm; D. 23 cm

50.4.190

Colorless lead glass, with a row of trifid ornaments around the edge; four oak leaves in center.
Ex coll: George S. McKearin
Comments: Fragments of this pattern and several variants have been found at the Sandwich factory site.
Parallels: Lee, Sandwich Glass, pl. 127; *McKearin, American Glass,* pl. 155, no. 1.

207 Bowl
New England
ca. 1830-1845
H. 4.8 cm; D. 26.4 cm

68.4.153

Colorless lead glass; circular bowl with oak leaf design around sides and center.
Ex colls: Louise S. Esterly; Dr. and Mrs. Charles W. Green.
Parallels: Lee, Sandwich Glass, pl. 126; *McKearin, American Glass,* pl. 155, no. 2.

*208 Another
D. 23.6 cm

61.4.105

Gift of Louise S. Esterly

209 Bowl
D. 18.1 cm

59.4.82

A variant with beaded edge.
Gift of Louise S. Esterly

210 Plate
Eastern United States
ca. 1830-1845
D. 15 cm

59.4.89

Colorless lead glass; leaf design
in sides and base around a central star.
Gift of Louise S. Esterly
Parallels: Lee, Sandwich Glass,
pl. 110, upper left.

211 Bowl
New England
ca. 1835-1850
H. 2 cm; D. 10.8 cm

67.4.61

Colorless lead glass; oak leaf
design around sides and in
center.
Gift of Mr. and Mrs. Harry A.
Snyder
Parallels: Lee, Sandwich Glass,
pl. 85, no. 4.

212 Plate
Midwest
ca. 1835-1850
D. 14 cm

68.4.390

*213 Another
D. 15.6 cm

63.4.69

Gift of Louise S. Esterly

Colorless lead glass; octagonal
with bull's-eye rim; row of par-
allel ellipses in sides; base with
oak leaves and acorns.
Ex coll: Louise S. Esterly
Comments: Same edge and rim
as no. 306.
Parallels: Lee, Sandwich Glass,
pl. 169, lower left; *McKearin,
American Glass,* pl. 143, no. 3;
Rose, nos. 354, 356; Rose,
James H. "Wheeling Lacy
Glass," *Antiques,* 69, no. 6, June
1956, p. 527.

214 Plate
New England
ca. 1830-1845
D. 13.8 cm

68.4.145

Amethyst glass; rim of peacock feathers; center with scrolled eyes pattern.
Ex colls: Louise S. Esterly; Dr. and Mrs. Charles W. Green
Comments: Numerous fragments of this pattern, in both clear and pale yellow, were found at the Sandwich factory site.
Published: Rose, no. 435.
Parallels: Keefe, John W. "American Lacy and Pressed Glass in The Toledo Museum of Art," *Antiques*, 100, no. 1, July 1971, p. 105, Fig. 3; *Lee, Sandwich Glass*, pl. 109, upper right; *McKearin, American Glass*, pls. 152, 153; *Rose*, no.437.

215 Another
D. 13.4 cm

67.4.24

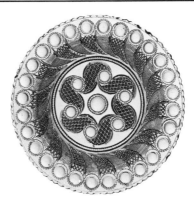

Colorless.
Gift of Mr. and Mrs. Harry A. Snyder

216 Another
D. 15.5 cm

68.4.187

*217 Another
D. 13.4 cm

59.4.97

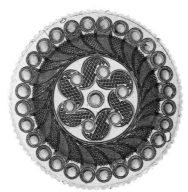

Lavender blue.
Ex colls: Louise S. Esterly; Dr. and Mrs. Charles W. Green

Pale yellow.
Gift of Louise S. Esterly

218 Another
D. 17.8 cm

68.4.413

*219 Another
D. 13.8 cm

58.4.73

Colorless.
Ex coll: Louise S. Esterly

Colorless.
Gift of Louise S. Esterly

220 Plate
D. 11 cm

50.4.192

A variant, light blue
Ex coll: George S. McKearin

221 Bowl
New England
ca. 1830-1845
H. 3.8 cm; D. (rim) 18.8 cm

68.4.150

Purple-blue glass; peacock
feathers around sides; scrolled
eyes in center.
Ex coll: Louise S. Esterly; Dr.
and Mrs. Charles W. Green
Comments: Extremely rare in
color.
Published: Rose, no. 173.
*Parallels: McKearin, American
Glass*, p. 358.

222 Compote
New England
ca. 1830-1845
H. 11.4 cm; D. 22.8 cm

58.4.59

Colorless lead glass; peacock
feathers in sides of bowl;
scrolled eyes in center; foot
pressed separately and joined
with a wafer.
Gift of Louise S. Esterly
Parallels: Lee, Sandwich Glass,
pl. 148.

223 Plate
New England
ca. 1830-1845
D. 20.3 cm

68.4.626

Light yellow glass; peacock
feather rim; thistles and scrolls
in center.
Ex coll: Louise S. Esterly
Comments: Fragments of this
pattern were found at the
Sandwich factory site.
Parallels: Lee, Sandwich Glass,
pl. 114, bottom; *McKearin,
American Glass,* pl. 152, no. 1.

*224 Another

58.4.78

Colorless.
Gift of Louise S. Esterly

---

225 Covered mustard pot
New England
ca. 1830-1845
H. (with cover) 5.1 cm; D. 7 cm

59.4.80

Colorless lead glass; cylindrical
with parallel peacock feathers
on sides and ear-shaped handle;
round flat lid with peacock
feathers on underside; cut out
for spoon.
Gift of Louise S. Esterly
Comments: This piece usually
has an underplate, missing in
this example.
Parallels: Keefe, John W.
"American Lacy and Pressed
Glass in The Toledo Museum
of Art," *Antiques,* 100, no. 1,
July 1971, p. 105, Fig. 3; *Lee,
Sandwich Glass,* pl. 114 (upper);
Rose, nos. 152, 154.

---

†226 Plate
New England
ca. 1830-1845
D. 13.3 cm

68.4.238

Colorless lead glass; rim with
peacock feathers silver-stained
yellow; star medallion in center.
Ex colls: Louise S. Esterly; Dr.
and Mrs. Charles W. Green
Comments: Fragments of this
pattern, with staining, have
been found at the Sandwich factory site.
Published: Green, Charles W.
"Little-Known Sandwich
Glass," *Antiques,* 38, no. 2,
Aug. 1940, p. 70, Fig. 4;
McKearin, American Glass, pl.
141, no. 4; *Rose,* no. 103.

227 Plate
New England
ca. 1830-1845
D. 15.6 cm

68.4.418

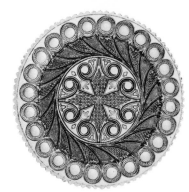

Colorless lead glass; rim with
peacock feathers; vines and
scrolls in center.
Ex colls: Louise S. Esterly;
Ruth Webb Lee
Parallels: Lee, Sandwich Glass,
pl. 109, lower right.

228 Tea plate
Midwest
ca. 1830-1845
D. 15 cm

58.4.68

Light blue glass; rim with flowers and circles; peacock feather
pattern in center.
Gift of Louise S. Esterly
Parallels: Lee, Sandwich Glass,
pl. 110, lower right; *Rose,*
no. 413.

229 Bowl
Midwest
ca. 1830-1845
H. 2.1 cm; D. 12.6 cm

68.4.434

Colorless lead glass; bull's-eye
rim; peacock feathers in sides;
scrolls and star in center.
Ex coll: Louise S. Esterly
Parallels: Rose, no. 385.

*230 Plate
D. 13 cm

68.4.391

Ex coll: Louise S. Esterly

231 Bowl
New England
ca. 1840-1850
H. 5.3 cm; D. (rim) 21.5 cm

50.4.193

Colorless lead glass; pattern of crossed peacock feathers alternating with diamonds and circles in sides; rayed center.
Ex coll: George S. McKearin
Comments: Fragments of this pattern have been found at the Sandwich factory site but it was probably made elsewhere as well. For a Midwestern version of the pattern, see below. These pieces also resemble the Ray design which appears in a M'Kee & Brother catalog of 1860. The pattern was apparently made for many years.
Parallels: Cross, Priscilla C. "The Boston & Sandwich Glass Company," *Antiques*, 7, no. 4, April 1925, Fig. 5, p. 184; *Lee, Sandwich Glass*, pl. 116.

*232 Another
D. 19.5 cm

58.4.65

Colorless.
Gift of Louise S. Esterly

*233 Another
D. 14.6 cm

63.4.147

Gift of Fletcher Ford and Sally Recker in memory of Lola Kincaid Ford

234 Compote
New England
ca. 1830-1845
H. 7.6 cm; D. 15.8 cm

68.4.433

Colorless lead glass; pattern of crossed peacock feathers alternating with diamonds and circles; rayed center; base pressed separately and joined with a wafer.
Ex coll: Louise S. Esterly
Comments: See above.
Parallels: Lee, *Sandwich Glass*, pl. 143, upper.

235 Bowl
Midwest
ca. 1840-1850
H. 5.3 cm; L. 18.8 cm

50.4.196

Dark green, nearly black glass; oval with pattern of crossed peacock feathers; diamond and circles; waffled center.
Ex coll: George S. McKearin
Published: McKearin, *American Glass*, no. 2, pl. 146.
Parallels: Rose, nos. 367, 370, 371.

*236 Another

50.4.197

Bluish-green.
Ex coll: George S. McKearin

*237 **Another**
L. 16 cm

58.4.67

Colorless.
Gift of Louise S. Esterly

*238 **Another**
D. 18.9 cm

60.4.798

Colorless.
Gift of Louise S. Esterly

239 **Another**
D. 10.9 cm

68.4.346

Colorless.
Ex colls: Louise S. Esterly; Dr.
E.R. Eller

240 **Another**
L. 24 cm

63.4.58

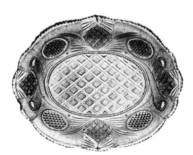

Colorless.
Gift of Louise S. Esterly

241 **Compote**
New England
ca. 1830-1845
H. 15.2 cm; D. 30.4 cm

58.4.61

Colorless lead glass; peacock
feathers and medallions around
sides of bowl; scrolled eyes in
center; vertically ribbed standard was pressed separately and
applied with a wafer.
Gift of Louise S. Esterly
Comments: Extremely rare as a
compote; see bowl below.
Published: Rose, no. 110, pl.
XXXI.

242 Bowl
New England
ca. 1830-1845
H. 5.7 cm; D. 30.3 cm

68.4.116

Colorless lead glass; four medallions with peacock feathers in sides; scrolled eyes in base.
Ex colls: Louise S. Esterly; Dr. and Mrs. Charles W. Green
Comments: This is one of the largest known pieces of lacy glass and is extremely rare, see compote above.
Parallels: Lee, Sandwich Glass, pl. 117; *Rose,* no. 133.

243 Bowl
New England
ca. 1830-1845
H. 4.8 cm; L. 25.4 cm

59.4.79

Colorless lead glass; rectangular with crossed peacock feathers and diamonds in sides and ends; peacock eyes and strawberry diamonds in base.
Gift of Louise S. Esterly
Parallels: Lee, Sandwich Glass, pl. 133; *Rose,* no. 183.

*244 Another
L. 30.8 cm

68.4.425

Colorless.
Ex coll: Louise S. Esterly

245 Bowl
Midwest
ca. 1830-1845
H. 3.4 cm; L. 20 cm

68.4.423

Colorless lead glass; rectangular, crossed cornucopias and shields in sides and ends; peacock eyes and leaves in base.
Ex coll: Louise S. Esterly
Comments: Extremely rare.
Parallels: Rose, no. 425, pl. XX.

246 Covered bowl
Midwest
ca. 1840-1850
H. (with cover) 14.4 cm;
D. 16 cm

68.4.486

Colorless lead glass; circular shape with peacock feather design around sides; lid with peacock feathers and crown knob.
Ex coll: Louise S. Esterly
Comments: See nos. 264, 265; this piece is so similar it must have been made by the same firm.

247 **Plate**
United States, possibly Europe
ca. 1840-1850
D. 20.4 cm

58.4.70

Colorless glass; circular; overall
pattern of crisscrossing lines re-
sembling a plaid.
Gift of Louise S. Esterly
Comments: Fragments of this
pattern were found at the
Sandwich factory site. Both this
plate and the one below look
newer than most 19th-century
pressed glass and show few
signs of wear. They may be late
European examples.
*Published: Innes, Pittsburgh
Glass*, Fig. 280.
Parallels: Keefe, John W.
"American Lacy and Pressed
Glass in The Toledo Museum
of Art," *Antiques*, 100, no. 1,
July 1971, Fig. 7, p. 107; *Lee,
Sandwich Glass*, pl. 106;
McKearin, American Glass, pl.
150; *Rose*, no. 313.

*248 **Another**
D. 15.5 cm

63.4.64

Colorless.
Gift of Louise S. Esterly

249 **Bowl**
New England
ca. 1840-1860
H. 3.3 cm; D. 15.5 cm

59.4.64

Opalescent glass with herringbone design around sides and center.
Gift of Louise S. Esterly
Comments: Fragments of this pattern were found at the site of the Boston & Sandwich Glass Company. The Museum has five similar pieces.
Parallels: Lee, Sandwich Glass, pl. 84; *McKearin, American Glass,* pls. 151, nos. 8, 162; *Rose,* no. 301.

*250 **Another**
D. 10.5 cm

67.4.25

Opalescent.
Gift of Mr. and Mrs. Harry A. Snyder

*251 **Another**
D. 15.4 cm

68.4.149

Amber.
Ex coll: Louise S. Esterly

*252 **Another**
D. 10.2 cm

68.4.331

Amethyst.
Ex coll: Louise S. Esterly

*253 **Another**
D. 12.8 cm

68.4.536

Amber.
Ex coll: Louise S. Esterly

*254 **Another**
D. 12.3 cm

68.4.543

Dark amethyst.
Ex coll: Louise S. Esterly

255 **Compote**
New England
ca. 1840-1860
H. 6.9 cm; D. 15.4 cm

63.4.89

Colorless glass with stippled herringbone design around sides and center; applied hollow standard.
Gift of Louise S. Esterly
Comments: See above.
Parallels: Lee, Sandwich Glass, pl. 139, upper; *McKearin, American Glass,* pl. 162; *Rose,* no. 303.

256 Bowl
United States
ca. 1835-1845
H. 3.8 cm; D. 18.6 cm

68.4.147

Light green glass; stippled princess feather medallion around sides; pairs of S-scrolls in base.
Ex coll: Louise S. Esterly; Dr. and Mrs. Charles W. Green
Comments: This glass is so crude that the piece could have been made in a bottle factory experimenting with pressing.

---

257 Bowl
Midwest
ca. 1840-1850
H. 3.2 cm; D. 16.8 cm

68.4.241

Light green glass; circular, coarsely stippled with princess feather medallions around sides.
Ex coll: Louise S. Esterly
Parallels: Lee, Sandwich Glass, pl. 91, top right; *Rose,* no. 448.

---

258 Bowl
Midwest
ca. 1830-1850
H. 4.1 cm; D. 19 cm

68.4.398

Colorless lead glass; circular, sides with alternating princess feather medallions and leafy branches; center with four-pointed star.
Ex coll: Louise S. Esterly
Parallels: McKearin, American Glass, pl. 158, no. 6; *Rose,* no. 343.

---

259 Bowl
Midwest
ca. 1830-1840
H. 2 cm; D. 10.8 cm

68.4.250

Light green glass; circular; coarsely stippled; rim with princess feather medallion, center with pinwheel design.
Ex colls: Louise S. Esterly; Dr. and Mrs. Charles W. Green
Parallels: Lee, Sandwich Glass, pl. 111, lower right; *McKearin, American Glass,* pl. 142, no. 6.

*260 Another
D. 11.8 cm

68.4.402

Colorless.
Ex coll: Louise S. Esterly

261 Bowl
New England
ca. 1830-1845
H. 4.7 cm; D. 25.3 cm

68.4.233

Colorless lead glass; circular, sides with four large princess feather medallions alternating with four heart/diamond designs; circular base with large sunburst.
Ex colls: Louise S. Esterly; Dr. and Mrs. Charles W. Green
Comments: Fragments of this pattern have been found at the site of the Sandwich factory. The design was also copied by the porcelain factory at Meissen, Germany, in the mid-19th century.
Published: Keyes, H.E. "Museum Examples of Sandwich Glass," *Antiques*, 34, No. 1, July 1938, p. 22, Fig. 8; *Lee, Sandwich Glass*, pl. 119; *McKearin, American Glass*, pl. 159, no. 1.
Parallels: Keefe, John W. "American Lacy and Pressed Glass in The Toledo Museum of Art, *Antiques*, 100, no. 1, July 1971, p. 105; *Rose*, pl. 30, no. 239.

262 Compote
New England
ca. 1835-1850
H. 10.8 cm; D. 16.3 cm

63.4.56

Colorless lead glass; with princess feather medallion in the bowl and a ribbed base pressed separately and joined with a wafer.
Gift of Louise S. Esterly
Parallels: Lee, Sandwich Glass, pl. 149, bottom.

263 Bowl
New England
ca. 1830-1845
H. 3.4 cm; L. 20.3 cm

68.4.396

Colorless lead glass; pattern of crossed cornucopias alternating with diamonds; princess feather medallions in base.
Ex coll: Louise S. Esterly
Published: Rose, no. 220.
Parallels: Lee, Sandwich Glass, pl. 98, lower.

†264 **Covered bowl**
Midwest
ca. 1840-1875
H. (with cover) 14.4 cm;
D. 16 cm

68.4.625

Opalescent blue glass; grape cluster on rim; sides with princess feather medallions and peacock feathers; transparent blue cover with princess feather medallions; grape clusters around rim and crown knob. *Ex colls:* Louise S. Esterly; The Metropolitan Museum of Art; Dr. and Mrs. Charles W. Green. *Comments:* May be unique in this color. In size, shape, and pattern, these seem to be identical to the Rochelle pattern pieces issued by Bakewell, Pears & Company of Pittsburgh in the 1870's. However, the character of the glass in this piece and the grape border seem earlier, and the Bakewell catalog may just demonstrate the longevity of this pattern. See also no. 246, a related bowl. *Published: Rose,* no. 109. *Parallels:* Keyes, H.E. "Museum Examples of Sandwich Glass," *Antiques,* 34, No. 1, July 1938, pp. 20-22; *Lee, Sandwich Glass,* pl. 155, upper; pl. 150.

*265 **Another**

68.4.488

Colorless.
Ex coll: Louise S. Esterly

266 **Covered vegetable dish**
New England
ca. 1830-1840
H. (with cover) 12.2 cm;
L. 26 cm

68.4.436

Colorless lead glass; oval shape; flat rim with grape clusters; sides with scrolls and princess feather medallions; matching lid with "D" shape handle. *Ex colls:* Louise S. Esterly; Dr. and Mrs. Charles W. Green *Comments:* Extremely rare. This pattern was copied in porcelain by the factory in Meissen, Germany, in the 1850's. *Parallels:* Keyes, H.E. "Museum Examples of Sandwich Glass," *Antiques,* 34, No. 1, July 1938, Fig. 3, p. 21 (Green Collection); *Lee, Sandwich Glass,* pl. 151, upper left, pl. 152; *McKearin, American Glass,* pl. 160, no. 1; *Rose,* no. 120.

*267 **Another**

68.4.409

Without grape clusters on rim.
Ex coll: Louise S. Esterly

268 Vegetable dish
Midwest
ca. 1830-1840
H. 5 cm; L. 25.5 cm

68.4.330

Colorless lead glass; oval; flat rim with S-scrolls; sides with thistles, lyres, and medallions.
Ex colls: Louise S. Esterly; Dr. and Mrs. Charles W. Green
Comments: Extremely rare; design copied from that of dishes above.
Parallels: Lee, Sandwich Glass, pl. 165; *Rose*, no. 414, pl. XXXII.

†269 Compote
New England
ca. 1830-1840
H. 15.2 cm; L. 26.8 cm

68.4.219

Amethyst glass; oval bowl with flat rim and design of scrolls and shields; joined while hot to a pressed base with leaf pattern.
Ex colls: Louise S. Esterly; George S. McKearin
Comments: The top of this compote is in virtually the same pattern as the covered vegetable dishes preceding, a pattern later copied by the porcelain factory at Meissen. Fragments of the pattern were found at the Sandwich factory site.
Published: Rose, no. 175.
Parallels: Keefe, John W. "American Lacy and Pressed Glass in The Toledo Museum of Art," *Antiques*, 100, no. 1, July 1971, Fig. 4; *Lee, Sandwich Glass*, pl. 147; *McKearin, American Glass*, pl. 161; *Rose*, nos. 211, 224, 226.

†*270 Another

68.4.351

Canary yellow.
Ex coll: Louise S. Esterly

***271 Another**

68.4.415

Colorless.
Ex coll: Louise S. Esterly

272   **Plate**
Probably New England
ca. 1835-1850
D. 13.9 cm

58.4.69

Opalescent glass; circular; design of linked circles with nine-pointed star in center.
Gift of Louise S. Esterly
Comments: Collectors today call this pattern Roman Rosette but its original name and manufacturer are not known. It was probably made in several factories in both the East and Midwest since it is relatively common and occurs in many sizes and colors. Fragments of the pattern were found at the Sandwich factory site.
Parallels: Lee, Sandwich Glass, pl. 84, upper right; *McKearin, American Glass,* pls. 132, no. 1, 151, no. 6, text, p. 357; *Rose,* nos. 170, 172, 174, 176, 179, 184.

*273   **Another**
D. 23.7 cm

68.4.111

Opalescent.
Ex colls: Louise S. Esterly;
Dr. and Mrs. Charles W. Green

*274   **Another**
D. 15.5 cm

68.4.186

Light amethyst.
Ex colls: Louise S. Esterly;
Dr. and Mrs. Charles W. Green

*275   **Another**
D. 15.5 cm

68.4.191

Amber.
Ex colls: Louise S. Esterly;
Mrs. Harlan Miller

*276   **Another**
D. 13.2 cm

68.4.537

Reddish amber.
Ex colls: Louise S. Esterly;
Dr. and Mrs. Charles W. Green

*277   **Another**
D. 13.6 cm

68.4.542

Dark amethyst.
Ex cofifi: Louise S. Esterly;
Dr. and Mrs. Charles W. Green

278 Bowl
Probably New England
ca. 1835-1850
D. 8.8 cm

59.4.87

Opalescent glass; circular
design of linked arches with a
nine-pointed star in center.
Gift of Louise S. Esterly
Comments: See above.
Parallels: Lee, Sandwich Glass,
pl 84, upper right; *McKearin,*
American Glass, pls. 132, no. 1,
151, no. 6, text, p. 357; *Rose,*
nos. 170, 172, 174, 176, 179, 184.

***279 Another**
D. 14.8 cm

60.4.806

Colorless.
Gift of Louise S. Esterly

***280 Another**
D. 10.3 cm

68.4.234

Colorless.
Ex coll: Louise S. Esterly

***281 Another**
D. 10.2 cm

68.4.354

Opalescent.
Ex coll: Louise S. Esterly

***282 Another**
D. 9.7 cm

68.4.355

Dark amber.
Ex coll: Louise S. Esterly

***283 Another**
D. 27 cm

68.4.380

Colorless.
Ex coll: Louise S. Esterly

***284 Another**
D. 10 cm

67.4.31

Colorless.
Gift of Mr. and Mrs. Harry A.
Snyder

***285 Another**
D. 8.8 cm

67.4.32

Colorless.
Gift of Mr. and Mrs. Harry A.
Snyder

286 Plate
New England
ca. 1835-1850
D. 13.6 cm

68.4.337

Opalescent glass; circular; design of linked circles with
eleven-pointed star in center.
Ex coll: Louise S. Esterly
Comments: This is a variation of
the Roman Rosette pattern, see
above.
Parallels: Rose, no. 184.

***287 Another**
D. 23.7 cm

61.4.106

Colorless.
Gift of Louise S. Esterly

†288 **Covered sugar bowl**
Probably Midwest
ca. 1835-1850
H.(with cover) 15.8 cm;
D.(at rim) 12.3 cm

68.4.473

Deep amethyst glass; cylindrical bowl with row of linked circles filling sides (Roman Rosette); domed lid with Roman Rosette pattern and mushroom knob.
Ex coll: Louise S. Esterly
Comments: This sugar bowl is thought to be a Midwestern variant of Roman Rosette.
Parallels: Lee, Sandwich Glass, pl. 156, upper left; *McKearin, American Glass,* pl. 163; *Rose,* nos. 402, 405.

289 **Covered bowl**
Probably Midwest
ca. 1835-1850
H.(with cover) 12.1 cm;
D. 18.1 cm

60.4.811

Colorless lead glass; circular, with Roman Rosette pattern around bowl and lid; double-domed lid has flat knob.
Gift of Louise S. Esterly
Comments: Rare. This and one in the Sandwich Museum are the only ones recorded.
Parallels: S.H.S., pp. 14-15.

290 **Bowl**
New England
ca. 1835-1850
D. 17.2 cm

68.4.424

Colorless lead glass; circular, with concentric circles of diamond-filled circles radiating out from center.
Ex coll: Louise S. Esterly
Parallels: Lee, Sandwich Glass, pl. 84, upper left; *Rose,* no. 177.

*291 **Another**
D. 14.2 cm

68.4.114

Opalescent.
Ex coll: Louise S. Esterly

292 **Pair of candlesticks**
Probably Midwest
ca. 1840-1850
H. 21.3 cm

65.4.34 A,B

Colorless lead glass; blown and pressed. Blown candle socket with metal interior cup; double knopped stem applied to a hollow pressed base with a Roman Rosette pattern around it.
Gift of Miss Gertrude Hoffman
Parallels: Innes, Pittsburgh Glass, Fig. 246.

293 Bowl
Midwest
ca. 1835-1850
H. 3.5 cm; D. 18 cm

50.4.210

Non lead glass of a pale puce
color; a series of crossed,
S-scrolls on sides alternating
with trefoils; in the center of
the base a lyre within a wreath
of leaf sprays.
Ex coll: George S. McKearin
*Published: McKearin, American
Glass*, pl. 144, no. 2.

294 Pane
New England, possibly Boston
& Sandwich Glass Company,
Sandwich, Massachusetts
ca. 1840-1860
L. 40.5 cm; W. 25.4 cm

66.4.80

Opalescent glass; design of ellipses and scrolls on side.
Gift of Dorothea Setzer
Comments: This pane was found
in Sandwich and is the largest
such pane known.

295 Bowl
New England
ca. 1835-1850
H. 3.5 cm; D. 15.5 cm

68.4.438

Colorless lead glass; hexagonal;
stippled sides with lunette
scrolls and leaves; hexagonal
base has a six-pointed star in
the center surrounded by six
diamonds and pairs of scrolls.
Ex coll: Louise S. Esterly
Parallels: Keyes, Homer E.
"Sandwich Lacy Glass," *Antiques*, 24, no. 2, August 1933,
p. 59, Fig. 9; *Lee, Sandwich
Glass*, pl. 87, bottom left; *Rose*,
no. 193.

296 Bowl
Probably Midwest
ca. 1835-1850
H. 2.5 cm; D. 13.5 cm

68.4.152

Light, cloudy blue glass; circular; with circles and medallions around sides; pairs of scrolls in base.
Ex coll: Louise S. Esterly

297 Plate
Probably Midwest
ca. 1835-1845
D. 13.1 cm

68.4.533

Colorless lead glass with an edge of scallops and points; circled rosettes in rim and a sunburst in center.
Ex coll: Louise S. Esterly
Comments: This is similar to two cup plate designs, *Lee and Rose*, nos. 204 and 205, but it is not exactly like either.
Parallels: Lee and Rose, nos. 204, 205.

298 Plate
Midwest
ca. 1835-1845
D. 15.2 cm

59.4.81

*299 Another
D. 17.5 cm

68.4.416

Colorless lead glass; circular shape with bull's-eye rim; sides with bands of S-scrolls; base with overlapping scales; star in center.
Gift of Louise S. Esterly

Colorless.
Ex coll: Louise S. Esterly

300 Tray
New England
ca. 1830-1845
L. 30 cm; W. 20 cm

68.4.406

Colorless lead glass; open chain rim and open handle at each end; fan and scroll design in center.
Ex coll: Louise S. Esterly
Comments: Extremely rare. This is one of the more difficult pieces to press due to the open handles and chain. Fragments of this pattern were found at the Sandwich factory site.
Parallels: Green, Charles W. "A Most Important Discovery at Sandwich," *Antiques*, 32, no. 2, Aug. 1937, p. 59, Fig. 4; Keefe, John W. "American Lacy and Pressed Glass in The Toledo Museum of Art," *Antiques*, 100, no. 1, July 1971, pp. 106-107; *Lee, Sandwich Glass*, pl. 163; *McKearin, American Glass*, pl. 154; *Rose*, no. 142, pl. XXVI.

301 Plate
New England
ca. 1830-1840
D. 15.5 cm

68.4.190

Soft cloudy blue glass; 12-sided
with 12 scallop shells forming
rim; stippled center with
lunettes and princess feather
medallions.
Ex coll: Louise S. Esterly
Comments: Unique in this color.
Fragments of this pattern in
colorless glass have been found
at the Sandwich factory site.
Published: Rose, no. 86.
Parallels: Ayers, Rose, "6-Inch
Tea Plates," *Antiques*, 20, no. 1,
July 1931, pp. 34, 35, Fig. 3d;
Keyes, H.E., "Museum Examples of Sandwich Glass," *Antiques*, 34, no. 1, July 1938, p.
22, Fig. 76; *Sandwich Glass*, pl.
87 upper right, and pl. 112,
lower right; *McKearin, American
Glass*, pl. 158, no. 2; *Rose*, nos.
129, 250.

*302 Another

63.4.67

Colorless.
Gift of Louise S. Esterly

303 Compote
New England
ca. 1830-1840
D. 15.5 cm; H. 8.8 cm

68.4.430

Colorless lead glass; top
pressed in the shell pattern as
pieces above, attached by a
wafer to a pressed hollow base.
Ex coll: Louise S. Esterly
Comments: See above.

304 **Whale oil lamp**
New England
ca. 1830-1835
H. 16.5 cm; D. (base) 7 cm

68.4.539

Colorless lead glass with inverted pear-shaped blown font
with surface ground; attached
by a wafer to pressed square
base with shell decoration.
Ex coll: Louise S. Esterly
Published: Wilson, Fig. 210,
p. 250.

305 **Tray**
New England
ca. 1830-1840
L. 24 cm; W. 19 cm

68.4.500

Colorless lead glass; shell
shape; open handle with rayed
pattern radiating from handle to
opposite edges.
Ex coll: Louise S. Esterly
Comments: Extremely rare.
Parallels: Lee, Sandwich Glass,
pl. 166, lower right; *Rose*, no.
80, pl. VIII.

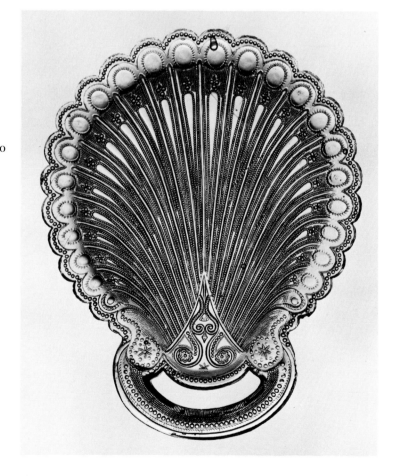

306 Plate
Midwest
ca. 1830-1845
D. 16.5 cm

68.4.524

Colorless lead glass; octagonal with bull's-eye rim, center with sailing ship; inscribed below "UNION."
Ex coll: Louise S. Esterly
Comments: This sailing ship may represent the *Constitution*. See no. 212.
Published: Innes, Pittsburgh Glass, Fig. 293.
Parallels: Keyes, H.E. "Sandwich Lacy Glass," *Antiques*, 24, no. 2, Aug. 1933, p. 58, Fig. 4; *Lee, Sandwich Glass*, pl. 170, right; *Rose*, no. 362.

307 Plate
Midwest
ca. 1830-1845
D. 15.4 cm

68.4.526

Colorless lead glass; octagonal with bull's-eye rim; center with paddle-wheel steamer.
Ex coll: Louise S. Esterly
Parallels: Innes, Pittsburgh Glass, Fig. 271; *Lee, Sandwich Glass*, pl. 170, left; *McKearin, American Glass*, pl. 143, no. 1; *Rose*, no. 363.

308 Bowl
New England
ca. 1830-1835
H. 3.8 cm; L. 15.8 cm

68.4.446

Colorless lead glass; oval with medallions in sides alternately showing sailing ship and an eagle.
Ex coll: Louise S. Esterly
Comments: The ship probably represents the U.S.F. *Constitution*, one of the United States' earliest naval vessels. There was a public outcry over a proposal to scrap the *Constitution* around 1830. See no. 168 above which has an identical center.
Parallels: Lee, Sandwich Glass, pl. 97, upper; *McKearin, American Glass*, pl. 128; *Rose*, no. 203.

309 Tray
New England
ca. 1830-1835
H. 2.6 cm; L. 17.8 cm

68.4.142

Colorless lead glass; rectangular with rim having a row of hearts and center a sailing ship with "U.S.F. CONSTITUTION" above.
Ex coll: Louise S. Esterly
Comments: At least one fragment of this tray was found at the Sandwich factory site and is in The Corning Museum of Glass collection. See note on preceding entry. The trays, nos. 158, 159 above, have identical rims.
Parallels: Lee, Sandwich Glass, pl. 167; *Rose,* no. 127.

310 Bowl
Possibly New England Glass Company, East Cambridge, Massachusetts
ca. 1840
H. 3 cm; D. 15.9 cm

59.4.88

Colorless lead glass; two oval vignettes in sides; a man plowing alternating with one oval with a ship and one with a glass factory; log cabin and cider barrel in center.
Gift of Louise S. Esterly
Comments: This bowl is fairly common and occurs in several sizes. Its origin is unknown, but the glass factory pictured on the bowl seems to be that of the New England Glass Company.
Parallels: Keefe, John W. "American Lacy and Pressed Glass in The Toledo Museum of Art", *Antiques,* 100, no. 1, July 1971, p. 104, Fig. 1; *Lee, Sandwich Glass,* pl. 89; *McKearin, American Glass,* pl. 141; *Rose,* no. 116; *Innes, Pittsburgh Glass,* Fig. 281.

311 Pane
Wheeling, West Virginia, glasshouse of John and Craig Ritchie
ca. 1831-1834
L. 17.8 cm; W. 12.8 cm

56.4.1

Colorless glass; rectangular with
a sidewheel steamer in center
below "J. & C. RITCHIE"; urns
and thistles on each side.
Comments: This pane is one of
eight found in a secretary in
1955. The Oglebay Mansion
Museum in Wheeling has
another one of the original
eight.
Published: Rose, James H.
"Wheeling Lacy Glass," *Antiques*, 69, no. 6, June 1956, p.
526.
Parallels: Innes, Pittsburgh Glass,
Fig. 306.

312 Bowl
Possibly Providence, Rhode
Island, Providence Flint Glass
Works
ca. 1830-1835
H. 3.8 cm; D. 20 cm

61.4.98

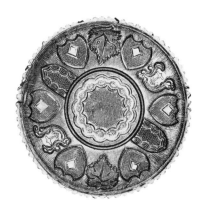

Colorless lead glass; scalloped
edge; fine ribbing around sides;
anchors and shields alternating
around sides; wreath in center.
Gift of Louise S. Esterly
Comments: The possible attribution to the Providence factory
is based on the resemblance
of this design to the seal of the
state of Rhode Island.
Parallels: Lee, Sandwich Glass,
pl. 94, lower right; *McKearin,
American Glass*, pl. 141; *Rose*,
no. 169.

313 **Bowl**
New England
ca. 1830-1845
H. 3.8 cm; D. 16.1 cm

59.4.65

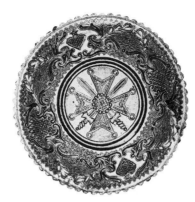

Pale, greenish glass; pressed in
a pattern of crossed swords.
Gift of Louise S. Esterly
Comments: Fragments of this
pattern were found at the
Sandwich factory site.
Parallels: Lee, Sandwich Glass,
pls. 85, 87; *McKearin, American
Glass,* pl. 158, no. 3, 158, no. 4,
158, no. 5; *Rose,* nos. 135, 139,
235.

*314 **Another**
D. 11.4 cm

68.4.335

Amethyst.
Ex colls: Louise S. Esterly;
Dr. and Mrs. Charles W. Green

*315 **Another**
D. 11 cm

68.4.336

Cobalt blue.
Ex colls: Louise S. Esterly;
Dr. and Mrs. Charles W. Green

*316 **Another**
D. 11.3 cm

68.4.338

Blue.
Ex colls: Louise S. Esterly;
Dr. and Mrs. Charles W. Green

*317 **Another**
D. 11.3 cm

68.4.339

Greenish-blue.
Ex coll: Louise S. Esterly

*318 **Another**
D. 11.2 cm

68.4.340

Blue.
Ex coll: Louise S. Esterly

*319 **Another**
D. 16.2 cm

68.4.435

Colorless.
Ex coll: Louise S. Esterly

320 Bowl
New England
ca. 1830-1845
H. 5 cm; D. 23.8 cm

59.4.60

Colorless lead glass; circular shape; egg and dart edge; cluster of acanthus leaves and tulips around sides; eight tulip blossoms radiating from center.
Gift of Louise S. Esterly
Comments: Fragments of this pattern were found at the Sandwich factory site.
Parallels: Lee, Sandwich Glass, pl. 131, lower; *McKearin, American Glass,* pl. 156, no. 3; *Rose,* no. 90, 140, 146, 188

*321 Another
D. 14 cm

59.4.86

Blue.
Gift of Louise S. Esterly

*322 Another
D. 19 cm

63.4.63

Colorless.
Gift of Louise S. Esterly

*323 Another
D. 18.9 cm

68.4.460

Blue.
Ex colls: Louise S. Esterly;
Dr. and Mrs. Charles W. Green

*324 Another
D. 15.9 cm

68.4.480

Blue.
Ex coll: Louise S. Esterly

325 Bowl
New England, or possibly Midwest
ca. 1830-1845
H. 5.1 cm; D. 27 cm

68.4.108

Colorless glass; rim of bull's-eyes and points; leaves and tulips in sides; eight tulips radiating from center.
Ex colls: Louise S. Esterly; Dr. and Mrs. Charles W. Green
Comments: As the bull's-eye rim is characteristic of midwestern glass, this may be a western version of the standard eastern pattern.
Parallels: Lee, Sandwich Glass, pl. 131, top.

326 Compote
New England
ca. 1830-1845
H. 12.3 cm: D.(rim) 22 cm

68.4.476

Colorless lead glass; circular bowl with egg and dart rim and standard tulip pattern; base pressed separately in the plume pattern and joined with a wafer. *Ex coll:* Louise S. Esterly *Comments:* Extremely rare as a compote although the tulip bowls by themselves are relatively common; see above. *Parallels: Lee, Sandwich Glass*, pl. 139, lower; *McKearin, American Glass*, pl. 162, no. 6.

327 Covered butter dish
New England
ca. 1830-1845
H.(with cover) 10.5 cm; D. 19 cm

68.4.444 a, b

Colorless lead glass; scalloped rim; base with tulip and leaves on sides; tulips radiating from center; dome-shaped cover with acorn knob; acanthus leaves and tulips around sides. *Ex coll:* Louise S. Esterly *Parallels: Lee, Sandwich Glass*, pl. 131; *McKearin, American Glass*, pl. 156, no. 3.

328 Bowl
New England, or possibly Midwest
ca. 1830-1845
H. 3.1 cm; D. 16 cm

58.4.71

Colorless lead glass; grape clusters and leaves around sides; tulip blossoms radiating from center.
Gift of Louise S. Esterly *Comments:* Only two of these are known. *Parallels: Rose*, no. 247; Rose, James H. "Unrecorded Rarities in American Glass," *Antiques*, 71, no. 2, Feb. 1957, p. 162.

329 Bowl
New England
ca. 1830-1845
H. 2 cm; D. 13.4 cm

63.4.75

*330 Another

58.4.64

Canary glass; leaves and blossoms around sides; tulips radiating from center.
Gift of Louise S. Esterly *Comments:* This is a variation of the standard tulip pattern.

Colorless.
Gift of Louise S. Esterly

†331 **Bowl**
Eastern United States
ca. 1830-1840
H. 3.6 cm; D. 24.3 cm

68.4.110

Bluish-gray glass; zigzag pattern on flat rim; swirl pattern in sides; quatrefoil in center.
Ex colls: Louise S. Esterly; Dr. and Mrs. Charles W. Green
Comments: Fragments of this pattern were found at the Sandwich factory site. Unique in this color.
Published: Rose, no. 205.
Parallels: Green, Charles W. "Little-Known Sandwich," *Antiques,* 38, no. 2, Aug. 1940, p. 71, Fig. 7; *Lee, Sandwich Glass,* pls. 115, 116; *McKearin, American Glass,* pl. 149.

*332 **Another**
D. 29.1 cm

59.4.83

Colorless.
Gift of Louise S. Esterly

333 **Another**
D. 22.8 cm

68.4.525

Pinkish.
Ex colls: Louise S. Esterly; Mrs. John J. Grossman

334 **Bowl**
Eastern United States, probably Philadelphia area
ca. 1830-1840
H. 3.5 cm; D. 25 cm

68.4.428

Colorless lead glass; zigzag pattern on flat rim; swirl pattern on sides; cinquefoil on a waffled background in center.
Ex colls: Louise S. Esterly; Dr. and Mrs. Charles W. Green
Comments: Fragments of this pattern were found at the Sandwich factory site.
Parallels: Keyes, H.E. "Museum Examples of Sandwich Glass," *Antiques,* 34, no. 1, July 1938, pp. 20-22; *Lee, Sandwich Glass,* pl. 123; *Rose,* no. 458.

Cup Plates

Cup plates are a fascinating anomaly in glass. Apparently used only in the United States from about 1825 to 1860,[1] they were produced in a limited range of materials, primarily American-made glass, but also in transfer-printed earthenware made in the Staffordshire potteries in England for export to the United States. Glass cup plates probably were among the first items to be produced by machine pressing. They were extremely popular and were made in a great variety of patterns. There are very few blown or mold-blown cup plates in existence, and there are none known in cut glass. Cup plates, used to hold the cup when a tea drinker drank his tea from his saucer, may have been used during a limited time, but Ruth Webb Lee and James Rose in 1948 identified more than 700 different cup plate molds which had been in use in the 19th century.[2] Unfortunately, no contemporary illustration of a cup plate in use has ever been found, although instructions for setting the table and using the plates are included in several etiquette books of the period.[3]

Designs in cup plates are even more varied than those in larger lacy pressed tablewares. Because they were so inexpensive, it must have been easy for the manufacturer to introduce different designs as soon as the public tired of one. Cup plates had disappeared from the scene almost entirely by 1860, however, and generally are not found in later pattern glass.

The Items in this section are arranged according to the classification system set forth in Ruth Webb Lee and James H. Rose's *American Glass Cup Plates of the Lacy Period*, 1948.

1. Shadel, Jane S. "Documented Use of Cup Plates in the Nineteenth Century," *Journal of Glass Studies* 13, 1971, pp. 128-133.
2. *Lee and Rose, Cup Plates*.
3. Beecher, Catherine. *Domestic Receipt Book*, New York, 1846, p. 246.

335 **Cup plate**
New England or possibly
Philadelphia
ca. 1830
D. 9.5 cm

60.4.694

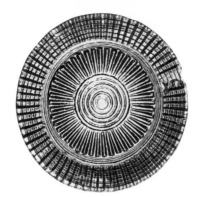

Colorless lead glass; very thick
with a waffled pattern.
Gift of Louise S. Esterly
Parallels: Lee and Rose, p. 70,
no. 13 Ex.

336 **Cup plate**
New England
ca. 1830
D. 8.4 cm

60.4.767

Colorless lead glass.
Gift of Louise S. Esterly
Comments: Fragments of this
pattern have been found at
Sandwich.
Parallels: Lee and Rose, p. 70,
no. 20.

337 **Cup plate**
Massachusetts, Boston &
Sandwich Glass Company,
Sandwich, or New England
Glass Company, Cambridge
ca. 1830
D. 8.5 cm

60.4.695

Colorless lead glass.
Gift of Louise S. Esterly
Parallels: Lee and Rose, p. 73,
no. 22.

338 **Cup plate**
Massachusetts, Boston &
Sandwich Glass Company,
Sandwich, or New England
Glass Company, Cambridge
ca. 1830
D. 9.2 cm

60.4.732

Colorless lead glass.
Gift of Louise S. Esterly
Parallels: Lee and Rose, p. 75,
no. 29.

339 Cup plate
Massachusetts, Boston &
Sandwich Glass Company,
Sandwich, or New England
Glass Company, Cambridge
ca. 1830
D. 8 cm

60.4.730

Colorless lead glass.
Gift of Louise S. Esterly
Parallels: Lee and Rose, p. 76,
no. 32.

340 Cup plate
Massachusetts, Boston &
Sandwich Glass Company,
Sandwich, or New England
Glass Company, Cambridge
ca. 1830
D. 8.2 cm

71.4.5

Colorless lead glass.
Parallels: Lee and Rose, pl. 6,
no. 44.

341 Cup plate
Boston & Sandwich Glass
Company, Sandwich, Mas-
sachusetts
ca. 1830
D. 8.9 cm

60.4.757

Colorless lead glass.
Gift of Louise S. Esterly
Parallels: Lee and Rose, p. 79,
no. 45.

342 Cup plate
Probably New England
ca. 1830
D. 8.9 cm

68.4.42

Black-amethyst lead glass.
Ex colls: Albert C. Marble;
Louise S. Esterly
Comments: Extremely rare.
Parallels: Lee and Rose, p. 79,
no. 46; *Rose*, no. 529.

343 Cup plate
Probably New England
ca. 1830-1845
D. 9.4 cm

60.4.722

Colorless lead glass.
Gift of Louise S. Esterly
Comments: Fragments of this
pattern have been found at the
Sandwich factory site.
Parallels: Lee and Rose p. 80,
no. 48.

344 Cup plate
Eastern United States
ca. 1830
D. 8.8 cm

60.4.697

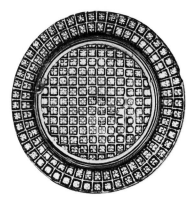

Colorless lead glass.
Gift of Louise S. Esterly
Parallels: Lee and Rose, p. 82,
no. 57.

345 Cup plate
Probably New England
ca. 1830
D. 8.8 cm

60.4.755

Colorless lead glass.
Gift of Louise S. Esterly
Parallels: Lee and Rose, p. 83,
no. 62A.

346 Cup plate
Probably Eastern United States
ca. 1830
D. 8.3 cm

60.4.756

Colorless lead glass.
Gift of Louise S. Esterly
Parallels: Lee and Rose, p. 84,
no. 65.

347   Cup plate
New England
ca. 1830
D. 8 cm

60.4.766

Colorless lead glass.
Gift of Louise S. Esterly
Parallels: Lee and Rose, p. 84,
no. 66.

348   Cup plate
Midwest, probably Benjamin
Bakewell, Pittsburgh
ca. 1830
D. 8.7 cm

71.4.6

Colorless lead glass.
Comments: The design of this
very thick plate is related to
that on Bakewell's patent knob.
See catalog no. 35.
Parallels: Lee and Rose, p. 85,
no. 70.

349   Cup plate
New England, possibly New
England Glass Company,
Cambridge, Massachusetts
ca. 1835-1850
D. 9.5 cm

55.4.10

Colorless lead glass.
Parallels: Lee and Rose, p. 94,
no. 78.
Gift of James M. Brown III

†350   Cup plate
New England, probably Boston
& Sandwich Glass Company,
Sandwich, or New England
Glass Company, Cambridge,
Massachusetts
ca. 1828-1830
D. 10 cm

68.4.41

Opaque light blue glass.
Ex coll: Louise S. Esterly
Comments: Only two or three
specimens of this plate are
known. At least one fragment
was found on the Sandwich factory site. See no. 442.
Parallels: Lee and Rose, p. 95,
no. 83; *Rose*, no. 542;
McKearin, American Glass,
p.178, no. 80.

351 **Cup plate**
Massachusetts, probably New
England Glass Company,
Cambridge, or Boston &
Sandwich Glass Company,
Sandwich
ca. 1830-1840
D. 9.4 cm

60.4.728

Fiery opalescent glass.
Gift of Louise S. Esterly
Parallels: Lee and Rose, p. 97,
no. 89.

352 **Cup plate**
Massachusetts, Boston &
Sandwich Glass Company,
Sandwich, or New England
Glass Company, Cambridge
ca. 1830-1840
D. 9.5 cm

60.4.770

Opalescent.
Gift of Louise S. Esterly
Parallels: Lee and Rose, p. 97,
no. 90.

353 **Cup plate**
New England, possibly New
England Glass Company,
Cambridge
ca. 1835-1845
D. 8.9 cm

65.4.65

Colorless lead glass.
Gift of Mrs. Leon S. Bard
Parallels: Lee and Rose, p. 98,
no. 95.

354 **Cup plate**
Eastern United States, possibly
Philadelphia
ca. 1830
D. 9.25 cm

50.4.229

Colorless lead glass.
Ex coll: George S. McKearin
Parallels: Lee and Rose, p. 99,
no. 97.

355 Cup plate
Probably Philadelphia
ca. 1830
D. 9 cm

60.4.735

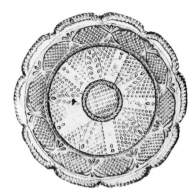

Colorless lead glass.
Gift of Louise S. Esterly
Parallels: Lee and Rose, p. 99,
no. 98.

†356 Cup plate
Probably Philadelphia, possibly
Union Glass Works
ca. 1830-1840
D. 8.1 cm

68.4.49

Deep amethyst lead glass.
Ex coll: Louise S. Esterly
Comments: Extremely rare.
Parallels: Lee and Rose, p. 99,
no. 99; *Rose*, no. 548.

357 Cup plate
Probably Philadelphia, possibly
Union Glass Works
ca. 1830-1840
D. 8.3 cm

60.4.706

Colorless lead glass.
Gift of Louise S. Esterly
Parallels: Lee and Rose, p. 100,
no. 100A.

358 Cup plate
Philadelphia area
ca. 1830-1840
D. 8.2 cm

60.4.771

Colorless lead glass.
Gift of Louise S. Esterly
Parallels: Lee and Rose, p. 100,
no. 101.

359 Cup plate
Philadelphia area
ca. 1830-1845
D. 8.8 cm

60.4.707

Colorless lead glass.
Gift of Louise S. Esterly
Parallels: Lee and Rose, p. 101,
no. 105.

360 Cup plate
Philadelphia area
ca. 1830-1845
D. 8.5 cm

60.4.709

Colorless lead glass.
Gift of Louise S. Esterly
Parallels: Lee and Rose, p. 107,
no. 107.

361 Cup plate
Eastern United States
ca. 1830-1840
D. 9.8 cm

65.4.70

Colorless lead glass.
Gift of Mrs. Leon S. Bard
Parallels: Lee and Rose, p. 103,
no. 109.

362 Cup plate
Midwest, probably Pittsburgh
ca. 1835-1850
D. 7.8 cm

65.4.72

Colorless lead glass.
Gift of Mrs. Leon S. Bard
Comments: This plate is unique
as far as is known.
Published: Rose, p. 142, no. 691,
pl. XXIV; Bilane, John E.
(comp.), *Cup Plate Discoveries
since 1948*; the Cup Plate Notes
of James H. Rose, New York ?
ca. 1971, p. 8.
Parallels: Lee and Rose, nos. 126
and 126A. This plate is 126B.

363 **Cup plate**
Midwest
ca. 1830-1845
D. 9.1 cm

60.4.754

Colorless lead glass.
Gift of Louise S. Esterly
Parallels: Lee and Rose, p. 112,
no. 127A.

364 **Cup plate**
Midwest, probably Pittsburgh
area
ca. 1830-1845
D. 7.6 cm

60.4.720

Colorless lead glass.
Gift of Louise S. Esterly
Parallels: Lee and Rose, p. 117,
no. 129.

365 **Cup plate**
Midwest, probably Pittsburgh
ca. 1830-1845
D. 8.6 cm

60.4.696

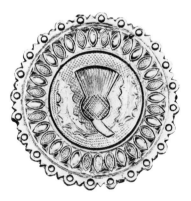

Colorless lead glass.
Gift of Louise S. Esterly
Parallels: Lee and Rose, p. 120,
no. 133.

†366 **Cup plate**
Midwest, probably Pittsburgh
area
ca. 1830-1845
D. 8.5 cm

68.4.45

Bright blue lead glass.
Ex coll: Louise S. Esterly
Parallels: Lee and Rose, p. 121,
no. 135A.

367 Cup plate
Midwest
ca. 1830-1845
D. 7 cm

50.4.230

Colorless lead glass.
Ex coll: George S. McKearin
Parallels: Lee and Rose, p. 124,
no. 145C.

368 Cup plate
Eastern United States
ca. 1835-1850
D. 6.8 cm

69.4.7

Colorless lead glass.
Gift of Mr. and Mrs. Harry A.
Snyder
Parallels: Lee and Rose, p. 124,
no. 146.

369 Cup plate
Midwest
ca. 1830-1845
D. 7 cm

60.4.742

Colorless lead glass.
Gift of Louise S. Esterly
Parallels: Lee and Rose, p. 125,
no. 147C.

370 Cup plate
Midwest
ca. 1830-1850
D. 7.6 cm

60.4.721

Colorless lead glass.
Gift of Louise S. Esterly
Parallels: Lee and Rose, p. 126,
no. 149.

371 Cup plate
Midwest
ca. 1830-1845
D. 9 cm

68.4.38

Colorless lead glass.
Ex coll: Louise S. Esterly
Parallels: Lee and Rose, p. 139,
no. 157.

372 Cup plate
Midwest
ca. 1835-1845
D. 7.4 cm

60.4.736

Colorless lead glass.
Gift of Louise S. Esterly
Parallels: Lee and Rose, p. 140,
no. 159B.

373 Cup plate
Midwest
ca. 1830-1845
D. 8.3 cm

60.4.741

Colorless lead glass.
Gift of Louise S. Esterly
Parallels: Lee and Rose, p. 141,
no. 160A.

374 Cup plate
Midwest
ca. 1830-1845
D. 8.7 cm

50.4.228

Colorless lead glass.
Ex coll: George S. McKearin
Parallels: Lee and Rose, p. 143,
no. 165.

375 Cup plate
Midwest
ca. 1830-1845
D. 8.2 cm

60.4.719

Colorless non-lead glass.
Gift of Louise S. Esterly
Parallels: Lee and Rose, p. 147,
no. 178B.

†376 Cup plate
Midwest
ca. 1830-1845
D. 9.5 cm

68.4.43

Deep blue lead glass.
Ex coll: Louise S. Esterly
Comments: Extremely rare in this
color.
Parallels: Lee and Rose, no. 183B;
Rose, no. 563; *McKearin, American Glass*, pl. 175, no. 6.

377 Cup plate
Midwest, probably Pittsburgh
ca. 1835-1850
D. 8.6 cm

60.4.762

Colorless lead glass.
Gift of Louise S. Esterly
Parallels: Lee and Rose, p. 165,
no. 203.

378 Cup plate
Midwest
ca. 1830-1845
D. 8.9 cm

60.4.760

Colorless lead glass.
Gift of Louise S. Esterly
Parallels: Lee and Rose, p. 166,
no. 206.

379 Cup plate
Midwest
ca. 1830-1845
D. 7.6 cm

60.4.744

Colorless lead glass.
Gift of Louise S. Esterly
Parallels: Lee and Rose, pp. 166-167, no. 208.

380 Cup plate
Midwest
ca. 1830-1845
D. 7.6 cm

60.4.745

Colorless lead glass.
Gift of Louise S. Esterly
Parallels: Lee and Rose, p. 167, no. 209.

381 Cup plate
R. B. Curling & Sons, Fort Pitt
Glass Works, Pittsburgh
ca. 1835-1845
D. 9.2 cm

71.4.7

Colorless lead glass.
Comments: Extremely rare.
Parallels: Lee and Rose, p. 167, no. 211.

382 Cup plate
Midwest
ca. 1830-1845
D. 9.2 cm

60.4.752

Colorless lead glass.
Gift of Louise S. Esterly
Parallels: Lee and Rose, p. 174, no. 216.

383 **Cup plate**
Philadelphia
ca. 1830-1845
D. 8.8 cm

60.4.704

Colorless lead glass.
Gift of Louise S. Esterly
Parallels: Lee and Rose, p. 178,
no. 226A.

384 **Cup plate**
Midwest
ca. 1830-1845
D. 7.8 cm

60.4.747

Colorless lead glass.
Gift of Louise S. Esterly
Parallels: Lee and Rose, p. 189,
no. 233A.

385 **Cup plate**
United States
ca. 1835-1850
D. 7.6 cm

60.4.759

Colorless lead glass.
Gift of Louise S. Esterly
Parallels: Lee and Rose, p. 189,
no. 235.

386 **Cup plate**
Eastern United States
ca. 1830-1840
D. 9 cm

60.4.753

Colorless lead glass.
Gift of Louise S. Esterly
Parallels: Lee and Rose, p. 191,
no. 243.

387 Cup plate
New England
ca. 1830-1845
D. 8.7 cm

60.4.750

Colorless lead glass.
Gift of Louise S. Esterly
Parallels: Lee and Rose, p. 193,
no. 245.

388 Cup plate
New England
ca. 1830-1845
D. 8.9 cm

60.4.749

Colorless lead glass.
Gift of Louise S. Esterly
Parallels: Lee and Rose, p. 193,
no. 246.

389 Cup plate
Probably Boston & Sandwich
Glass Company, Sandwich,
Massachusetts
ca. 1835-1850
D. 9.1 cm

67.4.54

Opalescent glass.
Gift of Mr. and Mrs. Harry A.
Snyder
Parallels: Lee and Rose, p. 195,
no. 255.

390 Cup plate
New England
ca. 1835-1850
D. 8.8 cm

60.4.751

Colorless lead glass.
Gift of Louise S. Esterly
Parallels: Lee and Rose, p. 204,
no. 267.

391 Cup plate
Massachusetts
ca. 1830-1845
D. 9 cm

60.4.729

Colorless lead glass.
Gift of Louise S. Esterly
Parallels: Lee and Rose, p. 206,
no. 271A.

392 Cup plate
Probably Boston & Sandwich
Glass Company, Sandwich,
Massachusetts
ca. 1830-1845
D. 8.8 cm

60.4.731

Colorless lead glass.
Gift of Louise S. Esterly
Parallels: Lee and Rose, p. 207,
no. 272.

393 Cup plate
Probably Boston & Sandwich
Glass Company, Sandwich,
Massachusetts
ca. 1835-1850
D. 8.9 cm

60.4.714

Colorless lead glass.
Gift of Louise S. Esterly
Parallels: Lee and Rose, p. 208,
no 275.

394 Cup plate
Eastern United States
ca. 1830-1845
D. 8.6 cm

60.4.733

Colorless lead glass.
Gift of Louise S. Esterly
Parallels: Lee and Rose, p. 208,
no. 278.

395 **Cup plate**
Midwest, probably Pittsburgh
ca. 1845-1855
D. 8.8 cm

75.4.37

Colorless lead glass.
Parallels: Lee and Rose, p. 223,
no. 315.

396 **Cup plate**
Massachusetts, probably Boston & Sandwich Company
ca. 1835-1850
D. 8.3 cm

60.4.725

*397 **Another**

60.4.761

*398 **Cup plate**
Eastern United States
ca. 1835-1850
D. 7.5 cm

65.4.73

Medium amethyst lead glass.
Gift of Louise S. Esterly
Parallels: Lee and Rose. p. 225,
no. 324.

Opalescent.
Gift of Louise S. Esterly

Colorless lead glass, similar
to 396.
Gift of Mrs. Leon S. Bard
Parallels: Lee and Rose, p. 226,
no. 326B.

399 **Cup plate**
Eastern United States, possibly
Boston & Sandwich Glass
Company, Sandwich,
Massachusetts
ca. 1840-1850

65.4.45

Colorless lead glass.
Gift of Mrs. Leon S. Bard
Parallels: Lee and Rose, p. 226,
no. 327.

400 **Cup plate**
Eastern United States
ca. 1840-1860
D. 8 cm

65.4.79

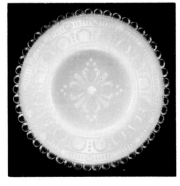

Opalescent lead glass.
Gift of Mrs. Leon S. Bard
Comments: Related to *Lee and
Rose*, nos. 327-330, but unrecorded.

401 Cup plate
United States
ca. 1835-1850
D. 8 cm

60.4.738

Colorless lead glass.
Gift of Louise S. Esterly
Parallels: Lee and Rose, p. 229,
no. 339.

402 Cup plate
Philadelphia area
ca. 1835-1850
D. 8.6. cm

60.4.726

Colorless lead glass.
Gift of Louise S. Esterly
Parallels: Lee and Rose, p. 231,
no. 343A.

403 Cup plate or honey dish
Eastern United States
ca. 1840-1850
D. 7.5 cm

60.4.740

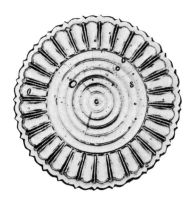

Colorless lead glass.
Gift of Louise S. Esterly
Parallels: Lee and Rose, p. 231,
no. 344.

404 Cup plate
United States
ca. 1835-1850
D. 7.7 cm

60.4.737

Colorless lead glass.
Gift of Louise S. Esterly
Parallels: Lee and Rose, p. 251,
no. 397.

405 Cup plate
New England, Boston &
Sandwich Glass Company or
New England Glass Company
ca. 1830-1835
D. 8.75

50.4.227

Colorless lead glass.
Ex coll: George S. McKearin
Parallels: Lee and Rose, p. 257,
no. 425.

406 Cup plate
Massachusetts
ca. 1830-1840
D. 8.5 cm

60.4.723

Colorless lead glass.
Gift of Louise S. Esterly
Parallels: Lee and Rose, p. 267,
no. 439.

407 Cup plate
New England, possibly Boston
& Sandwich Glass Company,
Sandwich, Massachusetts
ca. 1835-1845
D. 8.9 cm

60.4.724

Colorless lead glass.
Gift of Louise S. Esterly
Parallels: Lee and Rose, p. 267,
no. 439C.

408 Cup plate
New England
ca. 1835-1840
D. 9 cm

67.4.67

Greenish blue glass.
Gift of Mr. and Mrs. Harry A.
Snyder
Parallels: Lee and Rose, pl. 77,
no. 440.

409 Cup plate
Probably Boston & Sandwich
Glass Company, Sandwich,
Massachusetts
ca. 1835-1850
D. 8.8 cm

60.4.711

Medium blue glass.
Gift of Louise S. Esterly
Parallels: Lee and Rose. p. 268,
no. 440B.

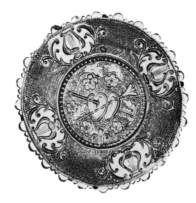

*410 Another

67.4.131.

Colorless.
Gift of Mr. and Mrs. Harry A.
Snyder

411 Cup plate
New England
ca. 1835-1845
D. 8.3 cm

60.4.768

Opalescent glass.
Gift of Louise S. Esterly
Parallels: Lee and Rose, p. 275,
no. 459B.

412 Cup plate
Probably Boston & Sandwich
Glass Company, Sandwich,
Massachusetts
ca. 1835-1850
D. 9 cm

50.4.226

Opalescent lead glass.
Ex coll: George S. McKearin
Parallels: Lee and Rose, p. 280,
no. 465J.

*413 Another

67.4.66.

Colorless.
Gift of Mr. and Mrs. Harry A.
Snyder

414 Cup plate
Probably Boston & Sandwich
Glass Company, Sandwich,
Massachusetts
ca. 1835-1850
D. 8.8 cm

67.4.132

Colorless lead glass.
Gift of Mr. and Mrs. Harry A.
Snyder
Parallels: Lee and Rose, 465S,
p. 281.

415 Cup plate
New England
ca. 1840-1860
D. 8.8 cm

63.4.53

Colorless lead glass.
Gift of Mrs. Helen Wormser
Parallels: Similar to *Lee and Rose*
no. 467, but unrecorded in this
variant with 58 scallops.

416 Cup plate
Probably Boston & Sandwich
Glass Company, Sandwich,
Massachusetts
ca. 1835-1850
D. 8.7 cm

63.4.51

Colorless lead glass.
Gift of Mrs. Helen Wormser
Parallels: Similar to *Lee and
Rose*, p. 281, no. 468, but with
58 scallops.

417 Cup plate
Eastern United States
ca. 1835-1850
D. 8.3 cm

60.4.718

Colorless lead glass.
Gift of Louise S. Esterly
Parallels: Lee and Rose, p. 302,
no. 537.

418 Cup plate
New England
ca. 1840-1852
D. 9. 1 cm

60.4.715

Colorless lead glass.
Gift of Louise S. Esterly
Comments: The bust on this
plate probably represents
Henry Clay.
Parallels: Lee and Rose, p. 313,
no. 563.

*419 Cup plate
Probably Boston & Sandwich
Glass Company, Sandwich,
Massachusetts
ca. 1840-1852
D. 9.2 cm

60.4.717

Colorless lead glass with bust of
Henry Clay.
Gift of Louise S. Esterly

Comments: Similar to plate
below but has rim of one large
and two small scallops.
Parallels: Lee and Rose, p. 313,
no. 564.

420 Cup plate
New England
ca. 1840-1852
D. 8.9 cm

60.4.710

Medium blue glass.
Gift of Louise S. Esterly
Comments: Henry Clay was a national figure from the 1820's
until his death in 1852, but his
1844 presidential campaign was
particularly hard-fought and
this plate may date from that
period.
Parallels: Lee and Rose, p. 314,
no. 565B.

421 **Cup plate**
New England
ca. 1844
D. 9.3 cm

60.4.780

Colorless lead glass.
Gift of Louise S. Esterly
Comments: See Comments re
Clay above.
Parallels: Lee and Rose, p. 314,
no. 566A.

422 **Cup plate**
Massachusetts, Boston &
Sandwich Glass Company or
New England Glass Company,
or possibly England
ca. 1837-1838
D. 9 cm

60.4.708

Colorless lead glass.
Gift of Louise S. Esterly
Comments: This plate was prob-
ably produced to mark Queen
Victoria's coronation in 1837.
Parallels: Lee and Rose, p. 317,
no. 576.

423 **Cup plate**
Union Glass Works, Philadel-
phia, or possibly Excelsior Glass
Works, South Camden, New
Jersey
ca. 1847-1848
D. 8.5 cm

68.4.37

Colorless lead glass.
Ex coll: Louise S. Esterly
Comments: Major Samuel
Ringgold was fatally wounded at
the Battle of Palo Alto, May 8,
1846, during the Mexican War
and was buried in Baltimore
with great honors that December.
Parallels: Lee and Rose, p. 320,
no. 586B.

424 Cup plate
Midwest
ca. 1840
D. 8.4 cm

60.4.705

Colorless lead glass.
Gift of Louise S. Esterly
Comments: This is probably a
souvenir of W. H. Harrison's
1840 Presidential campaign.
Parallels: Lee and Rose, p. 322,
no. 593.

425 Cup plate
Probably Midwest
ca. 1840
D. 9.0 cm

60.4.778

Colorless lead glass.
Gift of Louise S. Esterly
Comments: This is a souvenir of
W. H. Harrison's 1840 Presiden-
tial campaign.
Parallels: Lee and Rose, p. 322,
no. 596.

426 Cup plate
Philadelphia, possibly Union
Glass Works
ca. 1840
D. 8.5 cm

68.4.35

Colorless lead glass.
Ex coll: Louise S. Esterly
Comments: This is a souvenir of
W. H. Harrison's 1840 Presiden-
tial campaign.
Parallels: Lee and Rose, p. 326,
no. 601C; *McKearin, American
Glass*, p. 373, pl. 171.

427 Cup plate
Midwest
ca. 1835-1845
D. 8.8 cm

71.4.8

Colorless lead glass.
Comments: The ship is said to represent the U.S.F. *Constitution*.
Parallels: Lee and Rose, p. 328, no. 605.

428 Cup plate
Midwest, probably Pittsburgh
ca. 1835-1845
D. 9.0 cm

50.4.224

Colorless lead glass.
Ex coll: George S. McKearin
Parallels: Lee and Rose, p. 333, no. 605A.

429 Cup plate
New England
ca. 1840-1850
D. 9.0 cm

60.4.769

Colorless lead glass.
Gift of Louise S. Esterly
Parallels: Lee and Rose, p. 335, no. 610C.

430 Cup plate
Midwest, probably Pittsburgh
ca. 1830-1845
D. 8.9 cm

60.4.775

Colorless lead glass.
Gift of Louise S. Esterly
Parallels: Lee and Rose, p. 336, no. 612A.

431 Cup plate
Union Glass Works of Parke,
Campbell & Hanna, Pittsburgh
ca. 1836
D. 9.2 cm

68.4.36

Colorless lead glass.
Ex coll: Louise S. Esterly
Comments: Few of these plates
are known.
Parallels: Lee and Rose, p. 336,
no. 614; *Rose*, no. 665;
McKearin, American Glass, pl.
172.

---

432 Cup plate
Probably Midwest
ca. 1835-1850
D. 8.7 cm

69.4.6

Colorless lead glass.
Gift of Mr. and Mrs. Harry A.
Snyder
Parallels: Lee and Rose, p. 337,
no. 615A.

---

†433 Cup plate
Probably Boston & Sandwich
Glass Company, Sandwich,
Massachusetts
ca. 1829-1840
D. 8.8 cm

68.4.44

Violet-blue glass.
Ex coll: Louise S. Esterly
Comments: The ship on this plate
probably was copied from the
lithograph of the *Benjamin
Franklin* published by Senesel-
der Lithographic Co., Boston,
after the much-publicized visit
of the ship to Boston in 1828.
Parallels: Lee and Rose, p. 337,
no. 619; McKearin, Helen S.
"The *Benjamin Franklin* in
Glass and Print," *Antiques*, 54,
no. 1, July 1948, pp. 46-47.

*434 Another

50.4.223

Colorless.
Ex coll: George S. McKearin

*435 Cup plate
Probably Boston & Sandwich
Glass Company, Sandwich,
Massachusetts
ca. 1835
D. 8.9 cm

60.4.739

Colorless lead glass. Same design on plate below except rim
of 63 scallops.
Gift of Louise S. Esterly
Comments: The *Chancellor
Livingston* operated between

New York City and Providence,
R.I., and was decommissioned
in 1834. Fragments of this pattern have been found on the site
of the Sandwich factory.
Parallels: Lee and Rose, p. 340,
no. 631.

436 Cup plate
New England
ca. 1835
D. 8.8 cm

60.4.777

Colorless lead glass.
Gift of Louise S. Esterly
Comments: See preceding entry.
Fragments of this pattern have
been found on the site of the
Sandwich factory.
Parallels: Lee and Rose, p. 340,
no. 632A.

437 Cup plate
Probably Midwest
ca. 1850
D. 8.7 cm

60.4.727

Colorless lead glass.
Gift of Louise S. Esterly
Comments: This bridge is probably the suspension bridge over
the Ohio River at Wheeling,
West Virginia, built in 1849, the
longest such bridge in existence
at that time.
Parallels: Lee and Rose, p. 342,
no. 635; Keyes, H. E. "Interpreting the Sandwich Fragments," *Antiques*, 34, no. 3,
Sept. 1938, p. 133.

438 Cup plate
New England, probably Boston
& Sandwich Glass Company,
Sandwich, Massachusetts
ca. 1841-1850
D. 9.3 cm

60.4.773

Colorless lead glass.
Gift of Louise S. Esterly
Comments: The Bunker Hill
Monument was started in 1825
and finished in 1843 after a sub-
scription drive by a ladies' group
to raise money. Fragments of
this plate have been found at
Sandwich.
Parallels: Lee and Rose, p. 344,
no. 640.

439 Cup plate
New England, probably Boston
& Sandwich Glass Company,
Sandwich, Massachusetts
ca. 1841-1850
D. 8.9 cm

60.4.774

Colorless lead glass.
Gift of Louise S. Esterly
Comments: See note on Bunker
Hill Monument above.
Parallels: Lee and Rose, p. 345,
no. 643.

†440 Cup plate
New England, probably Boston
& Sandwich Glass Company,
Sandwich, Massachusetts
ca. 1841-1850
D. 9.3 cm

68.4.40

*441 Another

60.4.776

Emerald green glass.
Ex coll: Louise S. Esterly
Comments: Fragments of this
plate were found at the site of
the Sandwich factory. See note
on Bunker Hill Monument
above.
Parallels: Lee and Rose, p. 346,
no. 645A.

Colorless.
Gift of Louise S. Esterly

†442 **Cup plate**
Probably Boston & Sandwich
Glass Company, Sandwich, or
New England Glass Company,
Cambridge, Massachusetts
ca. 1830
D. 9.2 cm

68.4.39

Bluish-white opalescent glass.
Ex coll: Louise S. Esterly
Comments: This is an extremely
rare plate. See catalog nos. 53,
54 and 350.
Parallels: Lee and Rose, p. 347,
no. 650; *McKearin, American
Glass*, pl. 174, no. 30.

443 **Cup plate**
Midwest, probably Pittsburgh
ca. 1830
D. 7.8 cm

60.4.698

Colorless lead glass.
Gift of Louise S. Esterly
Parallels: Lee and Rose, p. 357,
no. 655.

444 **Cup plate**
Midwest, probably Pittsburgh
ca. 1830
D. 7.8 cm

50.4.220

Colorless lead glass.
Ex Coll: George S. McKearin
Parallels: Lee and Rose, p. 357,
no. 656.

445 **Cup plate**
New England, probably Boston
& Sandwich Glass Company,
Sandwich, Massachusetts
ca. 1831-1832
D. 9.0 cm

50.4.221

Colorless lead glass.
Ex coll: George S. McKearin
Comments: Possibly produced to
commemorate the Maine/
Canada boundary treaty of 1832.
Parallels: Lee and Rose, p. 359,
no. 661.

446 Cup plate
Eastern United States
ca. 1835-1845
D. 8.6 cm

60.4.701

Colorless lead glass.
Gift of Louise S. Esterly
Parallels: Lee and Rose, p. 360,
no. 666.

447 Cup plate
Probably Midwest
ca. 1835-1850
D. 7.7 cm

60.4.748

Colorless lead glass.
Gift of Louise S. Esterly
Parallels: Lee and Rose, p. 361,
no. 667A.

†448 Cup plate
Probably Pittsburgh
ca. 1830-1845
D. 8.8 cm

68.4.47

Medium blue glass.
Ex coll: Louise S. Esterly; Albert C. Marble
Comments: The only known
example in this color.
Parallels: Lee and Rose, p. 362,
no. 670A; *Rose,* no. 610;
McKearin, American Glass, pl.
180, no. 2.

*449 Another

55.4.8

Colorless.
Ex coll: George S. McKearin

450 Cup plate
Midwestern
ca. 1830-1845
D. 7.7 cm

60.4.713

Colorless lead glass.
Gift of Louise S. Esterly
Parallels: Lee and Rose, p. 363,
no. 672.

†451 **Cup plate**
R.B. Curling & Sons, Fort Pitt
Glass Works, Pittsburgh
ca. 1830-1845
D. 9.3 cm

68.4.46

Deep blue glass.
Ex coll: Louise S. Esterly
Comments: Very rare in this color.
Parallels: Lee and Rose, p. 365,
no. 676 B; *McKearin, American
Glass,* pl. 180, no 3.

*452 **Another**

60.4.716

Colorless.
Gift of Louise Esterly

---

453 **Cup plate**
Midwest
ca. 1835-1850
D. 8.0 cm

65.4.77

Colorless lead glass.
Gift of Mrs. Leon S. Bard
Parallels: Lee and Rose, p. 365,
no. 677A.

*454 **Cup plate**
Midwest
ca. 1835-1850
D. 8.1 cm

60.4.700

Colorless lead glass.
Gift of Louise S. Esterly
Parallels: Lee and Rose, p. 367,
no. 678.

---

455 **Cup plate**
Eastern United States
ca. 1845-1855
D. 8.8 cm

60.4.703

Colorless lead glass.
Gift of Louise S. Esterly
Parallels: Lee and Rose, p. 367,
no. 679.

---

456 **Cup plate**
Probably Midwest
ca. 1845-1855
D. 7.8 cm

50.4.222

Slightly amethystine lead glass.
Ex coll: George S. McKearin
Parallels: Lee and Rose, p. 367,
no. 680.

*457 **Another**

60.4.746

Colorless.
Gift of Louise S. Esterly

†458 **Cup plate**
Midwest, probably Pittsburgh
ca. 1840-1850
D. 9.5 cm

68.4.48

*459 **Another**

60.4.702

Blue glass.
Ex coll: Louise S. Esterly
Parallels: Lee and Rose, p. 370,
no. 686.

Colorless.
Gift of Louise S. Esterly

460 **Cup plate**
Midwest
ca. 1830-1845
D. 8.3 cm

50.4.225

Colorless lead glass.
Ex coll: George S. McKearin
Parallels: Lee and Rose, p. 375,
no. 691.

461 **Cup plate**
Probably Midwest
ca. 1840-1860
D. 8.5 cm

65.4.66

Colorless lead glass.
Gift of Mrs. Leon S. Bard
Parallels: Lee and Rose, p. 376,
no. 693.

462 **Cup plate**
New England
ca. 1850-1870
D. 8.4 cm

63.4.52

Colorless lead glass.
Gift of Helen R. Wormser
Parallels: Lee and Rose, p. 377,
no. 697.

463 Toddy plate
Midwest
ca. 1835-1850
D. 10.9 cm

65.4.62

Colorless lead glass.
Gift of Mrs. Leon S. Bard
Parallels: Lee and Rose, p. 382,
no. 802.

464 Toddy plate
United States
ca. 1835-1850
D. 10.9 cm

65.4.64

Colorless lead glass.
Gift of Mrs. Leon S. Bard
Parallels: Lee and Rose, p. 382,
no. 804.

465 Toddy plate
Eastern United States
ca. 1835-1850
D. 11.1 cm

65.4.61

Colorless lead glass.
Gift of Mrs. Leon S. Bard
Parallels: Lee and Rose, p. 388,
no. 806.

466 Toddy plate
Probably New England
ca. 1830-1845
D. 11.9 cm

65.4.59

*467 Another

68.4.403

Deep blue glass.
Gift of Mrs. Leon S. Bard
Parallels: Lee and Rose, p. 388,
no. 807; *Lee, Sandwich Glass*,
pl.111.

Colorless.
Ex coll: Louise S. Esterly

468 **Toddy plate**
Eastern United States
ca. 1835-1850
D. 11.0 cm

65.4.60

*469 **Another**

68.4.332

Colorless lead glass.
Gift of Mrs. Leon S. Bard
Parallels: Lee and Rose, p. 388,
no 808; *Lee, Sandwich Glass*, pl.
111.

Blue.
Ex coll: Louise S. Esterly

470 **Toddy plate**
United States
ca. 1840-1850
D. 10.4 cm

65.4.80

Colorless lead glass.
Gift of Mrs. Leon S. Bard
Parallels: Lee and Rose, p. 388,
no. 812.

Miniatures

I t was long supposed that lacy glass miniatures were salesmen's samples produced in small sizes to make it easier for traveling drummers to carry them. Since the miniature pieces do not match any of the patterns in the larger sizes and since no evidence whatsoever exists to document this custom, we may be fairly certain that they are, in fact, children's toys produced to use with doll houses or simply with dolls. Many fragments of the miniatures have been found on the site of the Sandwich factory and undoubtedly a number of them were made there. However, a study of Midwestern and European glass catalogs shows that a number were made elsewhere.

†471 **Washstand set**
Probably Boston & Sandwich
Glass Company, Sandwich,
Massachusetts
ca. 1835-1850
H. (pitcher) 6.5 cm;
D. (base) 2.8 cm
H. (bowl) 2.5 cm; D. 8. 1 cm

68.4.286

Cobalt blue glass; stippled, with
floral motifs.
Ex coll: Louise S. Esterly
Published: Rose, no. 484.
Parellels: Lee, Sandwich Glass,
pl. 80, no. 1; *S.H.S.*, pp. 16-17.

†*472 **Another**

68.4.287

Orange.
Ex coll: Louise S. Esterly
Published: Rose, no. 482.

†*473 **Another**

68.4.288

Green.
Ex coll: Louise S. Esterly
Published: Rose, no. 481.

---

†474 **Washstand set**
Probably Boston & Sandwich
Glass Company, Sandwich,
Massachusetts
ca. 1835-1850
H. (pitcher) 6.2 cm;
D. (base) 2.8 cm
H. (bowl) 2.5 cm; D. 7.5 cm

68.4.285

Opalescent glass; stippled, with
floral motifs.
Ex coll: Louise S. Esterly
Comments: Both this set and the
following one were assembled
separately from different deal-
ers.
Parallels: Lee, Sandwich Glass,
pl. 80, no. 1; *Rose*, nos. 481-489;
S.H.S., pp. 16-17.

†*475 **Another**

68.4.573

Colorless.
Ex coll: Louise S. Esterly

---

476 **Washstand set**
New England
ca. 1840-1860
H. (pitcher) 5.3 cm;
D. (base) 2.5 cm
H. (bowl) 2.3 cm; D. 7.8 cm

67.4.40

Colorless lead glass; cylindrical
pitcher; ten vertical panels
around sides.
Gift of Mr. and Mrs. Harry A.
Snyder
Parallels: Lee, Sandwich Glass,
pl. 80, no. 3; *S.H.S.*, pp. 15-16.

*477 **Pitcher**

68.4.623

Colorless.
Ex coll: Louise S. Esterly

*478 **Another**

68.4.282

Turquoise glass.
Ex coll: Louise S. Esterly

479 **Washstand set**
New England
ca. 1840-1860
H. (pitcher) 6.5 cm;
D. (base) 3.1 cm
H. (bowl) 2.3 cm; D. 7.8 cm

68.4.284

Cobalt blue glass; balustroid
pitcher; vertical panels around
body of both.
Ex coll: Louise S. Esterly
Parallels: Lee, Sandwich Glass,
pl. 80, no.3; *Rose,* nos. 479,
480, 485; *S.H.S.,* pp. 15-16.

*480 **Another**

68.4.289

Cobalt blue.
Ex coll: Louise S. Esterly

*481 **Another**

68.4.290

Opalescent.
Ex coll: Louise S. Esterly

*482 **Another**

68.4.569

Colorless.
Ex coll: Louise S. Esterly

*483 **Bowl**

68.4.277

Light blue opaque glass.
Ex coll: Louise S. Esterly

*484 **Bowl**

68.4.283

Pale yellow glass.
Ex coll: Louise S. Esterly

*485 **Pitcher**

68.4.306

Turquoise glass.
Ex coll: Louise S. Esterly

†486 **Covered tureen and tray**
Probably Boston & Sandwich
Glass Company, Sandwich,
Massachusetts
ca. 1835-1850
Tureen: H. (with cover and tray)
5.8 cm; L. 7.8 cm
Tray: W. 4.9 cm; L. 6.8 cm

68.4.292

Light yellow glass; stippled,
fans and scrolls on sides and lid;
matching tray.
Ex coll: Louise S. Esterly
Comments: The Museum has
nine tureens in this pattern with
several different covers and
trays. Fragments of tureens,
trays, and covers have been
found at the site of the Boston
& Sandwich Glass Company's
works.
Parallels: Lee, Sandwich Glass,
pl. 80, no. 12; *S.H.S.* , pp.
16-17.

†*487 **Another**

68.4.295

Cobalt blue glass.
Ex coll: Louise S. Esterly

†488 **Covered tureen and tray**
Probably Boston & Sandwich
Glass Company, Sandwich,
Massachusetts
ca. 1835-1850
Tureen: H. (with cover and tray)
5.7 cm; L. 7.9 cm
Tray: W. 4.8 cm; L. 6.7 cm

68.4.572

Colorless lead glass; stippled,
fans and scrolls on sides and lid;
matching tray.
Ex coll: Louise S. Esterly
Parallels: Lee, Sandwich Glass,
pl. 80, no. 12; *S.H.S.* pp. 16-17.

†*489 **Another**

68.4.293

Opalescent glass.
Ex coll: Louise S. Esterly

†490 **Covered tureen and tray**
Probably Boston & Sandwich
Glass Company, Sandwich,
Massachusetts
ca. 1835-1850
Tureen: H. (with cover and tray)
5.7 cm; L. 7.9 cm
Tray: W. 4.8 cm; L. 6.7 cm

68.4.570

Colorless lead glass; stippled,
fans and scrolls on sides and lid;
matching tray.
Ex coll: Louise S. Esterly
Parallels: Lee, Sandwich Glass,
pl. 80, no. 12; *S.H.S.*, pp. 16-17.

*491 **Tureen and cover**

68.4.296

Opalescent.
Ex coll: Louise S. Esterly

†492 **Covered tureen and tray**
Probably Boston & Sandwich
Glass Company, Sandwich,
Massachusetts
ca. 1835-1850
Tureen: H. (with cover and tray)
5.8 cm; L. 7.9 cm
Tray: W. 4.9 cm; L. 6.8 cm

68.4.291

Peacock blue glass; stippled,
fans and scrolls on sides and lid;
paneled tray.
Ex coll: Louise S. Esterly
Parallels: Lee, Sandwich Glass,
pl. 80, no. 12; *S.H.S.*, pp. 16-17.

†493 **Covered tureen and tray**
Probably Boston & Sandwich
Glass Company, Sandwich,
Massachusetts
ca. 1835-1850
Tureen: H. (with cover and tray)
5.8 cm; L. 7.9 cm
Tray: W. 4.9 cm; L. 6.8 cm

68.4.294

Opaque light blue glass; stippled fans and scrolls on sides
and lid; paneled tray.
Ex coll: Louise S. Esterly
Parallels: Lee, Sandwich Glass,
pl. 80, no 12; *S.H.S.*, pp. 16-17.

†494 **Covered tureen and tray**
Probably Boston & Sandwich
Glass Company, Sandwich,
Massachusetts
ca. 1835-1850
Tureen: H. (with cover and tray)
7.0 cm; L. 11 cm
Tray: W. 6.9 cm; L. 9.1 cm

68.4.622

Colorless lead glass; stippled
fans and scrolls on sides and lid;
matching tray.
Ex coll: Louise S. Esterly
Parallels: Lee, Sandwich Glass,
pl. 80, no. 2.

*495 **Another**

66.4.121

Gift of Arthur A. Houghton, Jr.

*496 **Tureen and cover**

68.4.297

Opaque blue glass.
Ex coll: Louise S. Esterly

497 **Oval tray**
New England
ca. 1840-1860
L. 6.6 cm; W. 4.8 cm

68.4.566

Colorless lead glass; twenty
square panels around sides; star
in oval base.
Ex coll: Louise S. Esterly
Comments: Trays similar to this
are sometimes found with tureens.

†498 **Salt**
New England
ca. 1835-1850
L. 4.6 cm; H. 2.0 cm

68.4.324

Light yellow glass; stippled,
with scroll pattern on sides and
base.
Ex colls: Louise S. Esterly; Dr.
and Mrs. Charles W. Green
Published: Rose, no. 503
Parallels: Lee, Sandwich Glass,
pl. 81, no. 3; *Rose,* nos. 498,
499, 504; *S.H.S.,* pp. 15-16.

†*499 **Another**

68.4.323

Clambroth.
Ex colls: Louise S. Esterly;
Dr. and Mrs. Charles W. Green

†*500 **Another**

68.4.325

Opaque blue.
Ex colls. Louise S. Esterly;
Mrs. Harry S. High

†*501 **Another**

68.4.326

Opalescent.
Ex colls: Louise S. Esterly;
Mrs. Harry S. High

†*502 **Another**

68.4.559

Colorless.
Ex coll: Louise S. Esterly

*503 Salt

66.4.120

A variant with rope rim on base, opalescent.
Gift of Arthur A. Houghton, Jr.

---

504 Footed salt
Probably Midwest
ca. 1835-1850
L. 4.5 cm; H. 2.1 cm

68.4.564

Colorless lead glass; stippled with shells on sides.
Ex coll: Louise S. Esterly

---

505 Sad iron
New England or Midwest
ca. 1850-1870
H. 2.5 cm; L. 3.4 cm

68.4.270

Green glass with a streak of red; triangular body with square handle on top.
Ex coll: Louise S. Esterly.
Comments: In the past, sad irons have been attributed to Sandwich, but the 1860 and 1868 M'Kee and Brothers catalogs list them as "Toy Sad Irons" at $4.75 per gross.
Parallels: M'Kee & Brother, *Prices of Glassware Manufactured by M'Kee & Brother* Pittsburgh (1860), 13th plate; M'Kee & Brothers, *Prices of Glassware Manufactured by M'Kee & Brothers* (1868), pl. 29; *S.H.S.* pp. 15-16.

*506 Another

68.4.271

Green.
Ex coll: Louise S. Esterly

*507 Another

68.4.272

Amethyst.
Ex coll: Louise S. Esterly

*508 Another

68.4.273

Ex coll: Louise S. Esterly

*509 Another

68.4.274

Pale yellow.
Ex coll: Louise S. Esterly

*510 Another

68.4.275

Opalescent.
Ex coll: Louise S. Esterly

*511 Another

67.4.38

Colorless.
Gift of Mr. and Mrs. Harry A. Snyder

512 Pitcher
New England
ca. 1835-1850
H. 4.5 cm; D. (base) 3.2 cm

68.4.586

Colorless lead glass; stippled, with scrolls and tulip on body; ear-shaped handle; base edge serrated.
Ex coll: Louise S. Esterly
Comments: Fragments of similar pieces have been found at the site of the Sandwich factory.
Parallels: Lee, Sandwich Glass, pl. 80, no. 4; *Rose,* nos. 510, 513, 518; *S.H.S.,* pp. 16-17.

*513 Another

68.4.54

Opalescent.
Gift of Mr. and Mrs. Harry A. Snyder

*514 Another

68.4.309

Amethyst.
Ex coll: Louise S. Esterly

515 Pitcher
New England
ca. 1835-1850
H. 4.3 cm; D. (base) 3.1 cm

68.4.308

Opalescent glass; stippled, with scrolls and tulips on body; ear-shaped handle; plain base edge.
Ex coll: Louise S. Esterly
Parallels: Lee, Sandwich Glass, pl. 80, no. 4; *Rose,* nos. 510, 513, 518; *S.H.S.* pp. 16-17.

*516 Another

68.4.322

Cobalt blue.
Ex coll: Louise S. Esterly

*517 Another

68.4.586

Colorless.
Ex coll: Louise S. Esterly

*518 Another

69.4.61

Gift of Mr. and Mrs. Harry A. Snyder

519 Pitcher
Possibly Midwest
ca. 1835-1850
H. 3.9 cm; D. (base) 3.2 cm

68.4.307

Amethyst glass; coarse cloth-like stippling; scroll pattern on sides; serrated base edge.
Ex coll: Louise S. Esterly
Comments: This pitcher is similar to others in the collection in design but is much more crude. One in the Sandwich Museum is the only other known example.
Parallels: S.H.S., pp. 16-17, bottom row.

520 Spillholder or goblet
New England or Midwest
ca. 1840-1870
H. 6.3 cm; D. (rim) 4.4 cm

68.4.279

Greenish-yellow glass.
Ex coll: Louise S. Esterly

*521 Another

69.4.12

Gift of Mr. and Mrs. Harry A.
Snyder

*522 Another

68.4.280

Opalescent.
Ex coll: Louise S. Esterly

*523 Another

69.4.13

Colorless.
Gift of Mr. and Mrs. Harry A.
Snyder

*524 Another

69.4.133

Amber.
Gift of Mr. and Mrs. Harry A.
Snyder

525 Spillholder
New England or Midwest
ca. 1840-1870
H. 4.6 cm; D. (rim) 3.6 cm

68.4.316

Pale yellow glass.
Ex coll: Louise S. Esterly
Parallels: S.H.S., pp. 15-16.

*526 Another

68.4.317

Turquoise.
Ex coll: Louise S. Esterly

*527 Another

68.4.582

Colorless.
Ex coll: Louise S. Esterly

*528 Another

67.4.29

Cobalt blue.
Gift of Mr. and Mrs. Harry A.
Snyder

529 Spillholder
New England or Midwest
ca. 1840-1870
H. 6.0 cm; D. (rim) 3.7 cm

68.4.281

Cobalt blue glass.
Ex coll: Louise S. Esterly

530 Spillholder
Probably Midwest
ca. 1840-1870
H. 4.8 cm; D. (rim) 4.8 cm

67.4.88

Colorless non-lead glass; pontil mark beneath hexagonal foot. Gift of Mr. and Mrs. Harry A. Snyder

531 Candlestick
New England or Pittsburgh
ca. 1840-1870
H. 4.2 cm

68.4.265

Amethyst glass; hexagonal stem and base.
Ex coll: Louise S. Esterly
Parallels: Lee, Sandwich Glass, pl. 83, no. 1; *Rose*, nos. 497, 500, 502, 505-508; *S.H.S.*, pp. 15-16; M'Kee & Brother *Prices of Glassware Manufactured by M'Kee & Brother* Pittsburgh, 1860, 13th plate; M'Kee & Brothers, *Prices of Glassware Manufactured by M'Kee & Brothers*, April 1, 1868, pl. 29.

*532 Another

68.4.266

Opalescent.
Ex coll: Louise S. Esterly

*533 Another

68.4.267

Cobalt blue.
Ex coll: Louise S. Esterly

*534 Another

68.4.268

Grayish blue.
Ex coll: Louise S. Esterly

*535   **Another**   Turquoise.
        68.4.269   *Ex coll:* Louise S. Esterly

*536   **Another**   Colorless.
        68.4.613   *Ex coll:* Louise S. Esterly

537   **Candlestick**   Colorless non-lead glass;
        United States or possibly   hexagonal stem and domed foot.
        Europe   *Ex coll:* Louise S. Esterly
        ca. 1840-1870
        H. 6.6 cm

        68.4.611

538   **Pair of candlesticks**   Yellow-green glass;
        New England   hexagonal socket, stem and
        ca. 1840-1870   foot.
        H. 5.2 cm   Gift of Mr. and Mrs. Harry A.
                                       Snyder
        67.4.50 A, B

539   **Pair of chamber sticks**   Colorless lead glass; hexagonal
        New England   socket, stem and foot with small
        ca. 1840-1870   handle.
        H. 3 cm   Gift of Mr. and Mrs. Harry A.
                                       Snyder
        67.4.89 A,B

540 Cup and saucer
Probably Boston & Sandwich
Glass Company, Sandwich,
Massachusetts
ca. 1835-1855
Cup and saucer: H. 3.3 cm;
Cup: D. (rim) 3.2 cm;
Saucer: D. 4.9 cm

67.4.37

Colorless lead glass; stippled;
tulip design on cup; ear-shaped
handle; circular saucer with rose
vine around rim.
Gift of Mr. and Mrs. Harry A.
Snyder
Comments: A cup and a saucer
half in this pattern are part of
the Esterly collection of
Sandwich fragments in the
Corning Museum collection.
Numerous other fragments of
similar cups and saucers have
been found at the site of the
Sandwich factory.
Parallels: Lee, Sandwich Glass,
pl. 80, no. 8; *Rose,* nos. 511, 512;
S.H.S., pp. 15-16.

*541 Another

68.4.311

Opalescent.
Ex coll: Louise S. Esterly

*542 Another

68.4.313

Blue.
Ex coll: Louise S. Esterly

*543 Another

68.4.318

Clambroth.
Ex coll: Louise S. Esterly

---

544 Cup and saucer
Probably Boston & Sandwich
Glass Company, Sandwich,
Massachusetts
ca. 1835-1850
Cup and saucer; H. 3.0 cm
Cup: D. (rim) 3.1 cm; Saucer:
D. 4.5 cm

68.4.608

Colorless lead glass; stippled;
tulip design on cup; rosette
handle; circular saucer with rose
vine around rim.
Ex colls: Louise S. Esterly; Dr.
and Mrs. Charles W. Green
Comments: Cups with the rosette
handle are extremely rare.
Published: Rose, no. 516.
Parallels: Lee, Sandwich Glass,
pl. 80, no. 9.

---

545 Cup and saucer
Midwest
ca. 1835-1850
Cup and saucer: H. 3.0 cm
Cup: D. (rim) 3.4 cm; Saucer:
D. 5.7 cm

68.4.310

Cobalt blue glass; stippled;
three shell motifs around sides
of handleless cup and saucer.
Ex coll: Louise S. Esterly
Published: Rose, no. 496.
Parallels: Lee, Sandwich Glass,
pl. 80, no. 7; pl. 82, no. 6; *Rose,*
nos. 494, 496.

*546 Another

68.4.607

Colorless.
Ex coll: Louise S. Esterly

547 Cup and saucer
Saucer, Midwest; cup probably
Europe
ca. 1835-1850
Cup and saucer: H. 3.3 cm
D. (cup) 5.2 cm;
D. (saucer) 5.7 cm

68.4.580

Colorless lead glass; stippled;
acanthus leaves around cup;
shell ornaments around saucer.
Ex coll: Louise S. Esterly
Comments: Saucer is identical to
those above; cup is considerably
more elaborate than other miniatures.

548 Cup and saucer
New England
ca. 1840-1870
Cup and saucer: H. 2.9 cm
Cup: D. (rim) 3.2 cm;
Saucer: D. 4.8 cm

68.4.315

Turquoise glass; cup and saucer
both paneled around sides.
Ex coll: Louise S. Esterly
Parallels: S.H.S., pp. 15-16.

*549 Another

68.4.583

Colorless.
Ex coll: Louise S. Esterly

*550 Saucer

68.4.327

Green.
Ex coll: Louise S. Esterly

551 Cup and saucer
New England
ca. 1840-1870
Cup and saucer: H. 2.7 cm;
Cup: D. (rim) 3.6 cm;
Saucer: D. 4.5 cm

68.4.563 a, b

Colorless lead glass; panels
around sides of cup and saucer.
Ex coll: Louise S. Esterly

552 Plate
New England
ca. 1830-1835
D.5.1 cm

68.4.597

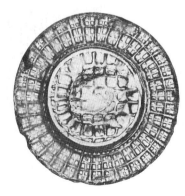

Colorless lead glass; unusually
thick; pontil mark on base.
Ex coll: Louise S. Esterly
Comments: This plate was dug
from the dump at the Sandwich
factory site by Francis Wynn.
This type is often used as a
small lamp base. See no. 787
Parallels: Lee, Sandwich Glass,
pl. 82, no. 5; *Rose,* no. 474.

553 Plate
Probably Midwest
ca. 1840-1860
D. 6.4 cm

68.4.621

Colorless lead glass.
Ex coll: Louise S. Esterly
Parallels: Lee, Sandwich Glass,
pl. 83, no. 3.

554 Plate
New England or Midwest
ca. 1840-1860
D. 5.1 cm

68.4.264

***555 Another**
68.4.604

Cobalt blue glass.
Ex coll: Louise S. Esterly
Parallels: Lee, Sandwich Glass,
pl. 82, no. 4.

Colorless.
Ex coll: Louise S. Esterly

556 Plate
New England or Midwest
ca. 1840-1860
D. 6.4 cm

65.4.76

Colorless lead glass.
Gift of Mrs. Leon S. Bard
Parallels: Lee, Sandwich Glass,
pl. 83, no. 4.

557 Plate
Probably Boston & Sandwich
Glass Company, Sandwich,
Massachusetts
ca. 1835-1850
D. 5.7 cm

67.4.47

***558 Another**
68.4.599

Colorless lead glass.
Gift of Mr. and Mrs. Harry A.
Snyder
Parallels: Lee, Sandwich Glass,
pl. 81, no. 7; *Rose,* nos. 472,
477.

This plate was excavated at the
site of the Sandwich factory.
Ex coll: Louise S. Esterly

*559 **Another**

68.4.257

Opalescent.
Ex coll: Louise S. Esterly

*560 **Another**

68.4.258

Amethyst.
Ex coll: Louise S. Esterly

---

561 **Plate**
Probably Boston & Sandwich
Glass Company, Sandwich,
Massachusetts
ca. 1835-1850
D. 5.7 cm

68.4.591

Colorless lead glass.
Ex coll: Louise S. Esterly
Parallels: Lee, Sandwich Glass,
pl. 81, no. 5.

---

562 **Plate**
New England or Midwest
ca. 1830-1850
D. 5.7 cm

68.4.263

*563 **Another**

68.4.589

Light green bubbly glass; ring of
table-rests on underside.
Ex coll: Louise S. Esterly
Comments: This variation, with
table-rests, has not been published before.

Colorless.
Ex coll: Louise S. Esterly

---

564 **Plate**
New England
ca. 1835-1850
D. 5.7 cm

68.4.260

*565 **Another**

68.4.592

Cobalt blue glass; beaded table
ring on base.
Ex coll: Louise S. Esterly
Comments: There are several variations of this pattern (see below).
Parallels: Lee, Sandwich Glass,
pl. 81, nos. 4, 5; pl. 83, no. 6;
Rose nos. 473, 476.

Colorless.
Ex coll: Louise S. Esterly

566 Plate
New England
ca. 1835-1850
D. 5.6 cm

68.4.259

Clambroth glass; rope table ring
on base.
Ex coll: Louise S. Esterly
Comments: There are several variations of this pattern (see above
and below).
Parallels: Lee, Sandwich Glass,
pl. 81, nos. 4,5; *Rose,* nos. 473,
476.

*567 Another

68.4.262

Opalescent.
Ex coll: Louise S. Esterly

*568 Another

67.4.34

Gift of Mr. and Mrs. Harry A.
Snyder

---

569 Plate
New England
ca. 1830-1850
D. 5.6 cm

68.4.616

Colorless lead glass; plain table
ring on base.
Ex coll: Louise S. Esterly
Comments: There are several variations of this pattern (see
above).
Parallels: Lee, Sandwich Glass,
pl. 81, nos. 4, 5; pl. 83, no. 5;
Rose, nos. 473, 476.

---

570 Plate
Midwest
ca. 1840-1860
D. 5.7 cm

68.4.261

Light blue glass.
Ex coll: Louise S. Esterly
Parallels: Lee, Sandwich Glass,
pl. 82, no. 6.

†571 **Plate**
New England
ca. 1830-1835
D. 5 cm

68.4.256

Opaque powder blue.
Ex colls: Louise S. Esterly; Dr.
and Mrs. Charles W. Green
Comments: Extremely rare.
Published: Lee, Sandwich Glass,
pl. 82, no. 3.
Rose, no. 475.

572 **Plate**
United States (?)
ca. 1840-1870
D. 6.5 cm

68.4.571

Colorless lead glass.
Ex coll: Louise S. Esterly

573 **Plate**
New England
ca. 1840-1870
D. 5.8 cm

68.4.588

Colorless lead glass; paneled.
Ex coll: Louise S. Esterly
Parallels: S.H.S., pp. 16-17.

574 **Plate**
Possibly Midwest
ca. 1840-1860
D. 6.5 cm

68.4.590

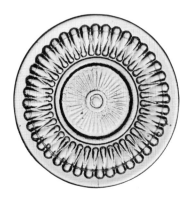

Colorless lead glass.
Ex coll: Louise S. Esterly

575 Plate
United States
ca. 1900
D. 6.7 cm

69.4.59

Colorless non-lead glass.
Gift of Mr. and Mrs. Harry A.
Snyder

576 Plate
United States or possibly Continental Europe
ca. 1840-1860
D. 6.7 cm

67.4.33

Colorless non-lead glass.
Gift of Mr. and Mrs. Harry A.
Snyder

577 Oval bowl
Midwest
ca. 1835-1850
L. 8.0 cm; H. 1.8 cm

68.4.593

Colorless lead glass; stippled;
pattern of shells and scrolls
around sides.
Ex coll: Louise S. Esterly
Parallels: Lee, Sandwich Glass,
pl. 81, no. 8.

578 Oval bowl
New England
ca. 1840-1870
L. 6.6 cm; H. 1.6 cm

68.4.319

Amethyst glass; paneled sides;
star in oval base.
Ex coll: Louise S. Esterly
Parallels: S.H.S., pp. 15-16.

*579 Another

68.4.320

Turquoise.
Ex coll: Louise S. Esterly

*580 Another

68.4.587

Colorless.
Ex coll: Louise S. Esterly

581 Circular bowl
New England
ca. 1835-1850
H. 2.3 cm; D. 4.2 cm

68.4.314

Opalescent glass; stippled; scroll
pattern on sides.
Ex coll: Louise S. Esterly
Parallels: Lee, Sandwich Glass,
pl. 80, no. 6; *Rose,* no. 490.

*582 Another

68.4.328

Opaque white with a blue
streak.
Ex coll: Louise S. Esterly

*583 Another

68.4.602

Colorless.
Ex coll: Louise S. Esterly

---

584 Oval bowl
Possibly Midwest
ca. 1835-1850
L. 7.4 cm; H. 1.3 cm

68.4.300

Light amethyst glass; coarsely
stippled; scroll design on sides.
Ex coll: Louise S. Esterly
Comments: Both this bowl and
the following one have uneven
rims, suggesting that the mold
shifted during the pressing process.

*585 Another

68.4.624

Colorless.
Ex coll: Louise S. Esterly

---

586 Oval bowl
New England
ca. 1835-1850
L. 7.5 cm; H. 1.5 cm

68.4.299

Clambroth glass; stippled;
scrolls and leaves on sides.
Ex coll: Louise S. Esterly
Parallels: Lee, Sandwich Glass,
pl. 81, no. 8; *Rose,* nos. 467,
468, 491; *S.H.S.,* pp. 16-17.

*587 Another

68.4.305

Opalescent.
Ex colls: Louise S. Esterly; Mr.
and Mrs. Harry S. High

*588 Another

68.4.301

Ex colls: Louise S. Esterly; Dr.
and Mrs. Charles W. Green

*589 Another

68.4.302

Pale yellow.
Ex colls: Louise S. Esterly; Dr.
and Mrs. Charles W. Green
Published: Rose, no. 491.

*590 Another

68.4.304

Green.
Ex colls: Louise S. Esterly; Dr.
and Mrs. Charles W. Green
Published: Rose, no. 467.

*591 Another

68.4.303

Amethyst.
Ex coll: Louise S. Esterly

*592 **Another**

68.4.609

Colorless.
Ex coll: Louise S. Esterly

---

593 **Oval bowl**
New England
ca. 1835-1850
L. 7.5 cm; H. 1.3 cm

68.4.298

Cobalt blue glass; stippled;
scrolls and leaves on sides.
Ex coll: Louise S. Esterly
Comments: One fragment of this
type is in the Esterly collection
of Sandwich fragments.
Parallels: Lee, Sandwich Glass, p.
275 (not illus.).

---

594 **Circular bowl**
Probably United States
ca. 1840-1860
H. 1.9 cm; D. 3.3 cm

67.4.41

Colorless lead glass; paneled.
Gift of Mr. and Mrs. Harry A.
Snyder

---

595 **Circular bowl**
Probably United States
ca. 1840-1860
H. 2.5 cm; D. 3.8 cm

67.4.63

Colorless lead glass; oval panels
on sides; top rim ground and
polished.
Gift of Mr. and Mrs. Harry A.
Snyder

---

596 **Circular bowl**
Probably United States
ca. 1840-1870
H. 5 cm; D. 3.4 cm

69.4.8

Greenish bubbly glass; waffle
and fan design on sides.
Gift of Mr. and Mrs. Harry A.
Snyder

597 Rectangular footed bowl
New England
ca. 1835-1850
L. 4.5 cm; H. 2.5 cm

68.4.598

Colorless non-lead glass; stippled sides with tulip design.
Ex coll: Louise S. Esterly
Comments: Extremely rare.
Parallels: Lee, Sandwich Glass, pl. 82, nos. 1-2; *S.H.S.*, pp. 16-17.

598 Hexagonal footed bowl
United States or possibly Continental
ca. 1835-1850
H. 2.3 cm; D. (rim) 3.2 cm

68.4.606

Colorless, non-lead glass; stippled; scrolls on sides.
Ex colls: Louise S. Esterly; Dr. and Mrs. Charles W. Green
Comments: Extremely rare.
Published: Rose, no. 501; *Lee, Sandwich Glass* (1947), pl. 80, no. 5.

599 Footed bowl
New England
ca. 1835-1850
H. 1.9 cm; D. (rim) 4.5 cm

68.4.615

Colorless lead glass; stippled; scrolls on sides.
Ex colls: Louise S. Esterly; Mrs. Harry S. High

600 Round footed bowl
New England
ca. 1840-1870
H. 3.3 cm; D. (rim) 5.1 cm

68.4.619

Colorless lead glass; paneled.
Ex coll: Louise S. Esterly
Parallels: S.H.S. pp. 16-17.

601 Tumbler or whiskey taster
New England
ca. 1840-1860
H. 4.5 cm

68.4.350

Whitish "clambroth" glass; cylindrical; lancet leaves around sides; top rim enameled with red blossoms and green leaves.
Ex coll: Louise S. Esterly
Parallels: Lee, Sandwich Glass, pl. 150, nos. 5, 7; *Rose*, nos. 158-162.

*602 Another

60.4.815

Clambroth.
Gift of Louise S. Esterly

*603 Another

60.4.818

Cobalt blue.
Gift of Louise S. Esterly

*604 **Another**

60.4.822

Opaque white.
Gift of Louise S. Esterly

*605 **Another**

67.4.27

Vaseline.
Gift of Mr. and Mrs. Harry A.
Snyder

*606 **Another**

67.4.28

Colorless.
Gift of Mr. and Mrs. Harry A.
Snyder

---

607 **Tumbler or whiskey taster**
New England
ca. 1840-1860
H. 4 cm

60.4.823

Vaseline glass; ten vertical
panels around sides; pontil
mark.
Gift of Louise S. Esterly

*608 **Another**

69.4.14

Gift of Mr. and Mrs. Harry A.
Snyder

*609 **Another**

69.4.62

Colorless.
Gift of Mr. and Mrs. Harry A.
Snyder

---

610 **Hat whimsy**
New England
ca. 1840-1860
H. 3.4 cm

60.4.824

Clambroth glass; top hat-shaped
with vertical panels around
crown; pontil mark on base.
Gift of Louise S. Esterly
Comments: This hat was made
from the same mold as the
tumblers, 607-609.

---

611 **Tumbler or whiskey taster**
Probably United States
ca. 1840-1860
H. 5 cm

68.4.349

Vaseline glass; cylindrical shape;
barred ovals around side.
Ex coll: Louise S. Esterly

612 Tumbler or whiskey taster
Probably United States
ca. 1840-1860
H. 4.3 cm

60.4.821

Light blue glass; vertical fluting around sides.
Gift of Louise S. Esterly

613 Covered sugar bowl
New England
ca. 1840-1860
Overall H. 5.3 cm

69.4.134

*614 Another

68.4.312

Colorless lead glass; paneled sides and lid.
Gift of Mr. and Mrs. Harry A. Snyder
Parallels: S.H.S., pp. 16-17.

Turquoise.
Ex coll: Louise S. Esterly

615 Mug
King, Son & Co., Cascade Glass Company, Pittsburgh, Pennsylvania
ca. 1875
H. 5 cm

74.4.160

Bluish-violet glass; grapevines and grapes around sides.
Bequest of Mrs. Jason Westerfield
Parallels: Innes, Pittsburgh Glass, p. 301.

616 Tumbler
United States or possibly Continent
ca. 1840-1860
H. 3.8 cm

68.4.276

Cobalt blue glass; barrel-shaped; Gothic arch around sides.
Ex colls: Louise S. Esterly; Dr. and Mrs. Charles W. Green

617 Compote
Probably Midwest or possibly
France
ca. 1850
H. 4.5 cm; D. 6 cm

69.4.9

Opaque light blue glass; ribbed
bowl; paneled stem; ribbed
foot.
Gift of Mr. and Mrs. Harry A.
Snyder
Comments: See no. 1503 which is
related.

618 Compote
New England
ca. 1835-1855
H. 4.9 cm; D. (rim) 4.7 cm

68.4.584

*619 Another

68.4.585

Colorless non-lead glass; stippled top with floral pattern;
knopped stem; round foot.
Ex colls: Louise S. Esterly; Dr.
and Mrs. Charles W. Green
Parallels: Lee, Sandwich Glass,
pl. 80, no. 10; *Rose,* no. 514, pl.
XXXI.

Ex coll: Louise S. Esterly

620 Toy cup
Midwest, probably Richards and
Hartley, Tarentum, Pennsylva-
nia
ca. 1870-1900
H. 4.5 cm; D. (rim) 5.2 cm

63.4.49

Colorless non-lead glass; lion's
head on each side.
Gift of Helen R. Wormser

621 Toy butter dish base
United States
ca. 1890
D. 8.4 cm

65.4.81A, B

Colorless non-lead glass with a
design of girls and boys, respectively, at work around sides.
Gift of Mrs. Leon S. Bard
Parallels: Lee and Rose, p. 401,
no. 895 is similar.

621 Toy butter dish base
United States
ca. 1890
D. 8.4 cm

65.4.81A, B

Colorless non-lead glass with a
design of girls and boys, respectively, at work around sides.
Gift of Mrs. Leon S. Bard
Parallels: Lee and Rose, p. 401,
no. 895 is similar.

622 Toy butter dish base
United States
ca. 1890
D. 8.5 cm

63.4.113

Colorless non-lead glass with a
design of boys at work around
sides.
Gift of Helen R. Wormser
Parallels: Lee and Rose, p. 401,
no. 895 is similar.

623 Toy saucer
United States
ca. 1870-1900
H. 1.8 cm; D. 9.3 cm

67.4.125

Amber glass.
Gift of Mr. and Mrs. Harry A.
Snyder
Parallels: Lee and Rose, p. 401,
no. 896.

***624 Miniature covered
butter dish**
Probably Midwest
ca. 1900-1930
H. (with cover) 6.1. cm;
D. 9.3 cm

74.4.95

Colorless non-lead glass in an
imitation cut glass design;
strawberry diamond pattern,
scalloped flange.
Gift of Ruth I. Roth

**625 Miniature covered
    butter dish**
Probably Midwest
ca. 1900-1930
H. (with cover) 8.6 cm;
D. 13.3 cm

74.4.96

Colorless glass.
Gift of Ruth I. Roth

**626 Miniature covered
    butter dish**
Probably Midwest
ca. 1900-1930
H. (with cover) 6.2 cm;
D. 9.4 cm

74.4.94

Colorless non-lead glass.
Gift of Ruth I. Roth

**627 Miniature covered
    butter dish**
United States, probably Midwest
ca. 1890-1900
H. 6.1 cm; D. 9.1 cm

79.4.165

Opalescent glass; pressed with a
pattern of diamonds; base with
scalloped rim.
Gift of Mr. and Mrs. William
Gelabert, Washington, D.C.

628 Pieplate
United States, Corning, New
York, Corning Glass Works,
1920's
H. 2.8 cm; D. 12.4 cm

79.4.94

Colorless glass; circular, marked
on base "PATENTED/PYREX/
May 27 1919"; on rim "25AA."
Gift of Otto Hilbert, Corning,
New York
Comments: This is a child's toy.

629 Loaf pan
United States, Corning, New
York, Corning Glass Works
1920's
H. 5 cm; L. 12.1 cm

79.4.95

Colorless glass; rectangular;
marked in base "PATENTED/
PYREX/May 27 1919" and on rim
"2½."
Gift of Otto Hilbert, Corning,
New York
Comments: This is a child's toy.

Salt Dishes, Lacy Type

Because salt has always been important in the human diet, it has frequently been accorded a place of honor on western tables. Saltcellars in the Middle Ages were impressive objects, often of silver gilt. In the late 18th and 19th centuries, salt was served in small cup-like salts in silver or glass, free-blown or mold-blown. With the advent of pressing in 1825, glass salts became much more popular because they could be produced cheaply, and glass sellers began to offer them in a great variety of designs. More than 400 different molds have been categorized by L. W. and D. B. Neal in their book on the subject.

After lacy glass went out of fashion, pressed salts continued to be made in simpler patterns, both to match table sets and in designs used only for salts. A few were made with covers to keep out dust and insects, but generally they were only open bowls. When salt shakers began to be used in the latter part of the 19th century, large open salts gradually declined in popularity. They were replaced at fashionable tables by individual salt dips.

Similar pressed salts were made and used on the Continent and are to be found in French and Scandinavian glass manufacturers' catalogs of the middle of the 19th century.

The salt dishes in this section are arranged according to the letter/number system of Logan W. and Dorothy B. Neal, *Pressed Glass. Salt Dishes of the Lacy Period, 1825-1850*, Philadelphia, 1962.

630 Salt dish
New England, probably New
England Glass Company
ca. 1830-1840
H. 5 cm; L. 7.6 cm

61.4.68

Colorless lead glass; rectangular
with a basket of fruit on one
side, birds and bird bath on the
other, and a single flower on
each end.
Gift of Louise S. Esterly
Parallels: Lee, Sandwich Glass,
pl. 71, no. 7; *Neal*, BB1, p. 17;
Rose, nos. 825, 827.

*631 Another

68.4.213

Opaque white.
Ex coll: Louise S. Esterly

632 Salt dish
New England, probably New
England Glass Company
ca. 1830-1840
H. 5 cm; L. 9.8 cm

68.4.342

Colorless lead glass; rectangular,
with a basket of fruit on one
side, birds and bird bath on the
other, and a single flower on
each end.
Ex coll: Louise S. Esterly
Comments: This large size is very
rare.
Parallels: Lee, Sandwich Glass,
pl. 71, no. 8; *McKearin, American Glass*, pl. 165, no. 5; *Neal*,
BB2, p. 18; *Rose*, no. 826.

†633 Salt dish
Massachusetts, Boston &
Sandwich Glass Company or
New England Glass Company
ca. 1830-1840
H. 5 cm; L. 7.7 cm

68.4.248

Emerald green; rectangular
shape, basket of flowers on each
side, lower part of sides stippled.
Ex coll: Louise S. Esterly
Comments: Very rare in this color;
fragments of this series were
found at the site of the Boston
& Sandwich factory.
Parallels: Lee, Sandwich Glass,
pl. 76, no. 1; *McKearin, American Glass*, pl. 168, no. 5; *Neal*,
BF1, p. 1; *Rose*, nos. 854-857.

634 Salt dish
Massachusetts, Boston &
Sandwich Glass Company or
New England Glass Company
ca. 1830-1840
H. 5 cm; L. 7.7 cm

68.4.201

Grayish blue glass; rectangular
shape; basket of flowers on each
side, on a stippled background.
Ex coll: Louise S. Esterly
Comments: Very rare in this color;
fragments in this pattern were
found at the site of the Boston
& Sandwich Glass factory.
Parallels: Lee, Sandwich Glass,
pl. 76, no. 1; *McKearin, American Glass*, pl. 168, no. 5; *Neal*,
BF1a, p. 2; *Rose*, nos. 854-857.

635 Salt dish
Massachusetts, Boston &
Sandwich Glass Company or
New England Glass Company
ca. 1830-1840
H. 5 cm; L. 7.5 cm

59.4.56

Colorless lead glass; rectangular
shape; basket of flowers on each
side; base with cross-hatched
pattern with ribbing at outer
edges.
Gift of Louise S. Esterly
Parallels: Lee, Sandwich Glass,
pl. 76, no. 1; *McKearin, American Glass,* pl. 168, no. 5; *Neal,*
BF1b, p. 3; *Rose,* nos. 854-857.

*636 **Another**

68.4.174

Opalescent.
Ex coll: Louise S. Esterly

*637 **Another**

68.4.124

Blue.
Ex coll: Louise S. Esterly

638 Salt dish
Massachusetts, Boston &
Sandwich Glass Company or
New England Glass Company
ca. 1830-1840
H. 4.5 cm; L. 7.3 cm

68.4.367

Opaque white glass; rectangular
shape; basket of flowers on each
side.
Ex coll: Louise S. Esterly
Comments: Very rare.
Parallels: Lee, Sandwich Glass,
pl. 76, no. 1; *McKearin, American Glass,* pl. 168, no. 5; *Neal*
BF1d, p. 5; *Rose,* nos. 854-857.

639 Salt dish
Massachusetts, probably Boston
& Sandwich Glass Company
ca. 1830-1840
H. 4.5 cm; L. 7.4 cm

68.4.87

Colorless lead glass; rectangular
shape; basket of flowers on each
side.
Gift of Mr. and Mrs. Harry A.
Snyder
Parallels: Lee, Sandwich Glass,
pl. 76, no. 1; *McKearin, American Glass,* pl. 168, no. 5; *Neal,*
BF1f, p. 7; *Rose,* nos. 854-857.

640 Salt dish
New England, possibly New
England Glass Company
ca. 1830-1840
H. 5 cm; L. 7.6 cm

61.4.71

Colorless lead glass; rectangular
shape; different compote of
flowers and fruit on each side;
thistle on one end and beehive
on other.
Gift of Louise S. Esterly
Parallels: Lee, Sandwich Glass,
pl. 70, no. 4; *McKearin, American Glass,* pl. 164, no. 9; *Neal,*
BH1, p. 16; *Rose,* no. 740.

641 **Salt dish**
Massachusetts, possibly Boston
& Sandwich Glass Company
ca. 1830-1840
H. 4.6 cm; L. 7.8 cm

68.4.249

Emerald green glass; rectangular
shape, with S-curved ends, concentric circles on base.
Ex coll: Louise S. Esterly
*Parallels: McKearin, American
Glass*, pl. 168, no. 1; *Neal*, BS2,
p. 9; *Rose*, no. 866.

*642 **Another**

68.4.130

Opalescent.
Ex coll: Louise S. Esterly

---

643 **Salt dish**
Massachusetts, Boston &
Sandwich Glass Company or
New England Glass Company
ca. 1830-1840
H. 4.5 cm; L. 7.7 cm

68.4.366

Violet blue glass; rectangular
shape with S-curved ends; star
and sunburst on base.
Ex coll: Louise S. Esterly
Comments: Fragments of this
pattern were found at the site of
the Boston & Sandwich Glass
factory.
*Parallels: McKearin, American
Glass*, pl. 168, no. 2; *Neal*, BS3,
p. 10; *Rose*, no. 865.

*644 **Another**

68.4.197

Opaque dark blue-gray.
Ex coll: Louise S. Esterly

*645 **Another**

61.4.82

Colorless.
Gift of Louise S. Esterly

---

646 **Salt dish**
United States or possibly France
ca. 1840
H. 4.8 cm; L. 7.6 cm

61.4.66

Colorless glass; rectangular with
a beaded ornament on each
side.
Gift of Louise S. Esterly
Parallels: Lee, Sandwich Glass,
pl. 73, no. 5; *Neal*, BS4, p. 12.

---

†647 **Salt dish**
New England, or perhaps
Bohemia
ca. 1830-1840
H. 5 cm; L. 7.5 cm

68.4.221

Colorless glass, ruby stained;
rectangular shape with S-curved
ends, sides with five-sided ornament.
Ex coll: Louise S. Esterly
Comments: Extremely rare, one other
known, in Met. Mus. of Art, N.Y.
Published: Neal, BS5, p. 13; *Rose*,
no. 861.
Parallels: Lee, Sandwich Glass,
pl. 73, no. 5; *McKearin, American Glass*, pl. 168, no. 3;
Charleston, Robert J. "A Glass
Pattern-Book of the Bieder-
meier Period," *International Congress on Glass Comptes Ren-
dus II*, 1965, p. 261, Fig. 4.

648 Salt dish
Stourbridge Flint Glass Works
of J. Robinson & Son,
Pittsburgh
ca. 1828-1835
H. 3.8 cm; L. 8.8 cm

59.4.73

Colorless lead glass; boat-
shaped; inscription on stern,
"J. ROBINSON & SON/PITTS-
BURGH," anchor and rope rim
on base.
Gift of Louise S. Esterly
Parallels: Neal, BT1, p. 19; *Rose,*
nos. 760, 761 and 762.

†649 Salt dish
Stourbridge Flint Glass Works
of John Robinson & Son,
Pittsburgh
ca. 1828-1835
H. 4.2 cm; L. 9.1 cm

64.4.88

Opaque white glass; boat-
shaped; inscription on stern,
"J. ROBINSON & SON/PITTS-
BURGH," anchor on plain base.
Comments: Unique in this color.
John Robinson received his first
patent for pressing in 1827 and
his sons are said to have formed
their own partnership by 1835.
Hence, the dating on this and
the previous salt.
Parallels: Neal, BT1a, p. 20.

†650 Salt dish
Stourbridge Flint Glass Works
of J. Robinson & Son,
Pittsburgh
ca. 1828-1835
H. 4.5 cm; L. 9.3 cm

50.4.216

Light cobalt blue glass; boat-
shaped; inscription on stern,
"PITTSBURGH."
Ex coll: George S. McKearin
Comments: Rare in this color.
Parallels: Neal, BT2, p. 21;
McKearin, American Glass, pl.
167, no. 3; *Rose,* no. 759; *Lee,*
Sandwich Glass, pl. 65, no. 5
(not illustrated).

***651 Another**

68.4.129

Darker blue.
Ex coll: Louise S. Esterly

652 Salt dish
Boston & Sandwich Glass Company, Sandwich, Massachusetts
ca. 1830-1835
H. 4.1 cm; L. 9.3 cm

68.4.347

Parallels: Lee, Sandwich Glass,
pl. 72, no. 1; *McKearin, Ameri-*
can Glass, pl. 167, no. 1; *Neal,*
BT4, p. 24; *Rose,* nos. 750, 757;
Short, Vincent, "Model for the
LAFAYET Salt?" *Antiques,* 72,
no. 2, Aug. 1957, p. 155.

Opalescent glass; boat-shaped;
inscription on paddle wheels,
"LAFAYET"; "B. & S./GLASS./
Cº." on stern; "SANDWICH" on
inside base, and "SANDWICH"
superimposed on scroll design
on underside.
Ex coll: Louise S. Esterly
Comments: See also following
salts; all variants are rare. Vincent Short suggests that the boat
represented is the *Lafayette,*
built at Mt. Holly, New Jersey,
in 1824 and used on the Nan-
tucket-Maine Coast Route. One
of the pioneer steamboats, it was
scrapped in 1835.

†653 **Salt dish**
Boston & Sandwich Glass Company, Sandwich, Massachusetts
ca. 1830-1835
H. 3.8 cm; L. 8.8 cm

68.4.358

Opaque purple-blue glass; boat-shaped; inscription "LAFAYET" on paddle wheels; "B. & S./GLASS./Cº." on stern; "SANDWICH" on inside base, scroll design on bottom.
Ex coll: Louise S. Esterly
Parallels: Lee, Sandwich Glass, pl. 72, no. 2; p. 261 (not illus.); *McKearin, American Glass*, pl. 167, no. 1; *Neal*, BT4d, p. 28; *Rose*, nos. 749 and 756; Short, Vincent, "Model for the LAFAYET salt?," *Antiques*, 72, no. 2, August 1957, p. 155.

*654 **Another**

59.4.72

Colorless.
Gift of Louise S. Esterly

†*655 **Another**

68.4.362

Cobalt blue.
Ex coll: Louise S. Esterly

†656 **Salt dish**
Boston & Sandwich Glass Company, Sandwich, Massachusetts
ca. 1830-1835
H. 3.8 cm; L. 9.1 cm

68.4.630

Opaque blue glass; boat-shaped; inscription: "LAFAYET" on paddle wheels; "B. & S./GLASS./Cº." on stern which lacks keel; "SANDWICH" on inside base; and "SAND-WICH" superimposed on scroll design on underside.
Ex coll: Louise S. Esterly
Comments: see no. 652 above.
Parallels: Lee, Sandwich Glass, pl. 72, no. 1; *McKearin, American Glass*, pl. 167, no. 1; *Neal*, BT5, p. 29; *Rose*, nos. 750 and 757; Short, Vincent, "Model for the LAFAYET salt?" *Antiques* 72, no. 2, Aug. 1957, p. 155.

†657 **Salt dish**
Probably Boston & Sandwich Glass Company, Sandwich, Massachusetts
ca. 1830-1835
L. 8.8 cm; H. 4.7 cm

68.4.176

Opaque pale blue glass; boat-shaped with "LAFAYET" on paddle wheels; two windows in stern.
Ex colls: Louise S. Esterly; Mr. and Mrs. Harry S. High
Comments: Very rare and may be unique in this color. Only four salts of this pattern were known in 1962.
Published: Neal, BT7, p. 32.
Parallels: Lee, Sandwich Glass, p. 261, no. 3A (not illus.); *Rose*, No. 755.

658 Salt dish
New England
ca. 1830-1840
H. 3.1 cm; L. 9.5 cm

68.4.125

Opalescent glass, boat-shaped; keel in front; square stern.
Ex coll: Louise S. Esterly
Parallels: Neal, BT9, p. 34.

659 Salt dish
Massachusetts, Boston & Sandwich Glass Company or New England Glass Company
ca. 1830-1840
H. 4.4 cm; L. 7.2 cm

59.4.71

Opaque powder blue glass; rectangular shape with charioteer in full gallop on sides and dolphins on ends, concentric circles on base.
Gift of Louise S. Esterly
Comments: Very rare.
Parallels: Lee, Sandwich Glass, pl. 71, no. 2; *Neal*, CT1, p. 35; *Rose*, nos. 858 and 864.

*660 Another

68.4.134

Opaque white.
Ex coll: Louise S. Esterly

661 Salt dish
Massachusetts, Boston & Sandwich Glass Company or New England Glass Company
ca. 1830-1840
H. 4 cm; L. 7.2 cm

68.4.96

Colorless lead glass; rectangular shape with charioteer on sides and dolphins on ends; scroll design on base.
Gift of Mr. and Mrs. Harry A. Snyder
Parallels: Neal, CT1a, p. 36.

662 Covered salt dish
Massachusetts, probably Boston & Sandwich Glass Company
ca. 1830-1840
H. (with cover) 8.3 cm;
L. 7.7 cm
Cover: H. 3.5 cm; L. 6.1 cm

68.4.156

Colorless lead glass; rectangular with a basket of flowers on each side; domed rectangular cover with pineapple knob, six-pointed star on base.
Ex coll: Louise S. Esterly
Comments: Very rare; an almost complete cover of this design is in the Esterly collection of fragments found at the Sandwich site.
Parallels: Lee, Sandwich Glass, pl. 69, no. 3; *McKearin, American Glass*, pl. 164, no. 5; *Neal*, CD2b, p. 40; *Rose*, no. 873.

663 Covered salt dish
Massachusetts, probably Boston
& Sandwich Glass Company
ca. 1830-1840
H. (with cover) 7.6 cm; L. 8 cm
Cover: H. 3.5 cm; L. 6.1 cm

68.4.179

Colorless lead glass, rectangular-
shaped with a lyre on each side;
domed, rectangular lid with
pineapple knob.
Ex coll: Louise S. Esterly
Parallels: Lee, Sandwich Glass,
pl. 69 (upper left and center);
McKearin, American Glass, pl.
164, no 1; *Neal,* CD3, p. 41;
Rose, nos. 874, 875.

†664 Covered salt dish
Massachusetts, probably Boston
& Sandwich Glass Company
ca. 1830-1840
H. (with cover) 7.9 cm;
L. 7.7 cm
Cover: H. 3.5 cm; L. 6.1 cm

68.4.166

Opaque blue-violet glass; rectangular shape with a lyre on
each side; ribbing on base;
domed rectangular lid with
pineapple knob.
Ex coll: Louise S. Esterly
Comments: Extremely rare; this
is the only salt of this design
published so far. The chief dif-
ference between this and the
preceding salt is the outer band
of ribbing on the base of this
one.
Parallels: Lee, Sandwich Glass,
pl. 69 (upper left and center);
McKearin, American Glass, pl.
164, no 1; *Neal,* CD4, p. 43;
Rose, nos. 874, 875.

665 Salt
New England
ca. 1830-1840
H. 5.4 cm; L. 7.8 cm

68.4.217

Purple-blue glass; rectangular
shape; sides with "crown" surrounded by stippling.
Ex coll: Louise S. Esterly
Comments: Fragments found at
the Sandwich site match this
salt.
*Parallels: McKearin, American
Glass,* pl. 169, no 1; *Neal,* CN1a,
p. 47; *Rose,* no. 867.

*666 Another

68.4.165

Opalescent.
Ex coll: Louise S. Esterly

*667 Another

61.4.80

Colorless.
Gift of Louise S. Esterly

†668 **Salt**
New England
ca. 1830-1840
H. 5.4 cm; L. 8 cm

68.4.211

Light green glass; rectangular shape, with "crown" on sides. *Ex coll:* Louise S. Esterly *Comments:* The base pattern of this salt differs slightly from the preceding ones, and the sides have less stippling. *Parallels: Neal*, CN1c, p. 49.

669 **Salt**
New England
ca. 1830-1840
H. 5 cm; L. 7.5 cm

61.4.76

Colorless lead glass; rectangular shape; eagle with olive branch and arrows on side; sheaf of wheat on ends.
Gift of Louise S. Esterly
Comments: Very rare.
Parallels: Lee, Sandwich Glass, pl. 70 (upper right); *Neal*, EE2, p. 76.

†670 **Salt dish**
Massachusetts, probably Boston & Sandwich Glass Company
ca. 1830-1840
H. 5 cm; L. 8 cm

68.4.226

Dark amber glass; trapezoidal form, two eagles with heads facing on each side; shield in center of sides; twelve-pointed star with center panel on base.
Ex coll: Louise S. Esterly
Published: Rose, no. 769.
Parallels: Lee, Sandwich Glass, pl. 76, no. 6; *McKearin, American Glass*, pl. 167, no. 2; *Neal*, EE3a, p. 78.

*671 **Another**

61.4.78

Colorless.
Gift of Louise S. Esterly

†*672 **Salt dish**
Massachusetts, possibly Boston & Sandwich Glass Company
ca. 1830-1845
H. 5.3 cm; L. 8 cm

68.4.218

Opaque white glass; rectangular shape; eagles facing each other on each side with shield in between; twelve-pointed star on base.
Ex colls: Louise S. Esterly; Mr. and Mrs. Harry S. High
Comments: Fragments of this

pattern have been found at the Sandwich site.
Published: Rose, no. 775.
Parallels: Lee, Sandwich Glass, pl. 76, no. 6; *McKearin, American Glass*, pl. 167, no. 2; *Neal*, EE3b, p. 79; *Rose*, nos. 773, 774, 775, 776, pl. XXIII.

†673 **Another**

68.4.223

†*674 **Another**

68.4.209

Opalescent glass.
Ex colls: Louise S. Esterly; Mr. and Mrs. Harry S. High

Purple-blue.
Ex colls: Louise S. Esterly; Mr. and Mrs. Harry S. High
Published: Rose, no. 776.

---

675 **Salt dish**
New England
ca. 1830-1840
H. 4 cm; L. 9.7 cm

68.4.118

Colorless lead glass; rectangular with cut corners; lyre-like design on long sides; fleur-de-lis on ends; American eagle on stippled base.
Ex coll: Louise S. Esterly
Parallels: McKearin, American Glass, pl. 164, no. 8; *Neal,* EE6, p. 82; *Rose,* no. 737.

---

676 **Salt dish**
New England
ca. 1830-1840
H. 4.1 cm; L. 9.2 cm

68.4.155

Colorless lead glass; rectangular shape with American eagle on each side.
Ex coll: Louise S. Esterly
Comments: Fragments of this pattern were found at the Sandwich site.
Parallels: Lee, Sandwich Glass, pl. 76, no. 5; *McKearin, Ameican Glass,* pl. 167, no. 5; *Neal,* EE7, p. 83; *Rose,* no. 771.

---

677 **Salt dish**
New England
ca. 1830-1840
H. 4.6 cm; D. 7.4 cm

68.4.230

Colorless lead glass; circular shape; three sailing ships alternating with three eagles around sides; circular base with eagle in center, floral pattern rim.
Ex coll: Louise S. Esterly
Comments: Very rare. This dish may have been produced during the 1830's when the threatened demolition of the U.S.F. *Constitution* produced a public outcry, and several pressed glass souvenirs depicting the frigate were produced.
Parallels: Lee, Sandwich Glass, pl. 75, no. 9; *McKearin, American Glass,* pl. 164, no. 3; *Neal,* EE8, p. 86; *Rose,* no. 741.

678 Salt
New England
ca. 1830-1840
H. 4.7 cm; D. 7.4 cm

68.4.344

Colorless lead glass; circular shape; three sailing ships alternating with three eagles on the sides; circular base with eagle in center, scalloped rim.
Ex coll: Louise S. Esterly
Comments: See above entry.
Parallels: Lee, Sandwich Glass, pl. 75, no. 7; *McKearin, American Glass,* pl. 164, no 4; *Neal,* EE8a, p. 87; Keyes, Homer E. and Carrick, Alice van Leer, "Notes on Historic Glass Cup Plates," *Antiques* 3, no. 1, Jan. 1923, p. 23.

679 Salt
New England
ca. 1830-1840
H. 3.9 cm; L. 7.2 cm

59.4.53

Colorless lead glass; rectangular shape; sides with three Gothic arches, ends with one arch.
Gift of Louise S. Esterly
Parallels: Neal, GA2, p. 90; *Rose,* no. 784. pl. XXIII (similar).

680 Salt dish
Probably Massachusetts, Boston & Sandwich Glass Company or New England Glass Company
ca. 1830-1840
H. 4.3 cm; L. 7.2 cm

68.4.198

Opalescent blue glass; rectangular shaped with four hearts above three Gothic arches on each side.
Ex coll: Louise S. Esterly
Parallels: Lee, Sandwich Glass, pl. 71, no. 1; *Neal,* GA4, p. 92.

*681 Another

69.4.56

Opaque light blue.
Gift of Mr. and Mrs. Harry A. Snyder

682 Salt dish
New England
ca. 1825-1830
H. 5.1 cm; L. 7.6 cm

68.4.253

Colorless lead glass; rectangular shape; one side with bust of Washington in an oval medallion; other with bust of man inscribed above, "LAFAYETTE"; grape leaf on base.
Ex coll: Louise S. Esterly; Mrs. Harry S. High
Comments: Only one published. Several other salts have similar portraits.
Published: Rose, no 799; *Neal,* HL1a, p. 117.

683 Salt dish
New England
ca. 1825-1830
H. 5.1 cm; L. 7.6 cm

68.4.254

Colorless lead glass; rectangular shape; one side with bust of man, inscribed above, "WASHINGTON," other with bust of man, inscribed above, "LAFAYETTE," grape leaf on base.
Ex coll: Louise S. Esterly
Comments: Extremely rare. Washington is clearly recognizable; Lafayette is not.
Parallels: Lee, Sandwich Glass, pl. 70, no. 1; *McKearin, American Glass,* pl. 164, no. 6; *Neal,* HL3, p. 119; *Rose,* no. 805.

684 Salt dish
United States
ca. 1835-1840
H. 4.1 cm; L. 7.3 cm

68.4.229

Colorless lead glass; rectangular shape; stippled sides with shell motif, ends of row of "hairpins"; base with an early railroad engine with smokestack, pulling one car inscribed "H. CLAY" beneath.
Ex coll: Louise S. Esterly
Comments: Extremely rare. Fragments of this pattern were found at the Sandwich site. The Lexington, Kentucky, Railroad, of which Henry Clay was a large shareholder, was built in the late 1830's and opened about 1838. This salt may commemorate that opening and, if so, is likely to be midwestern.
Parallels: Lee, Sandwich Glass, pl. 72, no. 4; *McKearin, American Glass,* pls. 170, no. 2 and 164, no 7; *Neal,* HL4, p. 120; *Rose,* no. 765.

685 Salt dish
Jersey Glass Company, near Jersey City, New Jersey
ca. 1830's
H. 5 cm; L. 7.5 cm

63.4.91

Light green glass; rectangular shape with basket of flowers on sides; inscribed on base, "JERSEY/GLASS CO./Nʳ. N.YORK."
Gift of Louise S. Esterly
Comments: Note similarity to the New England Glass Company salts, 696-699.
Parallels: Lee, Sandwich Glass, pl. 72; *McKearin, American Glass,* pl. 165, no. 1; *Neal,* JY2, p. 124; *Rose,* no. 801.

686 Salt dish
Probably Jersey Glass Company,
near Jersey City, New Jersey
ca. 1830-1840
H. 4.8 cm; L. 7.5 cm

68.4.200

Light green glass; rectangular
shape, fruit basket on each side;
sunburst on rectangular base.
Ex coll: Louise S. Esterly
Comments: The attribution is
based on the similarity of this
salt to the marked "Jersey City"
salts.
*Parallels: McKearin, American
Glass*, pl. 165, no. 4; *Neal*, JY2b,
p. 126.

---

687 Salt dish
Massachusetts, Boston &
Sandwich Glass Company or
New England Glass Company
ca. 1830-1840
H. 4.6 cm; L. 7.9 cm

59.4.58

Colorless glass; rectangular
shape; scroll and spear point de-
sign on ends.
Gift of Louise S. Esterly
Comments: Fragments of this
pattern were found at the
Sandwich site.
*Parallels: McKearin, American
Glass*, pl. 168, no. 6; *Neal*, LE1,
p. 127; *Rose*, nos. 869 and 870.

---

688 Salt dish
New England
ca. 1830-1840
H. 4.8 cm; L. 7.9 cm

68.4.131

Opaque violet glass; rectangular
shape with S-curved ends; spear
point and scroll design on ends,
ribbing on edge of base.
Ex coll: Louise S. Esterly
Comments: Fragments of this salt
were found at the site of the
Sandwich factory.
*Parallels: McKearin, American
Glass*, pl. 168, no. 6; *Neal*, LE2,
p. 129; *Rose*, nos. 869 and 870.

---

*689 Another

68.4.196

Opalescent.
Ex coll: Louise S. Esterly

---

690 Salt dish
Massachusetts, Boston &
Sandwich Glass Company or
New England Glass Company
ca. 1830-1840
H. 4.5 cm; L. 7.9 cm

68.4.360

Opalescent, medium blue glass;
rectangular shape with S-curved
ends; scroll and spear point design on ends, stippling on edge
of base.
Ex coll: Louise S. Esterly
Comments: Very rare in this color;
fragments of this design were
found at the Sandwich site.
*Parallels: McKearin, American
Glass*, pl. 168, no. 6; *Neal*, LE3,
p. 131; *Rose*, nos. 869 and 870.

691 Salt dish
New York, Mt. Vernon Glass
Company, Vernon, or Saratoga
Glass Works, Saratoga, or Bos-
ton & Sandwich Glass Com-
pany, Sandwich, Massachusetts
ca. 1830-1845
H. 4.4 cm; L. 7 cm

50.4.212

Dark, olive-green glass; rectangular shape with palmettes and
beaded scrolls on sides and
ends, scrolls on base.
Ex coll: George S. McKearin
Comments: Fragments of salts in
this design have been found at
the sites of all three factories
listed above. It is generally
thought that those in bottle glass
were made at the New York factories and those in flint glass at
Sandwich.
Parallels: Lee, Sandwich Glass,
pl. 70, no. 1B; *McKearin, American Glass,* pl. 169, no. 3; *Neal,*
MV1, p. 132; *Rose,* no. 790.

*692 Another

61.4.88

Colorless.
Gift of Louise S. Esterly

*693 Another

63.4.90

Red-amber.
Gift of Louise S. Esterly

*694 Another

68.4.132

Citron-colored.
Ex coll: Louise S. Esterly

695 Salt dish
New York, Mt. Vernon Glass
Company; Vernon, or Saratoga
Glass Works, Saratoga; or Bos-
ton & Sandwich Glass Com-
pany, Sandwich, Massachusetts
ca. 1835-1845
H. 4.1 cm; L. 6.9 cm

68.4.203

Cobalt blue glass; rectangular
shape with palmettes and beaded scrolls on sides and ends,
sunburst on base.
Ex coll: Louise S. Esterly
Comments: This is a rare variation of a relatively common pattern; see previous entry.
Parallels: Neal, MV1b, p. 134.

696 Salt dish
New England Glass Company,
Cambridge, Massachusetts
ca. 1826-1830
H. 5.1 cm; L. 7.8 cm

68.4.202

Fiery opalescent glass; rectangular with basket of fruit on each
side and flower on each end; inscription on base: "N.E. GLASS/
COMPANY/BOSTON."
Ex coll: Louise S. Esterly
Comments: Fragments of salts of
this design were found at the
Sandwich factory site. See also
the marked Jersey salt, no. 685,
and the similar salt no. 700.
Parallels: Lee, Sandwich Glass,
pl. 72, no. 9; *McKearin, American Glass,* pl. 165, nos. 2, 3;
Neal, NE1, p. 137; *Rose,* nos.
802, 803; McKearin, Helen,
"New England Glass Company
Invoices," *Antiques* 52, no. 4,
Oct. 1947, Fig. 4, p. 277.

697 Salt dish
New England Glass Company,
Cambridge, Massachusetts
ca. 1826-1830
H. 5 cm; L. 7.7 cm

68.4.361

Opaque white glass; rectangular with basket of fruit on each side; inscription on base: "N E GLASS/COMPANY/BOSTON." *Ex coll:* Louise S. Esterly *Comments:* Fragments of salts in this design were found at the Sandwich factory site. See also the marked Jersey salt, no. 685. *Parallels: Lee, Sandwich Glass,* pl. 72, no. 9; *McKearin, American Glass,* pl. 165, nos. 2, 3; *Neal,* NE1a, p. 138; *Rose,* nos. 802, 803. McKearin, Helen, "New England Glass Company Invoices," *Antiques,* 52, no. 4, Oct. 1947, Fig. 4, p. 277.

698 Salt dish
New England Glass Company,
Cambridge, Massachusetts
ca. 1826-1830
H. 5.1 cm; L. 7.5 cm

50.4.214

Colorless lead glass; rectangular with basket of fruit on each side, inscription on base: "N.E. GLASS/COMPANY/BOSTON." *Ex coll:* George S. McKearin *Comments:* Fragments of salts with this design were found at the Sandwich factory site. See also the marked Jersey salt, no. 685. *Parallels: Lee, Sandwich Glass,* pl. 72, no. 9; *McKearin, American Glass,* pl. 165, nos. 2, 3; *Neal,* NE2, p. 137; *Rose,* nos. 802, 803. McKearin, Helen, "New England Glass Company Invoices," *Antiques* 52, no. 4, Oct. 1947, Fig. 4, p. 277.

699 Salt dish
New England Glass Company,
Cambridge, Massachusetts
ca. 1826-1830
H. 5 cm; L. 7.2 cm

61.4.86

Colorless lead glass; rectangular with basket of fruit on each side; inscription on base: "N.E. GLASS/COMPANY/BOSTON." Gift of Louise S. Esterly *Comments:* Fragments of salts of this design were found at the Sandwich factory site. See also the marked Jersey salt no. 685. *Parallels: Lee, Sandwich Glass,* pl. 72, no. 9; *McKearin, American Glass,* pl. 165, nos. 2, 3; *Neal,* NE 4, p. 137; *Rose,* nos. 802, 803; McKearin, Helen, "New England Glass Company Invoices," *Antiques* 52, no. 4, Oct. 1947, Fig. 4, p. 277.

700   Salt dish
Probably New England Glass
Company, Cambridge, Mas-
sachusetts, or Jersey Glass
Company, Jersey City, New Jer-
sey
ca. 1826-1830
H. 4.8 cm; L. 7 cm

68.4.82

Light green glass; rectangular
with a basket of flowers on each
side, flower on each end and
sunburst on base.
Gift of Mr. and Mrs. Harry A.
Snyder
Comments: The attribution is
based on this salt's resemblance
to the marked salts, nos. 685,
696-699.
Parallels: Neal, NE 6, p. 143.

701   Salt dish
Probably Midwest
ca. 1830-1840
H. 3.4 cm; L. 8.3 cm

68.4.343

Colorless lead glass; trapezoidal
shape; scroll ornament on ends;
sunburst base.
Ex coll: Louise S. Esterly
Comments: Very rare.
Parallels: Neal, OG1a, p. 145;
Rose, no. 764, pl. XXIII.

702   Salt dish
Probably New England
ca. 1830-1835
H. 4.3 cm; L. 7.8 cm

61.4.69

Colorless lead glass; rectangular
shape; ends and base filled with
waffled pattern.
Gift of Louise S. Esterly
Published: Rose, no. 767.
Parallels: Neal, OG2, p. 147.

703   Salt dish
Eastern United States
ca. 1830-1840
H. 4 cm; L. 7.6 cm

61.4.70

Colorless lead glass; rectangular
shape; sides and ends with verti-
cal fluting; scroll design on base.
Gift of Louise S. Esterly
Published: Rose, no. 781.
Parallels: Neal, OG16, p. 162.

704   Salt dish
Probably Pittsburgh, Pennsylvania
ca. 1830-1840
H. 4.5 cm; L. 8.9 cm

68.4.252

Colorless lead glass; trapezoidal
shape; sides with circles and
peacock feathers; ends with
flower in a circle.
Ex coll: Louise S. Esterly
Comments: Very rare.
Parallels: Neal, OL9, p. 211;
Rose, no. 746, pl. XXII.

705 Salt dish
New England
ca. 1830-1840
H. 3.9 cm; L. 8.2 cm

68.4.357

Cobalt blue glass; oval shape; sides with heart enclosing diamonds, cornucopias and S-scrolls with diamonds alternating.
Ex coll: Louise S. Esterly
Comments: Very rare.
Parallels: Neal, OL11, p. 213; *Rose,* no. 818 (similar).

†706 Salt dish
New England
ca. 1830-1840
H. 3.5 cm; L. 8.5 cm

68.4.216

Citron-colored glass; oval shape; scalloped rim; sides with scroll, ends with heart, sunburst on base.
Ex coll: Louise S. Esterly
Comments: Extremely rare in this color.
Parallels: Lee, Sandwich Glass, pl. 75-8B; *Neal,* OL12, p. 214; *Rose,* nos. 817 and 818.

707 Salt dish
New England
ca. 1830-1840
H. 3.5 cm; L. 8.4 cm

59.4.55

Colorless glass; oval shape; sides with scroll; ends with hearts; bow design on base.
Gift of Louise S. Esterly
Parallels: Lee, Sandwich Glass, pl. 75, 8B; *Neal,* OL12a, p. 215; *Rose,* nos. 817 and 818.

708 Salt dish
New England
ca. 1830-1840
H. 3.1 cm; L. 8.3 cm

68.4.228

Cobalt blue glass; oval shape; sides with scroll; ends with hearts; bow and two rows of beading on base.
Ex coll: Louise S. Esterly
Parallels: Lee, Sandwich Glass, pl. 75, 8B; *Neal,* OL12b, p. 216; *Rose,* nos. 817 and 818.

*709 Salt dish
New England
ca. 1840
H. 4.5 cm; L. 8.5 cm

68.4.91

Colorless lead glass; oval shape; diamond waffle pattern on sides and oval base.
Gift of Mr. and Mrs. Harry A. Snyder
Parallels: Lee, Sandwich Glass, pl. 75, no. 3; *Neal,* OL14, p. 218.

†710 Another

68.4.135

Amethyst.
Ex colls: Louise S. Esterly; Mr. and Mrs. Harry S. High

711 **Salt dish**
New England
ca. 1830-1840
H. 4.8 cm; L. 8.8 cm

68.4.162

Amethyst glass; oval shape; sides and base with diamonds and beading.
Ex coll: Louise S. Esterly
Parallels: Lee, Sandwich Glass, pl. 68, no. 2; *Neal,* OL15, p. 219.

*712 **Another**

68.4.123

Clambroth.
Ex coll: Louise S. Esterly

†*713 **Another**

68.4.178

Opaque blue.
Ex coll: Louise S. Esterly

714 **Salt dish**
New England
ca. 1830-1840
H. 3.5 cm; L. 8.2 cm

61.4.79

Colorless lead glass; oval shape; sides with roman rosette design; sunburst base.
Gift of Louise S. Esterly
Parallels: Lee, Sandwich Glass, pl. 62, lower center; *Neal,* OL16, p. 220.

*715 **Another**

68.4.126

Red-amber.
Ex coll: Louise S. Esterly

716 **Salt dish**
New England
ca. 1830-1840
H. 3.8 cm; L. 8.1 cm

68.4.365

Opalescent glass; oval shape; roman rosette design with sunburst base.
Ex coll: Louise S. Esterly
Comments: Extremely rare.
Parallels: Lee, Sandwich Glass, pl. 69, no. 7; *Neal,* OL16a, p. 221; *Rose,* no. 809.

717 **Salt dish**
Probably Boston & Sandwich
Glass Company, Sandwich,
Massachusetts
ca. 1830-1845
H. 4.5 cm; L. 8.6 cm

68.4.170

Light amethyst glass; oval shape with C-scrolls on either side of a star on sides and ends; octagonal base with C-scrolls and diamonds.
Ex coll: Louise S. Esterly
Parallels: Lee, Sandwich Glass, pl. 70, no. 5; *McKearin, American Glass,* pl. 166, no. 6; *Neal,* OL17, p. 222.

*718 **Another**

59.4.57

Colorless.
Gift of Louise S. Esterly

719 **Salt dish**
Probably United States; possibly
Europe
ca. 1840-1860
H. 3.1 cm; L. 8.8 cm

68.4.348

Medium blue glass; oval shape,
pattern of stars and scrolls on a
stippled background; rectangular base with cut corners.
Ex coll: Louise S. Esterly
Comments: Very rare.
Parallels: Neal, OL20a, p. 228.

†*720 **Salt dish**
New England
ca. 1830-1840
H. 3.8 cm; L. 8.6 cm

68.4.158

Opaque white glass; oval shape,
sides with diamond-filled circles; oval base.
Ex colls: Louise S. Esterly; Mrs.
Harry S. High

Comments: Rare in this color.
Published: Rose, no. 837.
Parallels: Neal, OL22, p. 230.

721 **Another**

68.4.224

Purple blue.
Ex coll: Louise S. Esterly

722 **Salt dish**
Probably New England
ca. 1830-1840
H. 3.8 cm; L. 8.5 cm

61.4.87

Colorless glass; oval shape,
diamond-filled horseshoes on
ends.
Gift of Louise S. Esterly
Parallels: Neal, 001, p. 165.

†*723 **Another**

68.4.205

Reddish-amber.
Ex coll: Louise S. Esterly

724 **Another**

68.4.208

Amethyst.
Ex coll: Louise S. Esterly

725 **Salt dish**
New England
ca. 1830-1840
H. 4 cm; L. 9.5 cm

68.4.371

Colorless lead glass; rectangular
with diamonds on ends and
base.
Ex coll: Louise S. Esterly
Parallels: Neal, 004, p. 169; *Rose,*
no. 871.

726   Salt dish
New England
ca. 1830-1840
H. 3.8 cm; L. 9.1 cm

68.4.210

Opalescent glass; oval, four
hearts above panels of diamonds
on each side.
Ex colls: Louise S. Esterly; Mrs.
Harry S. High
Published: Rose, no. 816.
Parallels: Neal, 005, p. 171.

†727   Another

68.4.364

Opaque blue and white glass.
Ex coll: Louise S. Esterly

*728   Another

68.4.370

Opaque white glass.
Ex coll: Louise S. Esterly

*729   Another

68.4.372

Colorless glass.
Ex coll: Louise S. Esterly

---

730   Salt dish
United States, or possibly
Continent
ca. 1830-1845
H. 3.5 cm; L. 7.5 cm

63.4.95

Clambroth glass; octagonal with
a stepped base and scrolls on
sides.
Gift of Louise S. Esterly
Parallels: Neal, 0013, p. 179.

---

†731   Salt dish
New England
ca. 1830-1840
H. 5 cm; L. 8.4 cm

68.4.247

Colorless lead glass, oval with
cornucopias, scrolls, and diamonds around sides; part of design silver-stained yellow.
Ex coll: Louise S. Esterly
Comments: Extremely rare with
silver-stained decoration.
Parallels: Neal, OP1, p. 246.

---

732   Salt dish
New England
ca. 1830-1840
H. 5 cm; L. 8.4 cm

68.4.139

Colorless lead glass; oval, with
cornucopias, scrolls and diamonds around sides, scrolls and
a row of beading on base.
Ex coll: Louise S. Esterly
Parallels: Neal, OP1a, p. 247.

733 Salt dish
Probably New England
ca. 1830-1840
H. 4.9 cm; L. 8.2 cm

68.4.214

Purple-blue glass; oval; diamond pattern on body; four paw feet.
Ex coll: Louise S. Esterly
Comments: Fragments of this design were found at the site of the Sandwich factory.
Parallels: Lee, Sandwich Glass, pl. 76, no. 9; *McKearin, American Glass,* pl. 166, no. 4; *Neal,* OP2, p. 249; *Rose,* no. 807.

734 Salt dish
New England
ca. 1830-1840
H. 4.8 cm; L. 8.1 cm

68.4.137

Opalescent glass; oval; diamond pattern around body.
Ex colls: Louise S. Esterly; Mrs. Harry S. High
Comments: Fragments of this design were found at the Sandwich factory site.
Parallels: Lee, Sandwich Glass, pl. 76, no. 9, *McKearin, American Glass,* pl. 166, no. 4; *Neal,* OP2a; *Rose,* no. 807.

735 Salt dish
New England
ca. 1830-1840
H. 5 cm; L. 8.1 cm

61.4.73

Colorless lead glass; oval; diamond pattern around body; four paw feet.
Gift of Louise S. Esterly
Comments: Fragments of this design were found at the Sandwich factory site.
Parallels: Lee, Sandwich Glass, pl. 76, no. 9; *McKearin, American Glass,* pl. 166, no.4; *Neal,* OP2b, p. 251; *Rose,* no. 807.

†736 Salt Dish
Probably New England
ca. 1830-1840
H. 4.8 cm; L. 8.9 cm

68.4.121

Opaque, mottled blue and white glass; rectangular; diamond design on each side.
Ex coll: Louise S. Esterly
Comments: Extremely rare in this color.
Parallels: Lee, Sandwich Glass, pl. 67, no. 5; *Neal,* OP17, p. 267.

†*737 Another

68.4.171

Opaque white.
Ex coll: Louise S. Esterly

†*738 Another

68.4.173

Opalescent dark blue.
Ex coll: Louise S. Esterly

***739 Another**

68.4.220

Opalescent.
Ex coll: Louise S. Esterly

76

288

264

100

102

269

270

331

54

157

136

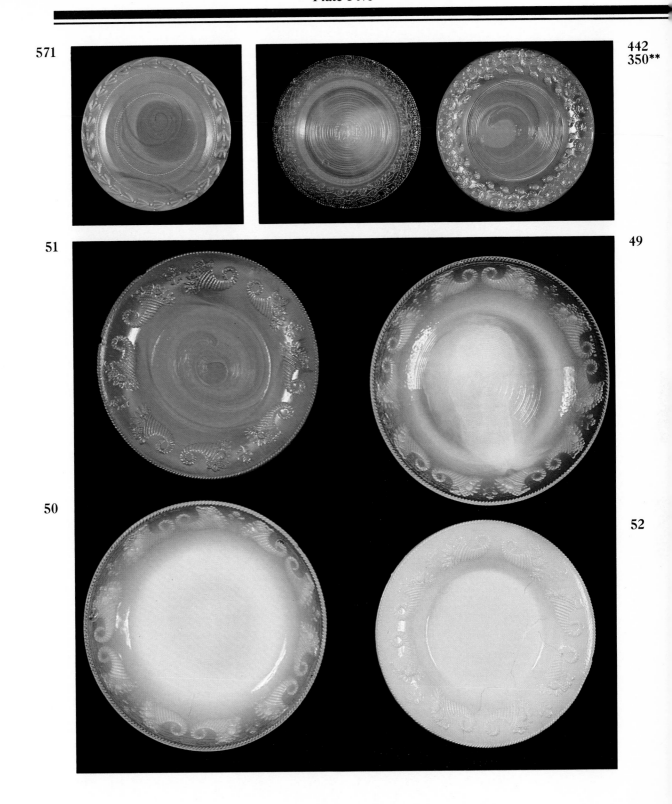

571

442
350**

51

49

50

52

**Center

440
458
448
433

366
451

356
376

*494
490
493
489
486
488
492
**487

*499
501
500
498
502

*471
474
472
475
473

*Clockwise from top
**Center

*731
126
226

647

**668

771

633

706

713

710

*Clockwise from top
**Center

673

**664

670

672

674

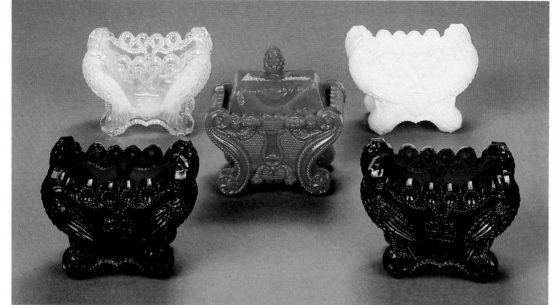

*742
720
723
749
755
**774

944
727

*Clockwise from top
**Center

**736

738

737

*655
653
657
649
656
**650

*Clockwise from top
**Center

867

844

790
788

853
850
854
849
852
848

891
890
892
893

869
870
871
873
872

975
976
977
974

1179

919

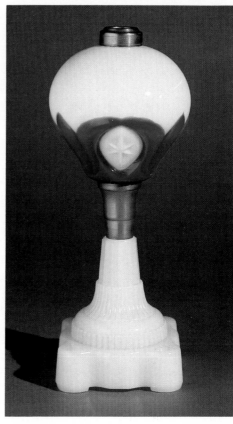

1401

1468

*1427

1428

1426

*Center

1512

1507

1459
1463
1464
1462
1461

1477

1475

1534

1530

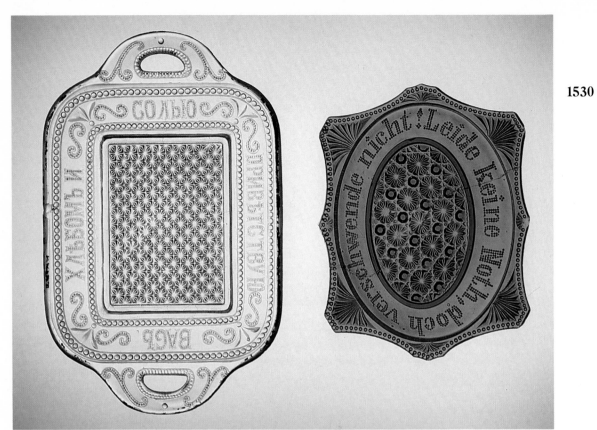

1535

740 **Salt dish**
Possibly Midwest
ca. 1835-1850
H. 4.8 cm; L. 8.9 cm

60.4.808

Colorless lead glass; oval;
diamond-filled hearts on sides
and ends.
Gift of Louise S. Esterly
Comments: Very rare.
Parallels: Neal, OP18, p. 268.

741 **Salt dish**
Probably Midwest; possibly
Continent
ca. 1835-1850
H. 6.1 cm; L. 8.9 cm

68.4.255

Colorless lead glass; oval with
diamond-filled circles on sides;
octagonal foot.
Ex coll: Louise S. Esterly
Comments: Extremely rare.
Parallels: Neal, OP22, p. 272;
Rose, no. 795, pl. XXII.

†742 **Salt dish**
Providence Flint Glass Works,
Providence, Rhode Island
ca. 1831-1833
H. 5.6 cm; L. 7.6 cm

68.4.159

Blue glass; rectangular; shield
and double-headed eagle on
each end; "PROVIDENCE" on
base.
Ex coll: Louise S. Esterly
Comments: Fragments of this design have been found at the
Sandwich factory site.
Parallels: Lee, Sandwich Glass,
pl. 72; *McKearin, American
Glass,* pl. 167, no. 4; *Neal,* PE1,
p. 305; *Rose,* no. 798, p. 151;
Wilson, pp. 286-288.

*743 **Another**

68.4.408

Colorless.
Ex coll: Louise S. Esterly

744 **Salt dish**
New England, probably Providence Flint Glass Works, Providence, Rhode Island
ca. 1831-1833
H. 5.6 cm; L. 7.6 cm

68.4.180

Colorless lead glass; rectangular
shape with a double-headed
eagle and shield on each end;
leaf on base.
Ex coll: Louise S. Esterly
Comments: Very rare; attribution
is based on this salt's similarity
to the two salts marked "PROV-
IDENCE," above.
Parallels: Lee, Sandwich Glass,
pl. 76, no. 4A; *McKearin, American Glass,* pl. 167, no. 6; *Neal,*
PE1a, p. 306; *Rose,* no. 806.

745 Salt
New England
ca. 1830-1840
H. 3.2 cm; L. 8.5 cm

68.4.140

Colorless lead glass; oval with peacock feathers around sides; bow on base in two rows of beading.
Ex coll: Louise S. Esterly
Comments: Very rare.
Parallels: Neal, PO 3, p. 281; *Rose*, no. 792.

746 Salt dish
New England
ca. 1830-1840
H. 3.5 cm; L. 9.8 cm

68.4.119

Light green glass; oval with peacock feathers around sides; sunburst on base.
Ex colls: Louise S. Esterly; Mrs. Harry S. High
Comments: Extremely rare in this color; fragments of this design were found at the Sandwich factory site.
Parallels: McKearin, American Glass, pl. 166, no. 5; *Neal*, PO4, p. 282.

*747 Another

68.4.133

Cobalt blue.
Ex coll: Louise S. Esterly

748 Salt dish
New England
ca. 1830-1840
H. 3.5 cm; L. 9.5 cm

61.4.81

Colorless lead glass; oval with peacock feathers around sides; eight-pointed star on base.
Gift of Louise S. Esterly
Parallels: Lee, Sandwich Glass, pl. 68, rt. center; *McKearin, American Glass*, pl. 166, no. 5; *Neal*, PO5, p. 283; *Rose*, no. 797.

†749 Another

68.4.164

Opalescent blue.
Ex coll: Louise S. Esterly

750 Salt dish
Midwest, probably Pittsburgh
ca. 1830-1840
H. 6.7 cm; L. 9.5 cm

68.4.117

Colorless lead glass; oval with peacock feathers around sides; sixteen bull's-eyes underneath base.
Ex coll: Louise S. Esterly
Comments: Very rare.
Parallels: Lee, Sandwich Glass, pl. 75, no. 5; *McKearin, American Glass*, pl. 170, no. 9; *Neal*, PP1, p. 291; *Rose*, no. 793.

751 **Salt dish**
New England
ca. 1830-1845
H. 4.9 cm; D. 8 cm

61.4.77

Colorless lead glass; circular
with peacock eyes around sides;
pedestal foot, with concentric
rings on bottom.
Gift of Louise S. Esterly
Parallels: Neal, PP2, p. 292.

752 **Salt dish**
New England
ca. 1830-1840
H. 5.1 cm; D. 8 cm

68.4.222

Opaque purple glass; circular
with peacock eyes around sides;
circular foot with sunburst beneath.
Ex coll: Louise S. Esterly
Parallels: Neal, PP3, p. 296.

753 **Salt dish**
United States or possibly France
ca. 1840-1850
H. 5.6 cm; D. 8.2 cm

60.4.807

Colorless glass; round shape
with elaborate scroll pattern.
Gift of Louise S. Esterly
Comments: The only salt in this
pattern published.
Published: Neal, RD36, p. 347.

754 **Salt dish**
Probably Midwest
ca. 1830-1845
H. 3.8 cm; D. 7.7 cm

68.4.160

Amethyst glass; circular with
diamond-filled arches around
sides.
Ex coll: Louise S. Esterly
Comments: Extremely rare.
Parallels: Neal, RD12, p. 320.

†*755 **Salt dish**
Massachusetts, New England
Glass Company or Boston &
Sandwich Glass company
ca. 1830
H. 5 cm; D. 7.7 cm

68.4.246

Light opaque silver-blue glass;
circular with leaves and
bouquets around sides; round
scalloped foot.
Ex coll: Louise S. Esterly
Comments: Extremely rare.
Parallels: Lee, Sandwich Glass,
pl. 69, nos. 6, 8; *McKearin,
American Glass*, pl. 164, no. 2;
Neal, RP3, p. 350, *Rose*, nos.
847, 848, 849.

756 **Salt dish**
Massachusetts, Boston &
Sandwich Glass Company or
New England Glass Company
ca. 1830-1845
H. 5.7 cm; D. 7.8 cm

68.4.194

Colorless lead glass; circular
with Gothic arches around sides
of bowl.
Ex coll: Louise S. Esterly
Comments: Very rare.
Parallels: Neal, RP7, p. 355.

757 **Salt dish**
New England
ca. 1835-1850
H. 4.6 cm; D. 7.3 cm

61.4.85

Colorless lead glass; circular
with Gothic arches on sides.
Gift of Louise S. Esterly
Parallels: Neal, RP9, p. 357.

758 **Salt dish**
New England
ca. 1835-1845
H. 5.1 cm; L. 8 cm

61.4.84

Colorless lead glass; rectangular;
scrolls on sides; heart and club,
respectively, on ends.
Gift of Louise S. Esterly
Comments: Very rare.
Published: Rose, no. 778.
Parallels: Lee, Sandwich Glass,
pl. 74, no. 6; *Neal,* SC1, p. 386.

759 **Salt dish**
New England, or possibly
Europe
ca. 1830-1840
H. 4.4 cm; L. 8.1 cm

61.4.91

Cobalt blue glass; trapezoidal,
with scrolls on sides and diamond waffle pattern on ends
and base.
Gift of Louise S. Esterly
Comments: Very rare.
Parallels: Neal, SC5, p. 390.

760 **Salt dish**
Probably New England
ca. 1830-1840
H. 4.5 cm; L. 7.5 cm

68.4.225

Pale green glass; rectangular;
heart design on sides; stylized
tulip on ends.
Ex coll: Louise S. Esterly
*Parallels: McKearin, American
Glass,* pl. 169, no. 2; *Neal,* SC7,
p. 392; *Rose,* no. 766.

*761 **Another**

59.4.59

Colorless.
Gift of Louise S. Esterly

762 Salt dish
Probably New England
ca. 1830-1840
H. 5 cm; L. 8.5 cm

61.4.74

Colorless lead glass; rectangular,
with strawberry diamond and
fans on sides.
Gift of Louise S. Esterly
Parallels: Lee, Sandwich Glass,
pl. 74, no. 4; *McKearin, American Glass*, pl. 166, no. 3; *Neal*,
SD2a, p. 438.

763 Salt dish
New England
ca. 1840
H. 5 cm; L. 7.8 cm

59.4.54

Cobalt blue glass; rectangular
with serpentine sides filled with
strawberry diamonds.
Gift of Louise S. Esterly
Parallels: Neal, SD4a, p. 441.

764 Salt dish
New England, possibly Boston
& Sandwich Glass Company,
Sandwich, Massachusetts
ca. 1830-1845
H. 5.2 cm; L. 8 cm

68.4.84

Colorless lead glass; rectangular,
with serpentine sides filled with
strawberry diamonds.
Gift of Mr. and Mrs. Harry A.
Snyder
Comments: This seems to be an
unlisted variant.
Parallels: Lee, Sandwich Glass,
pl. 74, no. 1; *Neal*, SD4, p. 440,
or SD4e, p. 445.

765 Salt dish
New England, possibly Boston
& Sandwich Glass Company,
Sandwich, Massachusetts
ca. 1830-1840
H. 5.4 cm; L. 7.3 cm

68.4.136

Pale green glass; rectangular,
with diamond design on sides
and ends.
Ex colls: Louise S. Esterly; Mrs.
Harry S. High
Comments: Fragments of this design were found at the Sandwich
site.
Parallels: Lee, Sandwich Glass,
pl. 74, no. 3B (not illus.);
McKearin, American Glass, pl.
166, no. 2; *Neal*, SD7, p. 449.

*766 Another

68.4.177

Amber.
Ex coll: Louise S. Esterly

*767 Another

68.4.199

Red-amber.
Ex coll: Louise S. Esterly

*768 Another

68.4.352

Blue.
Ex coll: Louise S. Esterly

769 Salt dish
New England
ca. 1830-1840
H. 5.1 cm; L. 6.7 cm

68.4.206

Pink glass; rectangular, with diamond design on sides and
ends.
Ex coll: Louise S. Esterly
Parallels: Neal, SD9, p. 452.

770 Salt dish
New England
ca. 1830-1840
H. 5.6 cm; L. 8.2 cm

68.4.181

Colorless glass in the shape of a
sleigh.
Ex coll: Louise S. Esterly
Comments: Extremely rare.
Parallels: Lee, Sandwich Glass,
pl. 74, no. 9; *Neal*, SH1, p. 425;
Rose, no. 758.

†771 Salt dish
United States or possibly Finland or Denmark
ca. 1835-1850
H. 4.2 cm; L. 7.5 cm

68.4.215

Dark green glass; rectangular
with a shell on each side and
end.
Ex coll: Louise S. Esterly
Comments: Extremely rare in this
color. Before the 1972 flood,
Corning Museum photographic
files contained a photograph of a
salt which appeared to be like
this one, sent by the National
Museum of Helsinki and made
at the Nuutajarvi glass house,
Finland.
Parallels: Neal, SL1, p. 403; Larsen, Alfred, Peter Riismøller,
Mogens Schlüter, *Dansk Glas
1825-1925*, Copenhagen: Ny &
Nordisk Forlag Arnold Busck,
1974, Fig. 362, p. 286.

772 Salt dish
United States
ca. 1835-1850
H. 4.5 cm; L. 7.5 cm

50.4.217

Light green glass; rectangular
with a shell on each side.
Ex coll: George S. McKearin
Comments: May be unique in
this color.
Parallels: Neal, SL10, p. 414.

773   Salt dish
New England
ca. 1830-1840
H. 4 cm; L. 8.2 cm

68.4.172

Light green glass; rectangular
with shell on each side and
stylized leaf on each end.
Ex coll: Louise S. Esterly
Comments: Very rare in this color.
Parallels: Lee, Sandwich Glass,
pl. 73; *Neal,* SL11, p. 415.

†774   Salt dish
New England
ca. 1830-1845
H. 5 cm; L. 8 cm

68.4.122

Purple-blue glass; rectangular
with "hairpin" design on each
end.
Ex coll: Louise S. Esterly
Comments: Fragments of this design were found at the Sandwich
factory site. Extremely rare in
this color.
Published: Rose, no. 871.
Parallels: Lee, Sandwich Glass,
pl. 66, no. 7A; *Neal,* SL14,
p. 418; *McKearin, American
Glass,* pl. 170, no. 1.

*775   Another

68.4.363

Opalescent.
Ex coll: Louise S. Esterly

776   Salt dish
Probably New England
ca. 1830-1840
H. 4.5 cm; L. 8.2 cm

61.4.72

Colorless glass; rectangular with
shell on sides and acorn and oak
leaves on ends.
Gift of Louise S. Esterly
Published: Rose, no. 780.
*Parallels: McKearin, American
Glass,* pl. 170, no. 3; *Neal,* SL17,
p. 423.

777   Salt dish
Probably New England
ca. 1830-1845
H. 7 cm; L. 8.2 cm

68.4.157

Colorless lead glass; rectangular,
with shell on sides and acorn
and oak leaves on ends; pedestal
base.
Ex coll: Louise S. Esterly
Published: Rose, no. 779.
Parallels: Lee, Sandwich Glass,
pl. 75, no. 4; *McKearin, American Glass,* pl. 170, no. 7; *Neal,*
SL18, p. 424.

778 Salt dish
New England or possibly
Denmark
ca. 1830-1845
H. 4.3 cm; L. 7.6 cm

59.4.69

Amber glass; trapezoidal shape;
design resembling stag's head on
sides and ends.
Gift of Louise S. Esterly
Comments: Fragments of this de-
sign were found at the Sandwich
factory site.
*Parallels: McKearin, American
Glass,* pl. 169, no. 6; *Neal,* SN1,
p. 427; Larsen, Alfred, Peter
Riismøller, Mogens Schlüter,
Dansk Glas 1825-1925,
Copenhagen: Ny & Nordisk
Forlag Arnold Busck, 1974,
Fig. 365, p. 288.

*779 Another

68.4.85

Colorless.
Gift of Mr. and Mrs. Harry A.
Snyder

*780 Another

69.4.57

Blue.
Gift of Mr. and Mrs. Harry A.
Snyder

781 Salt dish
United States
ca. 1830-1840
H. 5.1 cm; L. 7.6 cm

68.4.232

Colorless glass in the shape of a
wagon.
Ex coll: Louise S. Esterly
Comments: Very rare.
Parallels: Lee, Sandwich Glass,
pl. 74, no. 8; *Neal,* WN1, p. 463;
Rose, no. 768.

782 Salt dish
United States
ca. 1830-1840
H. 5.2 cm; L. 7.6 cm

68.4.231

Colorless glass in the shape of a
wagon.
Ex coll: Louise S. Esterly
Comments: May be unique.
Published: Neal, WN2, p. 465.

Lighting Devices and Vases

Even after the advent of machine pressing, standing pieces such as lighting devices, vases, and compotes continued to be made with machine-pressed bases and blown tops or, more rarely, with blown bases added to machine-pressed tops. A further development was to press top and bottom simultaneously but separately and join them while hot with a disc of glass. In this way a large number of patterns and color combinations could be made with only a few molds for bases and a variety of candle sockets, lamp fonts, and vase tops. Even though this was a great saving in the manufacture of molds, partly blown and partly pressed pieces continued to be manufactured through mid-century.

In the 1860's, lamps were often joined with a metal collar and plaster cement while cold, instead of being joined while hot in the glass factory. It is probable that the joining in this case was done by the seller rather than the manufacturer. It may be that the glass factories shipped boxes of lamp fonts and lamp stems to various retailers who then joined them according to the style favored in their area. By 1876, Atterbury in Pittsburgh was advertising that the company could at last produce lamps pressed in one part and thus much stronger.[1]

For lamps and candlesticks pressed in one piece, or in patterns which match other tablewares, see the sections on lacy glass and later tablewares.

1. *Innes, Pittsburgh Glass*, p. 325.

783 Lamp
New England, probably
Thomas Cains' Phoenix Glass
Works
ca. 1830-1840
H. 25 cm; D. 12.3 cm

70.4.72

Colorless lead glass; spherical
blown font with a horizontal air
trap; attached to a quatrefoil
pressed base, ribbed under-
neath.
Gift of Mr. and Mrs. Kenneth
Wakefield
Parallels: Wilson, Fig. 182, p.
225; Bassett, Preston R. "The
Evolution of the American Glass
Lamp," *The Rushlight*, 33, no. 1,
Feb. 1967, Fig. 11, p. 1468.

784 Lamp
New England, probably
Thomas Cains' Phoenix Glass
Works
ca. 1830-1840
H. 17.4 cm; D. 12.3 cm

72.4.31

Colorless lead glass; spherical
blown font with everted collar
and horizontal air trap attached
by wafer to quatrefoil stepped
base with ribbing on underside.
Gift of Preston R. Bassett
Published: The Toledo Museum
of Art. *New England Glass Company 1818-1888*, Toledo, Ohio:
Museum, 1963, no. 190, p. 73.
Parallels: Bassett, Preston R.
"The Evolution of the American
Glass Lamp," *The Rushlight*, 33,
no. 1, Feb. 1967, Fig. 11, p.
1468.

785 Lamp
New England
ca. 1827-1835
H. 17.3 cm; D. (base) 8.7 cm

72.4.41

Colorless lead glass; blown font
attached by double wafer to
button-knopped stem; attached
by wafer to pressed cup plate
turned upside-down to form a
flat circular foot with an outer
circle of fans and inner band of
ribbing; rough pontil mark.
Gift of Preston R. Bassett
Comments: This was originally a
whale oil lamp with a drop-in
burner.
*Parallels: McKearin, American
Glass*, pl. 190, no. 6; *Wilson*,
Fig. 212c; Bassett, Preston R.
"The Evolution of the American
Glass Lamp," *The Rushlight*, 33,
no. 1, Feb. 1967, Fig. 17, p.
1470.

786 Lamp
New England
ca. 1827-1835
H. 17.5 cm; D. (base) 9.6 cm

50.4.295

Colorless lead glass; free-blown;
inverted pear-shaped font; attached to a pressed cup plate
base.
Ex coll: George S. McKearin
Comments: This cup plate is attributed by Ruth Webb Lee and
James H. Rose to the New England Glass Company or the Boston & Sandwich Glass Com-
pany.
Parallels: Lee and Rose, no. 32;
McKearin, American Glass, pp.
377 ff.

787 Whale oil lamp
New England
ca. 1827-1835
H. 10.8 cm; D. (base) 5.3 cm

68.4.538

Colorless lead glass with spherical blown font; applied straight
stem and applied pressed
circular foot with a waffle
design.
Ex coll: Louise S. Esterly
Comments: See no. 552, a miniature cup plate identical to the
base of this lamp.
*Parallels: McKearin, American
Glass,* pl. 189, no. 15.

†788 Lamp
Probably Cambridge, Mas-
sachusetts, New England Glass
Company; possibly Boston &
Sandwich Glass Company
ca. 1830-1840
H. 20.5 cm; D. (base) 8 cm

68.4.496

Opaque white glass; spherical
blown font; joined by a triple
wafer to a pressed base which is
a hollow stepped square having a
basket of flowers on each side
and a lion's head at each top
corner.
Ex coll: Louise S. Esterly
*Parallels: McKearin, American
Glass,* pls. 193, no. 2; 196, nos. 7
and 9; *Wilson,* p. 254; *Rose,* no.71.

789   Pair of lamps
New England Glass Company,
Cambridge, Massachusetts
ca. 1830-1840
H. 28.2 cm; D. (base) 8 cm

73.4.125 A,B

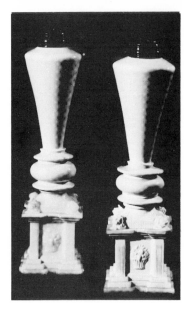

Opaque white glass with conical
blown font attached to a pressed
square base with a basket of
flowers on each side and a lion's
head on each top corner; inside
the base, opposite the bottom, is
an impressed inscription,
"NEG/ER:SR."
Comments: It is not known what
the initials "ER:SR" indicate, but
it has been suggested that they
refer to Enoch Robinson, an of-
ficial of the company. These
lamps, with and without initials
and with fonts of different
shapes, occur in white, colorless,
and a streaky blue glass. See below.
Parallels: The Toledo Museum
of Art, *The New England Glass
Company, 1818-1888*, Toledo,
Ohio: Museum, 1963, p. 70;
Wilson, pp. 254, 257; *McKearin,
American Glass*, pls. 193, 196.

†790   Lamp
Probably Cambridge, Mas-
sachusetts, New England Glass
Company; possibly Boston and
Sandwich Glass Company.
ca. 1830-1840
H. 19.2 cm; D. (base) 7.6 cm

68.4.495

Opaque light blue glass; spherical blown font; joined by a triple
wafer to a pressed base which is
a hollow stepped square having a
basket of flowers on each side
and a lion's head at each top
corner.
Ex coll: Louise S. Esterly
Comments: Extremely rare in this
color. An 1825-1828 account
book of the Boston & Sandwich
Glass Company in the library of
The Edison Institute lists "lion
head lamps."
Published: Wilson, Fig. 215C.
*Parallels: McKearin, American
Glass*, pls. 193, no. 2; 196, nos. 7
and 9; *Wilson* p. 254; *Rose*, no. 71.

791   Lamp
Probably Cambridge, Mas-
sachusetts, New England Glass
Company; possibly Boston &
Sandwich Glass Company
ca. 1830-1840
H. 19.5 cm; D. (base) 7.8 cm

72.4.43

Opaque white glass; spherical
blown font; joined by a triple
wafer to a pressed base which is
a hollow stepped square having a
basket of flowers on each side
and a lion's head at each top
corner.
Gift of Preston R. Bassett
*Parallels: McKearin, American
Glass*, pls. 193, no. 2; 196, nos. 7
and 9; *Wilson*, p. 254; *Rose*, no.
71.

792 Lamp
Probably Cambridge, Massachusetts, New England Glass
Company; possibly Boston &
Sandwich Glass Company
ca. 1830-1840
H. 24.3 cm; D. (base) 7.9 cm

72.4.44

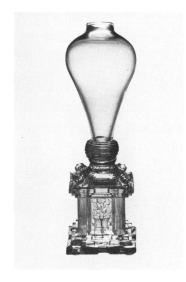

Colorless glass; inverted baluster-shaped blown font; joined by
a triple wafer to a pressed base
which is a hollow stepped square
having a basket of flowers on
each side and a lion's head at
each top corner.
Gift of Preston R. Bassett
*Parallels: McKearin, American
Glass*, pls. 193, no. 2; 196, nos. 7
and 9; *Wilson*, p. 254; *Rose*, no. 71.

793 Lamp
New England
ca. 1830-1840
H. 21.2 cm; D. (base) 12.4 cm

68.4.510

Colorless lead glass with a blown
spherical font attached to a
pressed hollow tripodal base
with C-scrolls resting on circular
hollow plinth, ribbed underneath.
Ex coll: Louise S. Esterly

794 Lamp
New England
ca. 1830-1840
H. 34.8 cm; D. (base) 12.4 cm

72.4.73

Colorless lead glass; baluster-
shape chimney blown and
roughly ground on outside to
produce gray matte finish;
blown spherical font attached by
a bladed knop to pressed
tripodal base with three
C-scrolls upright on circular hollow plinth, ribbed underneath.
Gift of Preston R. Bassett

795 Pair of lamps
New England
ca. 1830-1835
H. 17 cm; D. (base) 10.8 cm

61.4.96 A,B

Colorless lead glass; inverted
pear-shaped blown font; ground
to gray matte finish and painted
with spray of leaves; attached to
a pressed tripodal base with
C-scrolls; three paw feet.
Gift of Louise S. Esterly

796 Candlestick
New England
ca. 1830-1835
H. 17.7 cm; D. (base) 10.8 cm

68.4.511

Colorless lead glass; vertically
ribbed and fluted socket
attached by bladed knop to
tripodal base with C-scroll on
each side; three paw feet.
Ex coll: Louise S. Esterly
Parallels: Lee, Sandwich Glass,
pl. 178 (illustrates socket);
McKearin, American Glass, pl.
192, no. 3, pl. 191, no. 4 and 191,
no. 6 (illustrates socket); pl. 192,
no. 2 (illustrates base).

797 Candlestick
New England
ca. 1830-1835
H. 17.5 cm; D. (base) 10.8 cm

68.4.512

Colorless lead glass; socket
decorated with row of peacock
feathers around sides above row
of vertical flutes; attached by
wafer to tripodal base with a
C-scroll on each side; three paw
feet.
Ex coll: Louise S. Esterly
Published: Wilson, Fig. 240, p.
277.
Parallels: Lee, Sandwich Glass,
pl. 177, top; pl. 179, top (illustrates the sockets); *McKearin,*
American Glass, pl. 192, no. 1 (illustrates sockets); pl. 192, no. 2
(illustrates base); *Rose,* no. 83.

798 Candlestick
New England
ca. 1830-1835
H. 22.4 cm; D. (base) 10.8 cm

63.4.71

Colorless lead glass; pressed socket attached to a mold-blown ribbed stem above a pressed tripodal base with a C-scroll on each side; three paw feet.
Gift of Louise S. Esterly
Published: Wilson, Fig. 240, p. 277.

799 Lamp
New England
ca. 1830-1840
H. 28 cm

50.4.243

Colorless lead glass; font and baluster stem blown; attached by a wafer to a pressed three-step square base, ribbed underneath.
Ex coll: George S. McKearin
Parallels: McKearin, American Glass, pl. 191, no. 5.

800 Candlestick
New England
ca. 1830-1840
H. 26.5 cm; D. (base) 12.4 cm

62.4.44

Colorless lead glass with a blown candle socket; attached by a wafer to a blown stem and a pressed three-step square base, ribbed underneath.
Gift of Mr. and Mrs. Elliot A. Wysor
Parallels: McKearin, American Glass, pl. 191, no. 5.

801 Candlestick
New England
ca. 1830-1840
H. 23.5 cm; D. (base) 11.6 cm

68.4.51

Slightly purplish glass; cylindrical blown socket with blown stem; attached by a wafer to a pressed three-step square base, ribbed underneath.
Parallels: McKearin, American Glass, pl. 191, no. 5.

802 Candlestick
New England
ca. 1830-1840
H. 16.6 cm; D. (base) 13.3 cm

69.4.68

Colorless lead glass; ribbed and stippled socket with gadrooning around lower third; attached by a wafer to a pressed three-step square base, ribbed underneath.
Gift of Mr. and Mrs. Harry A. Snyder
Published: Wilson, p. 278, Fig. 241 center.
Parallels: McKearin, American Glass, pl. 191, nos. 4, 5 and 6.

803 Candlestick
New England
ca. 1830-1840
H. 17cm; D. (base) 13.5 cm

69.4.67

Colorless lead glass; ribbed and stippled socket with gadrooning around lower third; attached by a wafer to a pressed, hollow quatrefoil standard with five steps.
Gift of Mr. and Mrs. Harry A. Snyder
Comments: See nos. 806, 807 for objects with same base.
Published: Wilson, p. 278, Fig. 241, left.
Parallels: McKearin, American Glass, pl. 191, nos. 4, 5 and 6.

804 Candlestick
New England
ca. 1830-1840
H. 18 cm; D. (base) 12 cm

69.4.69

Colorless lead glass; ribbed and stippled socket with gadrooning around lower third; attached by a wafer to a pressed, hollow standard with a square base.
Gift of Mr. and Mrs. Harry A. Snyder
Published: Wilson, p. 278, Fig. 241, right.
Parallels: McKearin, American Glass, pl. 191, nos. 4, 5 and 6.

805 Pair of candlesticks
New England
ca. 1830-1840
H. 24.5 cm; D. (base) 12.1 cm

61.4.100 A,B

Colorless lead glass; ribbed and stippled socket with gadrooning around lower third; attached by a wafer to a hollow, mold-blown stem, attached by a knop to a hollow, pressed standard.
Gift of Louise S. Esterly
Parallels: McKearin, American Glass, pl. 191, no. 4.

806 Compote
New England
ca. 1830-1840
H. 21.6 cm; D. 23 cm

70.4.2

Colorless lead glass; hemispherical blown bowl with engraved swags and tassels; attached by a wafer to a hollow pressed quatrefoil standard with five steps.
Comments: See above, no. 803 for candlestick with same pressed foot; and no. 807 for lamp with same foot.

807 Lamp
New England
ca. 1830-1840
H. 32 cm; D. (base) 13.6 cm

72.4.74

Colorless lead glass; blown baluster-shape font; attached by three wafers to hollow blown stem; attached by three wafers to pressed columnar stem and hollow quatrefoil foot.
Gift of Preston R. Bassett
Comments: See candlestick, no. 803, and compote, no. 806 for objects with same pressed foot.
Parallels: McKearin, American Glass, pl. 191, no. 6; pl. 193, no. 1.

808 Lamp
New England
ca. 1830-1840
H. 21.1 cm; D. (base) 9.5 cm

72.4.38

Colorless lead glass; trumpet-shape mold-blown font with flutes on lower half; attached by a bladed knop to pressed hollow domed base with a scroll design.
Gift of Preston R. Bassett
Comments: See lamps below.
Parallels: Lee, Sandwich Glass, pl. 191; *McKearin, American Glass,* pl. 190, no. 3.

809 Lamp
New England
ca. 1830-1840
H. 20.3 cm; D. (base) 8.6 cm

72.4.39

Colorless lead glass; inverted mold-blown font with flutes on lower half; attached by a bladed knop to pressed hollow domed base formed by a row of vertical fluting and a row of rosettes, ending in circular scalloped ring.
Gift of Preston R. Bassett
Comments: See lamps above and below.
Published: Bassett, Preston R. "The Evolution of the American Glass Lamp," *The Rushlight* 33, no. 1, Feb. 1967, p. 1470, Fig. 16.
Parallels: Lee, Sandwich Glass, pl. 191; *McKearin, American Glass,* pl. 190, no. 3.

810 Lamp
New England
ca. 1830-1840
H. 26.7 cm; D. (base) 11 cm

72.4.40

Colorless lead glass; mold-blown font with flutes on lower half; attached by triple wafer to spherical blown stem; attached by triple wafer to hollow stepped pressed base formed of one row of vertical fluting and two rows of rosettes, ending in circular scalloped ring.
Gift of Preston R. Bassett
Comments: See lamps above and below.
Published: Bassett, Preston R. "The Evolution of the American Glass Lamp," *The Rushlight*, 33, no. 1, Feb. 1967, p. 1470, Fig. 15.

811 Lamp
New England
ca. 1830-1840
H. (with chimney) 43.2 cm;
D. (base) 11.0 cm

66.4.39

Colorless lead glass; with a blown bulbous chimney, roughly ground to a matte finish; trumpet-shaped font with molded flutes on lower half and cut strawberry diamond and fan decoration above; attached by triple wafer to spherical blown stem; attached by triple wafer to hollow stepped pressed base formed of one row of vertical fluting and two rows of rosettes ending in circular scalloped ring.
Gift of Mrs. Jason Westerfield

812 Lamp
Possibly Union Glass Company, Philadelphia, Pennsylvania or New England Glass Company, Cambridge, Massachusetts
ca. 1830-1840
H. 24.2 cm; D. (base) 10.6 cm

72.4.37

Colorless lead glass; blown spherical font with cut decoration of cross-hatched diamonds and ellipses and cut fans; attached by two wafers to bulging hollow stem with notched cutting; attached by wafer to pressed stem and stepped standard with circles of rosettes, above square base with rosettes on underside.
Gift of Preston R. Bassett
Comments: See no. 814.
Parallels: Lee, Sandwich Glass, pl. 191.

813 Pair of lamps
Possibly Union Glass Company,
Philadelphia, Pennsylvania or
New England Glass Company,
Cambridge, Massachusetts
ca. 1830-1840
H. 28.3 cm; W. (at base) 10.1 cm

71.4.81 A,B

Colorless lead glass; blown conical font with cut arches and fans
above cut vertical flutes; attached to a blown stem, attached by a wide bladed flange
to a pressed square base.
Comments: These lamps *appear*
to be identical but B is signifi-
cantly heavier and has a plug of
pinkish glass inside base while A
has four knobbed feet. The
lamps were from the collection
of a descendant of Richard
Synar who was a founder of the
Union Glass Company in
Philadelphia and had worked
previously at the New England
Glass Company in Cambridge,
Massachusetts.
Parallels: Lee, Sandwich Glass,
pl. 191.

814 Lamp
Possibly Union Glass Company,
Philadelphia, Pennsylvania or
New England Glass Company,
Cambridge, Massachusetts
ca. 1830-1840
H. 34 cm; D. (base) 10.6 cm

61.4.97

Colorless lead glass with an inverted pear-shaped blown font
and cut decoration of fans and
diamonds; attached by a wafer
to a hollow square stepped standard with circles of rosettes
above square base with rosettes
on underside.
Gift of Louise S. Esterly
Comments: See no. 812.
Parallels: Lee, Sandwich Glass,
pl. 191.

815 Lamp
Probably Midwest
ca. 1830-1840
H. 13.2 cm; D. (base) 10.1 cm

66.4.36

Colorless lead glass with a flat-
tened spherical blown font; attached by a double wafer to a
pressed four-sided hollow standard ribbed on the inside.
Gift of Mrs. Jason Westerfield.

816 Lamp
New England or Pittsburgh area
ca. 1820-1830
H. 25.1 cm;
D. (base) 8.3 x 8.5 cm

72.4.36

Slightly purplish glass; blown
font having cut decoration of
diamonds and fans alternating
with circles and flutes around
sides; attached by wafer to
straight hollow blown stem with
hollow knop in center; attached
by wafer to hand-pressed square
base with fluted design underneath.
Gift of Preston R. Bassett
Comments: See also lamps above
for similar cutting. The base of
this lamp is similar to many
made in New England and illustrated in the first section of this
book, but the cutting is like that
on the mug attributed to
Pittsburgh in CMG's collection,
no. 55.4.58 (not shown in this
catalog).
*Parallels: McKearin, American
Glass*, pls. 50, 51; *Wilson*, pp.
225-226.

817 Compote
Midwest or possibly Bohemia
ca. 1840-1850
H. 20 cm; L. (bowl) 23.6 cm

55.4.55

Colorless non-lead glass; ovoid
blown bowl with cut pattern of
diamonds and leaves; attached
by a wafer to a tooled stem and
an octagonal pressed foot.
Ex coll: George S. McKearin
Published: McKearin, Helen and
George S. *200 Years of American
Blown Glass*, Garden City, N.Y.:
Doubleday, 1950, pl. 18;
McKearin, American Glass, pl. 51.

818 Lamp
New England
ca. 1830-1840
H. 17.7 cm; D. (base) 7.5 cm sq.

72.4.71

Font blown of green glass attached by a wafer to pressed
colorless standard with straight
solid stem above three circular
and two square steps.
Gift of Preston R. Bassett
*Parallels: McKearin, American
Glass*, pl. 190.

819 Lamp
New England
ca. 1830-1840
H. 23.5 cm; D. (base) 10.7 cm

72.4.72

Colorless lead glass with a blown font roughly ground, with painted decoration of blue and green flowers; attached by a triple wafer to pressed hollow standard with columnar stem; three stepped circles atop square base.
Gift of Preston R. Bassett

820 Lamp
New England
ca. 1825-1840
H. 26.6 cm; D. (base) 8.9 cm

66.4.37

Colorless lead glass; blown inverted baluster-shape font with cut flutes around lower part; attached by a wafer to pressed columnar stem and circular stepped hollow base, ending in a square plinth.
Gift of Mrs. Jason Westerfield
Published: Wilson, Fig. 211, p. 250.

821 Lamp
New England, possibly Thomas Cains' Phoenix Glass Works
ca. 1830-1840
H. 18.2 cm; D. (foot) 10.8 cm

72.4.34

Colorless lead glass; inverted baluster-shaped blown font with horizontal air-trap; attached by wafer to pressed hollow base with columnar stem; three stepped circles and square plinth.
Gift of Preston R. Bassett
Parallels: Wilson, Fig. 190, p. 228.

822 Lamp
Probably New England
ca. 1820-1830
H. 13.2 cm; D. (base) 7.0 cm

72.4.69

Colorless lead glass; blown font with sloping shoulders and up-standing collar; attached by a wafer to pressed standard with columnar stem and circular stepped hollow base, ending in a square plinth.
Gift of Preston R. Bassett
Parallels: McKearin, American Glass, pl. 189, nos. 2, 14, 23.

823 Lamp
New England
ca. 1830-1840
H. 18.0 cm; D. (base) 10.7 cm

72.4.70

Aquamarine glass; blown conical font attached by bladed knop to pressed standard which has fluted stem, three circular steps and square base with rounded corners.
Gift of Preston R. Bassett
Comments: Extremely rare in this color.
Parallels: McKearin, American Glass, pl. 190.

824 Lamp
New England
ca. 1825-1835
H. 8.8 cm; D. (base) 5.7 cm

62.4.38

Colorless lead glass; spherical blown font applied by a wafer to a pressed straight stem and round foot.
Ex coll: Mrs. A. J. Wiesner
Parallels: McKearin, American Glass, pl. 189, nos. 16, 19.

825 Lamp
New England
ca. 1830-1840
H. 24.6 cm; D. (base) 8 cm

65.4.40

Colorless lead glass; inverted pear-shaped blown font; attached by a bladed knop to a pressed base ribbed underneath.
Gift of Earl A. Betz
Parallels: Rose, pl. VII, no. 94 (candlestick with same base).

826 Lamp
New England
ca. 1830-1840
H. 27.2 cm; D. (base) 12.5 cm

72.4.75

Colorless lead glass; inverted baluster-shaped blown font; attached by bladed knop to pressed square hollow base formed of Gothic arch motifs at four corners.
Gift of Preston R. Bassett
Comments: Base form very rare.
Parallels: Hough, Walter. *Collection of Heating and Lighting Utensils in the United States National Museum*, Washington. U.S. Gov't. Printing Office 1928, pl. 61, no. 4; *Lee, Sandwich Glass*, pl. 191 (center).

827 Lamp
New England, or possibly Pittsburgh area
ca. 1830-1840
H. 24.4 cm; D. 7.7 cm

72.4.35

Colorless lead glass; spherical blown font; attached by a triple wafer to blown hollow inverted baluster-shape stem; attached by triple wafer to pressed hollow four-tiered base ending in square plinth.
Gift of Preston R. Bassett
Comments: The font and stem of this lamp are standard New England type, but the "cascade" pressed base is associated with Pittsburgh.
Published: Bassett, Preston R. "The Evolution of the American Glass Lamp," *The Rushlight* 33, no. 1, Feb. 1967, p. 1470, Fig. 15.
Parallels: McKearin, American Glass, pl. 200, no. 32.

828 Pair of candlesticks
United States
ca. 1830-1850
H. 21.3 cm

50.4.241 A,B

Colorless lead glass with a
pressed diamond-patterned
socket with ribbed lower half;
attached by a tooled stem to a
pressed octagonal base.
Ex coll: George S. McKearin
*Parallels: McKearin, American
Glass*, pls. 190, 192.

829 Lamp
New England
ca. 1830-1835
H. 16.2 cm; D. (base) 5.7 cm

68.4.540

Colorless lead glass with a blown
inverted pear-shaped font attached to a square, double-
domed hollow base, with pattern of ribbings and dots on
underside.
Ex coll: Louise S. Esterly
Parallels: Lee, Sandwich Glass,
pl. 189 (right center); *McKearin,
American Glass*, pl. 190, no. 2.

830 Lamp
New England
ca. 1830-1840
H. 28 cm; D. (base) 13.0 cm

68.4.462

*831 Another
As above

68.4.463

Colorless lead glass; spherical
shape; blown font; blown stem
joined by wafer to hollow
pressed quatrefoil base; four
paw feet.
Ex coll: Louise S. Esterly

832   Lamp
Probably New England
ca. 1825-1840
H. 13.5 cm; D. (base) 6.5 cm
square

80.4.69

Colorless lead glass; vertically ribbed, mold-blown font with metal drop-in double whale-oil burner; square pressed base stippled underneath.
Bequest of Donald F. Clark
Comments: This combination of mold-blowing and pressing is rare.

833 Pair of vases
Three-Printie-Block pattern
United States
Mid-19th century
H. 26 cm; D. (at rim) 11.5 cm

50.3.231 A,B.

Amethyst glass; pressed in two parts; conical bowl with six vertical panels, each having three round depressions; attached by a wafer to a hollow, hexagonal standard.
Ex coll: George S. McKearin
Parallels: McKearin, American Glass, pl. 201, nos. 42, 43; pl. 197, no. 6; pl. 202, no. 53; *Lee, Sandwich Glass*, pl. 192, right.

*834 Another
Probably after 1875

68.4.478

Bluish-purple, pressed in one part.
Ex coll: Louise S. Esterly
Comments: As nos. 834 and 835 have been pressed in one piece, they must date from after 1875 and may be of 20th-century manufacture.

*835 Another
As above

68.4.479

See comment above.

*836 Lamp
H. 25.8 cm

68.4.451

Amethyst. In the same pattern, with square base.
Ex coll: Louise S. Esterly

837 Another
As above

68.4.452

838 Another
Probably after 1875
H. 20.3 cm

68.4.453

Pressed in one part with hexagonal base.
Ex coll: Louise S. Esterly

839 **Another**
As no. 838

68.4.454

As nos. 838 and 839 have been pressed in one piece, they must date from after 1875 and may be of 20th-century manufacture.

840 **Lamp**
Four-Printie-Block pattern
New England
Mid-19th century
H. 18.2 cm

68.4.466

841 **Another**
As above

68.4.467

Vaseline yellow glass; conical font with rounded top; six panels around sides, each with four circular depressions diminishing in size from top to bottom; joined by a wafer to a hollow hexagonal standard.
Ex coll: Louise S. Esterly
Parallels: McKearin, American Glass, pl. 201, no. 44.

842 **Vase**
Four-Printie-Block pattern
H. 30.4 cm

68.4.556

Bright blue.
Ex coll: Louise S. Esterly

843 **Vase**
Tulip pattern
Probably New England
ca. 1850
H. 23.8 cm; D. (at rim) 14 cm

50.4.232

Yellowish-green vaseline glass;
pressed in two pieces and joined
by a wafer; octagonal bowl with
petaled rim; hollow octagonal
stem.
Ex coll: George S. McKearin
Comments: Flint enameled
earthenware vases of the same
shape were made at Bennington,
Vermont.
Parallels: Lee, Sandwich Glass,
pl. 198, no. 2, *McKearin, American Glass,* pl. 201, no. 4; *Rose,*
nos. 253, 255 and 257, *SHS.* p. 21.

†*844 **A pair**

50.4.233 A,B.

Violet-blue with opaque white
marbleizing.
Ex coll: George S. McKearin

*845 **A pair**

58.4.76A,B

Amethyst.
Gift of Louise S. Esterly

*846 **Another vase**

68.4.333

Vaseline.
Ex coll: Louise S. Esterly

847 **Vase**
United States
Mid-19th century
H. 20.5 cm; D. (base) 9.5 cm

60.4.825

Opalescent white glass; pressed
tulip-shaped top with eight vertical panels around sides;
applied straight stem and round
flat foot with polished pontil
mark.
Gift of Louise S. Esterly
Comments: See tulip vases above.

†848 **Vase**
Loop pattern
New England
Mid-19th century
H. 28 cm; D. (base) 6.5 cm

59.4.94

Light amethyst glass; conical
top; six oval loops around sides;
attached by a wafer to a hollow
hexagonal standard above a hollow square foot.
Gift of Louise S. Esterly
*Parallels: McKearin, American
Glass,* pl. 197, nos. 1, 3; Lee,
Sandwich Glass, pl. 192, left.

†*849 **Another**

68.4.558

Blue.
Ex coll: Louise S. Esterly

†850 **Lamp**
In the same pattern
H. 24.8 cm

68.4.464

Greenish-blue.
Ex coll: Louise S. Esterly

851 **Another**
H. 25 cm

68.4.552

Amethyst.
Ex coll: Louise S. Esterly

†*852 **Another**
H. 26.2 cm

72.4.77

Amber.
Gift of Preston R. Bassett

†*853 **Lamp**
H. 21.7 cm

68.4.469

Ex coll: Louise S. Esterly

†*854 **Another**
As above

68.4.470

855 **Pair of candlesticks**
Petal and Loop pattern
New England
Mid-19th century
H. 17.7 cm; D. (base) 10.8 cm

61.4.62 A,B

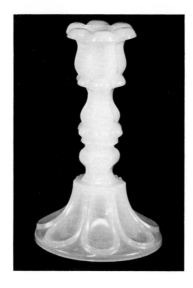

Whitish-clambroth glass; hexagonal candle socket with six petals around rim above a baluster stem; joined by a wafer to a hollow, pressed, dome-shaped standard with seven loops around it.
Gift of Alderman F. Gleason
Parallels: Lee, Sandwich Glass, pl. 182, no. 4; *McKearin, American Glass*, pl. 200, no. 35; *Rose*, no. 258; Watkins, Lura Woodside, "Positively Sandwich," *Antiques*, 27, no. 4, April 1935, Fig. 6, p. 134.

*856 **Another**

61.4.111

Opaque turquoise blue.
Gift of Louise S. Esterly

*857 **Another**

67.4.51

Colorless.
Gift of Mrs. John F. Staub

*858 **A pair**

63.4.72 A,B

Translucent lavender blue glass.
Gift of Louise S. Esterly

*859 **Another**

68.4.507

Medium blue.
Ex coll: Louise S. Esterly

*860 **Another**

68.4.508

As above.

*861 **Another**

68.4.534

Bluish gray.
Ex coll: Louise S. Esterly

*862 **Another**

68.4.535

As above.

*863 **Another pair**

69.4.58 A,B.

Vaseline glass.
Gift of Mr. and Mrs. Harry A. Snyder

864 Vase
Loop pattern
New England
Mid-19th century
H. 24.8 cm; D. (base) 10.8

68.4.468

Green glass; conical bowl; fluted rim; vertical loops around sides; joined by a wafer to a hollow hexagonal standard.
Ex coll: Louise S. Esterly
Comments: See above for other "looped" vases with different bases.
Parallels: Lee, Sandwich Glass, pl. 198, left; *McKearin, American Glass,* pl. 199, no. 19.

865 Vase
Loop pattern
New England
ca. 1840-1860
H. 27.4 cm; D. (base) 8 cm

68.4.628

Amethyst bubbly glass; conical top; sides with Loop pattern, twisted into a spiral; joined by a wafer to hexagonal baluster standard.
Ex colls: Louise S. Esterly; Mrs. John J. Grossman
Parallels: McKearin, American Glass, pl. 197, no. 1b.

866 Vase
New England
ca. 1840-1860
H. 28.2 cm; D. (base) 7.9 cm

68.4.557

Amethyst glass; conical top with fluted rim; two rows of flat panels around body, separated by vertical molding; joined by a wafer to hollow octagonal standard on square plinth.
Ex coll: Louise S. Esterly
Parallels: McKearin, American Glass, pl. 198, no. 15; *Rose,* no 270.

†867   **Pair of compotes**
Loop pattern
New England
Mid-19th century
H. 11.4 cm; D. (base) 10.4 cm

68.4.421 A,B

Amethyst glass; conical shape
bowl with seven-petal rim; attached by a wafer to a hollow
hexagonal standard with seven
loops around sides.
Ex coll: Louise S. Esterly
Parallels: *S.H.S.*, p. 21, lower
center.

868   **Candlestick**
New England
ca. 1840-1860
H. 22.5 cm; D. (base) 8.6 cm

68.4.529

Opaque blue socket with
acanthus leaves; attached by a
wafer to an opaque white hour-
glass standard, also with acanthus leaves; above hexagonal
base.
Ex coll: Louise S. Esterly
Parallels: Lee, Sandwich Glass,
pl. 187, no. 3.

†869   **Pair of lamps**
New England
ca. 1830-1845
H. 32.5 cm; D. (base) 10.3 cm

63.4.73 A,B

Opaque white font; vertically
decorated with acanthus leaves
and with a ring of petals at bottom; attached by a wafer to an
opaque blue pear-shaped standard with acanthus leaves ending in a square stepped base.
Gift of Louise S. Esterly
Parallels: Lee, Sandwich Glass,
pl. 193, center; *McKearin, American Glass,* pl. 194, no. 1; *Rose,*
no. 105.

†*870   **Another**

68.4.375

Light green font, white base.
Ex coll: Louise S. Esterly

†*871   **Another**

68.4.376

Opaque white.
Ex coll: Louise S. Esterly

†*872   **Another**

68.4.629

Blue font, white base.
Ex coll: Louise S. Esterly

†*873   **Another**

72.4.88

Colorless.
Gift of Preston R. Bassett

874 Pair of candlesticks
New Bedford, Massachusetts,
Mount Washington Glass
Company
ca. 1869-1880
H. 16.8 cm

50.4.234. A,B

Opaque white glass; pressed in
two pieces and joined while hot;
twelve-paneled socket with scalloped rim; attached by a wafer
to a standard having S-scrolled
dolphin shaft on a circular scalloped base.
Ex coll: George S. McKearin
Comments: The Museum has
three fragments of a candlestick,
identical except for color, which
were excavated on the site of the
Mount Washington Glass Company's factory, under the site of
the 1880 ten-pot furnace. These
fragments seem to have been
pressed in the same mold as the
whole candlestick. However, at
least one fragment of this pattern was also found at the
Sandwich factory site.
Published: Wilson, Fig. 295.
Innes, Fig. 469.

*****875 Fragments**
As above

68.4.11

Opaque blue.
Gift of Mr. and Mrs. Kauko
Kahila

876 Pair of candlesticks
New England
ca. 1840-1860
H. 26.4 cm; D. (base) 9.3 cm

62.4.46 A,B

Lotus-shaped socket of blue
glass; joined by a blue wafer to a
stem formed of a grayish glass
dolphin with tail up on a square
plinth.
Published: Wilson, fig. 248, p.
294.
Parallels: Lee, Sandwich Glass,
pl. 184.

*877 **Candlestick**
New England
ca. 1840-1850
H. 26 cm

68.4.554

878 **Another**
As above

68.4.555

Colorless lead glass; inverted pear-shaped socket, decorated with shells and tiny dolphins; joined by wafer to a standard in the form of a dolphin with its tail in the air; mounted on hollow square base.
Ex colls: Louise S. Esterly; Dr. and Mrs. Charles W. Green
Comments: This style of dolphin candlestick may be Midwestern.
Parallels: Lee, Sandwich Glass, pl. 184, right; *McKearin, American Glass*, pl. 204, no. 65; *Rose*, no. 326.

879 **Candlestick**
New England
ca. 1840-1860
H. 18.9 cm; D. (base) 7.8 cm

61.4.109

Amethyst glass; inverted bell-shaped socket attached by a wafer to octagonal pear-shape standard on a square plinth; Ground and polished base.
Gift of Louise S. Esterly
Parallels: McKearin, American Glass, pl. 197, no. 8; *Rose*, no. 254.

880 **Pair of candlesticks**
Probably Midwest
ca. 1850-1870
H. 19.4 cm; D. (base) 10 cm

62.4.45 A,B

Transparent deep blue glass;
pressed in two parts; hexagonal
socket attached by a wafer to a
hexagonal hollow columnar stem
and hexagonal foot.
Parallels: Lee, Sandwich Glass,
pl. 185, no. 3; *McKearin, American Glass*, pl. 200, no. 29; *Rose*,
no. 309.

*881 **Another**

59.4.78 A,B

Deeper blue.
Gift of Louise S. Esterly

*882 **Another candlestick**

68.4.455

Amethyst.
Ex coll: Louise S. Esterly

*883 **Another**
As above
68.4.456

884 **Vase**
New England
ca. 1840-1860
H. 29.5 cm

59.4.84

Light yellow glass; conical
shape; fluted rim; pressed in
two parts and attached by
bladed knop to hollow hexagonal base.
Gift of Louise S. Esterly
Parallels: Lee, Sandwich Glass,
pl. 198, no. 3; *McKearin, American Glass*, pl. 200, no. 34.

*885 **Another**

68.4.553

Amethyst.
Ex coll: Louise S. Esterly

886 **Pair of candlesticks**
Probably New England
ca. 1840-1860
H. 17.8 cm; D. (base) 9.2 cm

63.4.77 A,B

Opaque light blue glass; hexagonal urn-shaped socket above
stem composed of three
hexagonal-shape knops above a
hollow hexagonal base.
Gift of Louise S. Esterly
Parallels: Lee, Sandwich Glass,
pl. 183 (left).

887 **Whale oil lamp**
United States
ca. 1840-1850
H. 13.4 cm; D. (base) 6 cm

59.4.92

Opalescent white glass; pressed
in two parts with an octagonal
font attached by a wafer to hollow hexagonal standard and
base.
Gift of Louise S. Esterly

888 **Candlestick**
Probably New England
ca. 1845-1860
H. 14.4 cm; D. (base) 8 cm

63.4.76

Opaque light blue glass with
darker striations; lotus-shaped
socket attached by wafer to hollow tapered columnar stem
above stepped base.
Gift of Louise S. Esterly
Comments: Possibly unique form.
Published: Rose, no. 194.
Parallels: Lee, Sandwich Glass,
pl. 187, left (same base).

889 **Candlestick**
United States
1850-1870
H. 18.6 cm; D. (base) 10.0 cm

63.4.83

Canary-colored glass; lotus-
shaped socket joined by wafer to
solid columnar section; joined
by wafer to hollow columnar
standard with round base.
Gift of Louise S. Esterly

†890 **Candlestick**
New England
ca. 1840-1860
H. 22 cm; D. (base) 9 cm

64.4.83

Opaque blue glass; petal-form
socket applied by a wafer to a
columnar stem on a double-
stepped square base.
Parallels: Lee, Sandwich Glass,
pl. 186 (center).

†*891 **Pair of candlesticks**

68.4.385 A,B

Green socket, white base.
Ex coll: Louise S. Esterly

†*892 **Candlestick**

68.4.481

Blue.
Ex coll: Louise S. Esterly

†*893 **Another**
As above

68.4.482

894 **Lamp**
New England
ca. 1840-1860
H. 24.3 cm; D. (base) 8.4 cm

66.4.38

Colorless lead glass; hexagonal
font with a stylized tulip on each
side; hexagonal baluster stem
and foot.
Gift of Mrs. Jason Westerfield
*Parallels: McKearin, American
Glass,* pl. 204, no. 69.

895 **Lamp (fragment)**
New England
ca. 1840-1850
H. 24 cm; D. (rim) 12.3 cm

67.4.112

Colorless lead glass; conical
bowl with a round flat rim;
ground and polished; attached
by a wafer to a columnar hollow
stem and square stepped base.
Gift of Dorothea S. Setzer
Comments: This piece is obviously cut down from a broken
lamp, the upper half of the font
being ground off. See also nos.
897, 898. below, for similar
lamps.
*Parallels: McKearin, American
Glass,* pl. 194, nos. 2 and 3.

896 Candlestick
Probably New England
ca. 1840-1860
H. 13 cm; D. (base) 6.2 cm

68.4.138

Opaque light blue glass; hexagonal socket with flat rim; six-sided stem ending in three round steps; hollow, square base.
Ex coll: Louise S. Esterly
Parallels: Lee, Sandwich Glass, pls. 180 (left center), 181 (center), and 187 (left).

897 Lamp
New England
ca. 1830-1850
H. 31.1 cm; D. (base) 10.3 cm

68.4.374

898 Another
As above

68.4.377

Opaque white font; row of vertical panels around sides; attached by a wafer to an opaque blue columnar stem above a stepped square hollow base.
Ex coll: Louise S. Esterly
Parallels: McKearin, American Glass, pl. 194, no. 2; *Rose,* no. 106.

899 Lamp
United States
ca. 1850
H. 21 cm; D. (base) 8.6 cm

68.4.384

Opalescent glass; six-panel pear-shaped font with burning fluid wick tubes; attached by a wafer to hexagonal stepped standard.
Ex coll: Louise S. Esterly
Parallels: Lee, Sandwich Glass, pl. 193, left (lamp with same base).

900 Lamp
New England
ca. 1840-1860
H. 27.7 cm; D. (base) 8.5 cm

68.4.457

Deep amethyst glass; hexagonal font; fitted with a metal two-wick burning fluid burner; six sides, each with a raised circle above an ellipse; joined by a wafer to a hollow square plinth base.
Ex coll: Louise S. Esterly
Parallels: McKearin, American Glass, pl. 198, no. 12 (font) and pl. 203, no. 64 (base), pl. 202, no. 51 (vases); *Rose,* no. 302 (vases).

***901 Another**
As above

68.4.458

***902 Vase**
In the same pattern
Probably after 1875
H. 21.9 cm

68.4.494

Green, with hexagonal base.
Ex coll: Louise S. Esterly
Comments: As this vase and those below have been pressed in one piece, they must date from after 1875 and may be of 20th-century manufacture.

903 Another
H. 18.8 cm

68.4.490

Bright green.
Ex colls: Louise S. Esterly; Mrs. John J. Grossman
Comments: See above.

904 Another
H. 18.8 cm

68.4.491

Comments: See above.

***905 Another**

68.4.550

Amethyst.
Ex coll: Louise S. Esterly
Comments: See above.

***906 Another**
As above

68.4.551

907 Vase
New England
ca. 1840-1860
H. 23.6 cm; D. (base) 8.7 cm

68.4.465

Bluish-green glass; conical top with fluted top rim; six side panels, each with a heart design; joined by a wafer to a hexagonal baluster stem.
Ex coll: Louise S. Esterly
Parallels: Lee, Sandwich Glass, pl. 199, left.

908 Lamp
New England
ca. 1830-1850
H. 25.5 cm

50.4.260

Colorless lead glass; free-blown font cut into panels, each panel decorated with engraving; attached to a pressed, hexagonal hollow standard base which has been ground and polished on all surfaces.
Ex coll: George S. McKearin
Published: McKearin, American Glass, pl. 194, no.6.

909 Lamp
New England
ca. 1840-1850
H. 27 cm; D. (base) 8.6 cm

68.4.459

Amethyst glass; conical font with eight vertical panels around sides; attached by a wafer to short straight stem above hollow cube base with square plinth.
Ex coll: Louise S. Esterly
Parallels: McKearin, American Glass, pl. 203, no. 62.

910 Lamp
New England
ca. 1840-1860
H. 16.7 cm; D. (base) 6.8 cm

68.4.471

Violet-blue glass; conical font
with two whale oil wick tubes;
six panels around sides, each
decorated with two circles; flaring hexagonal standard.
Ex colls: Louise S. Esterly; Edward McGowan
Comments: An unpublished variant of a standard pattern.

911 Lamp
New England
ca. 1840-1860
H. 26.2 cm; D. (base) 7.8 cm

68.4.477

Bluish-green glass; conical font
with six vertical panels around
sides; attached by wafer to octagonal baluster standard on
square base.
Ex coll: Louise S. Esterly
Parallels: McKearin, *American Glass*, pl. 198, no. 13.

912 Lamp
Probably New England
ca. 1840-1860
H. 25.9 cm; (base) 7.5 cm x 7. 8
cm

72.4.78

Colorless lead glass with a double whale oil burner attached to
top of inverted baluster-shaped
font; attached by wafer to
pressed paneled stem and
square hollow base.
Gift of Preston R. Bassett
Parallels: Russell, pl. 51;
McKearin, American Glass, pls.
195, no. 4 and 197, no. 10.

913 Lamp
Probably Cambridge, Massachusetts; New England Glass Company
ca. 1847-1870
H. 24.0 cm; D. (base) 9.7 cm

72.4.79

Colorless lead glass with font pressed in a pattern of large protruding diamonds; attached by wafer to hexagonal pressed stem and foot.
Gift of Preston R. Bassett
Comments: Joseph Magoun of the New England Glass Company in 1847 patented a process to eliminate the mold seams on top of the font. This lamp seems to have been pressed under that patent.
Parallels: McKearin, American Glass, pl. 204, no. 69; *Russell*, pl. 50.

914 Lamp
Probably Cambridge, Massachusetts; New England Glass Company
ca. 1847-1865
H. 28.1 cm; (base) 8.6 cm. sq.

72.4.80

Pale green glass with a double whale oil burner attached to top of eight-sided font; attached by a wafer to an eight-sided baluster stem above a square base.
Gift of Preston R. Bassett
Parallels: McKearin, American Glass, pl. 197, no. 10; *Russell*, p. 101, pl. 51 (same standard).

915 Candlestick
Probably Midwest
ca. 1840-1860
H. 21.8 cm

50.4.235

Dark olive-green glass with free-blown socket attached to pressed hexagonal base.
Ex coll: George S. McKearin
Parallels: McKearin, American Glass, pl. 200, no. 33.

916 Candlestick
Probably Midwest
ca. 1840-1860
H. 23.8 cm

50.4.236

Cobalt blue glass; free-blown
socket; attached to pressed hex-
agonal standard.
Ex coll: George S. McKearin
*Parallels: McKearin, American
Glass*, pl. 200, no. 33.

917 Lamp
United States, probably Midwest, possibly New England
ca. 1865-1875
H. 60.1 cm

79.4.101

Base pressed of opaque white
glass; attached by a brass collar
to a ruby overlay blown font with
cut decoration; a kerosene
burner and a blown chimney
and shade.
Comments: Pressed bases of this
type are found both in New
England and the Midwest.
Parallels: Lee, Sandwich Glass,
pl. 194.

918 Lamp
United States, probably Midwest
ca. 1860-1880
H. 58.4 cm

80.4.47

Colorless pressed font attached
by a brass collar to an opaque-
white hollow pressed square
base. Blown shade; brass burner
converted for electricity.
Comments: See preceding lamp
for similar base and correct type
of chimney.
Parallels: Russell, p. 186.

†919 **Lamp**
Pittsburgh, Pennsylvania; Atterbury & Company
1862-1870
H. 26.8 cm; D. (font) 11.7 cm

76.4.20

Blown font of opaque white glass with an outer shell of blue glass covering the lower part; inscription around base of font "PATENTED MARCH 4 & JUNE 3, 1862" with "2" in the inside bottom of the font; attached by a brass collar and screw to a pressed hollow base of white glass with columnar stem and a square fluted base.
Ex coll: Mr. and Mrs. Kenneth Wakefield
Comments: This design was patented by J. S. Atterbury and James Reddick and had to do with the method of manufacture, i.e., a combination of blowing and pressing which produced the two-colored "bas-relief" design.
Parallels: Russell, pp. 169, 170.

920 **Lamp**
Pittsburgh, Pennsylvania, Atterbury & Company
ca. 1868-1880
H. 27 cm; D. (font) 10.2 cm

51.4.719

Mold-blown colorless font; connected with a brass collar to an opaque white pressed base and stem; bottom of font has inscription, "PATENTED SEPTEMBER 29, 1868," as does brass collar; kerosene burner stamped on handle, "PAT. FEB. 19, 1865/ HOLMES, BOOTH & HAYDEN."
Gift of Mrs. R. C. Woods
Comments: Patent date on the lamp is that of a screw socket patented by Atterbury. Holmes, Booth & Hayden was a maker of lamp parts in Waterbury, Connecticut.
Parallels: Innes, Pittsburgh Glass, pp. 320-321; *Russell*, p. 229.

921 **Lamp**
Pittsburgh, Pennsylvania, Ripley & Company
ca. 1870-1880
H. (with globes) 49.8 cm

76.4.40

Colorless and whitish "clambroth" glass and brass; two globular fonts on either side of a cylindrical match safe with lid; joined by a brass collar to a cast bronze four-sided pedestal; brass kerosene burner on each font; colorless chimneys.
Gift of Preston R. Bassett
Comments: Patented September 20, 1870. This lamp also appears in blue and with two different styles of pressed glass base.
Parallels: Innes, Pittsburgh Glass, pp. 64, 65; Peterson, Arthur G. *American Glass Patents and Patterns*, Sanford, Fla.: author, 1973, pp. 171, 172; *Revi*, p. 292.

Later Glass ca. 1840-1920

Although several different sizes and shapes of tableware might have been made in one pattern in the early days of glass pressing, matching table sets do not appear until the 1840's. The earliest objects were primarily serving pieces such as bowls and plates in many sizes, salts, and a few individual small dishes like cup plates and small sauce dishes. Probably because of the difficulty in controlling the thickness of the rim before the invention of the cap ring around 1830, drinking vessels were not made. Eventually, by 1837, it became possible to make tumblers[1] and by 1849 glassware was produced in matching table sets with goblets and wineglasses in various sizes, tumblers, and a variety of serving dishes. Since there are no printed catalogs until the 1850's, the earliest evidence for the production of pressed glass in matching sets and for the names of the patterns lies in advertisements and order books.

Lura Woodside Watkins discusses at some length orders of glassware sent by the New England Glass Company to the West Coast in 1849.[2] The only pattern names in these orders are Ashburton and Flute, but there are no illustrations. In 1853, the New England Glass Company exhibited 130 pieces of Sharp Diamond pattern pressed glassware at the New York Crystal Palace exhibition.[3] A Montreal retailer advertised the following patterns in Boston & Sandwich glassware in 1852: "Punty Bowls, Spangle and Pannel [sic] Dishes, Spangle Bitter Bottles, Astor and Revere Champagne goblets, Gothic, Arch, and Ashburton Lemonade, Astor and Ashburton Wines. . . . Tumblers in great variety and pattern. . . ."[4]

As discussed in the introduction, "lacy" stippled glassware was less prevalent by the mid-1840's, fire-polishing had changed mold requirements, and the new non-stippled glass produced in sets was becoming popular. Existing illustrated catalogs date primarily from the 60's and 70's.[5] After 1860, therefore, we can more certainly make attributions of existing glass to specific factories and know what types of glasswares were made. However, by no means were all pieces of glass produced in this period made in matching sets. We still find odd plates, butter dishes, and other shapes which seem to have no matching pieces but date stylistically from the late 40's or after.

In the early part of the nineteenth century, most of the novelty pieces produced were individual items made by a workman who was either working on his own time or perhaps simply tired of making the standard item for that day. By the third quarter of the century, however, pressed novelties were being produced as regular factory wares. The greatest boost to the production of novelties was the Centennial of 1876 in Philadelphia. Fortunately, many of these objects are documented because they were patented.

During the same period, the patenting of pressed glass designs became habitual with manufacturers. Although not all patterns were patented, perhaps most of the novelties were recorded because the glassmaker feared they would be copied if they became popular. Even after the Centennial Exposition ended, production of novelties such as the animal-covered dishes continued in favor, and historical items were made to commemorate historical events such as Dewey's battle of Manila in the Spanish-American War (no. 1223).

Pressed glass tableware made after about 1845 is included in the following section, arranged chronologically and by designs wherever possible.

1. *Watkins, Pressed Glass*, pp. 150-151.
2. *Watkins, Pressed Glass*, pp. 158-159.
3. Wilson, Kenneth M. *New England Glass and Glassmaking*, 1972, p. 325.
4. Kaellgren, C. Peter. "Glass Used in Canada: A Survey from the Early Nineteenth Century to 1940 Using Primarily Ontario Evidence," *Material History Bulletin*, National Museum of Man, Ottawa, Fall, 1976, p. 15. The advertisement quoted is from the *Hamilton Daily Spectator and Journal of Commerce*, Sept. 25, 1852.
5. Lowell Innes discusses several catalogs of Pittsburgh companies in his book, *Pittsburgh Glass, 1797-1891—A History and Guide for Collectors*, 1976. Kenneth Wilson discusses the Cape Cod Glass Company's production of pressed glass in *New England Glass and Glassmaking*.

922 Sauce dish
United States
ca. 1850-1870
D. 10.4 cm

65.4.74

Colorless lead glass with horizontal ribbing around sides.
Gift of Mrs. Leon S. Bard
Parallels: Lee and Rose, p. 401, no. 885.

923 Plate
Midwest
ca. 1840-1860
D. 15.4 cm

59.4.96

Medium amethyst glass; triple band just inside edge and around base.
Gift of Louise S. Esterly

924 Compote
Midwest
ca. 1840-1860
H. 11.7 cm; D. (at rim) 20.9 cm

68.4.71

Colorless lead glass, pressed bowl with an edge of alternating scallops and points and a ring around the sides, sunburst in base; applied blown baluster stem containing an air bubble; pontil mark underneath foot.
Gift of Lowell Innes
Published: Innes, Early Glass, p. 47; *Innes, Pittsburgh Glass*, Fig. 230.

925 Plate
Midwest
ca. 1840-1860
D. 14.5 cm

68.4.113

Light green glass.
Ex coll: Louise S. Esterly
Comments: See above.
Parallels: Innes, Pittsburgh Glass, Fig. 265.

926 Plate
Midwest
ca. 1840-1860
D. 12.6 cm

63.4.80

Light blue glass.
Gift of Louise S. Esterly
Parallels: Innes, Early Glass,
p. 48.

927 Bowl
New England, or possibly
Europe
ca. 1850-1870
H. 5.5 cm; L. 31 cm; W. 23.5
cm

60.4.812

Brilliant green glass; horizontal
fluting on sides and waffle design in base.
Gift of Louise S. Esterly
Comments: This is the only bowl
of this size and color recorded.
The smaller bowls, see below,
are common in colorless glass
and they occur in blue, as well.
James Rose, in correspondence
with the author, expressed the
opinion that the large green bowl
is probably European and, on
the basis of design, that seems
likely, but a wooden model of
salts of the same design, sup-
posedly from the Boston &
Sandwich Glass Company, was
sold at auction in 1975 (Richard
E. Bourne, Hyannis,
Masaachusetts, Oct. 24-25,
1975, Lot 133).

928 Bowl
L. 18.4 cm

59.4.76

Dark amber with star in base.
Gift of Louise S. Esterly

*929 Bowl
L. 13.1 cm

63.4.86

Dark amber.
Gift of Louise S. Esterly

*930 Salt
L. 8.2 cm

61.4.93

Blue.
Gift of Louise S. Esterly

*931 **Another**

61.4.95

Amber.
Gift of Louise S. Esterly

932 **Another**

68.4.207

Amethyst.
Ex coll: Louise S. Esterly

933 **Salt dish**
Midwest, or possibly Europe
ca. 1840-1870
H. 6 cm; D. (rim) 7.7 cm

68.4.161

Opalescent glass; capstan shape
with a band of diamonds around
the ground and polished top
rim.
Ex coll: Louise S. Esterly
Comments: See salts below,
which are similar.
Parallels: Lee, Sandwich Glass,
pl. 69, no. 5.

934 **Salt dish**
Midwest, or possibly Europe
ca. 1840-1870
H. 9 cm; D. (rim) 8.2 cm

68.4.369

Opalescent glass with yellow
silver stain; capstan shape; top
rim ground and polished
Ex coll: Louise S. Esterly
Comments: See also salts above,
and below, which are similar.
Parallels: Lee, Sandwich Glass,
pl. 69, no. 6.

935 **Salt dish**
Probably M'Kee & Brothers,
Pittsburgh
ca. 1850-1870
H. 6 cm; D. (rim) 9 cm

68.4.163

Canary yellow glass; capstan
shape.
Ex coll: Louise S. Esterly
Parallels: Dyer, Walter A. "The
Pressed Glassware of Old
Sandwich," *Antiques*, No. 2,
Feb. 1922, p. 59; *Lee, Sandwich
Glass*, pls. 69, center left, and
73, lower right; M'Kee &
Brothers, *Prices of Glassware
Manufactured by M'Kee &
Brothers* (Pittsburgh, April 1,
1868), pl. 29.

*936 **Another**

68.4.368

Turquoise.
Ex coll: Louise S. Esterly; Mr.
and Mrs. Harry S. High

937 **Salt dish**
United States
ca. 1840-1860
H. 3.8 cm; D. 7.8 cm

61.4.92

Cobalt blue glass; octagonal,
with egg and dart molding on
top rim.
Gift of Louise S. Esterly

*938 **Another**

61.4.83

Colorless.
Gift of Louise S. Esterly

939 **Salt dish**
Probably United States
ca. 1850-1870
H. 5.1 cm; L. 7.3 cm

63.4.94

Transparent greenish glass; four
feet.
Gift of Louise S. Esterly
Comments: See below, for similar
salt.

940 **Salt dish**
Probably United States
ca. 1850-1870
H. 4.5 cm; L. 7.3 cm

68.4.227

Opalescent glass; ground and
polished base.
Ex coll: Louise S. Esterly
Comments: See salts above and
below, for similar salts.

941 **Salt dish**
Probably United States
ca. 1850-1870
H. 4.2 cm; L. 8 cm

68.4.195

Cobalt blue glass; checkered
pattern on base.
Ex coll: Louise S. Esterly
Comments: See above, for similar
salt.

942 **Salt dish**
Probably United States
ca. 1850-1870
H. 4.6 cm; L. 8 cm

68.4.175

Greenish-yellow glass; with cut
grooves in ground and polished
top edge.
Ex coll: Louise S. Esterly
Comments: A wooden model of a
salt of this design (purportedly
Sandwich) was sold at Richard
Bourne's auction house, Hyan-
nisport, Massachusetts, Oct. 24,
25, 1975, no. 411.

943 **Salt dish**
Probably United States
ca. 1850-1870
H. 3.4 cm; L. 8.4 cm

61.4.90

Emerald green glass; six knobs
around sides and ends.
Gift of Louise S. Esterly

†944 **Salt dish**
Probably United States
ca. 1850-1870
H. 5.1 cm; L. 8.3 cm

68.4.359

Mottled opaque blue and white
glass.
Ex coll: Louise S. Esterly

*945 **Another**

61.4.94

Light green.
Gift of Louise S. Esterly

*946 **Another**

63.4.92

Opalescent.
Gift of Louise S. Esterly

947 **Salt dish**
Probably United States
ca. 1850-1870
H. 4 cm; L. 9 cm

68.4.204

Opaque cream colored glass.
Ex colls: Louise S. Esterly; W.
Stanley Curtis

948 **Salt dish**
Probably United States
ca. 1850-1870
H. 3.5 cm; L. 8.3 cm

68.4.120

Amethyst glass.
Ex coll: Louise S. Esterly

949 Salt dish
Probably New England
ca. 1845-1865
H. 6.8 cm; D. (rim) 7.3 cm

67.4.62

Colorless lead glass; six panels
around body; circular hollow
foot with six loop designs.
Gift of Mr. and Mrs. Harry A.
Snyder
Comments: The original name of
this pattern is not known.
Parallels: Lee, E.A.P.G., pp.
27-30; *S.H.S.,* pp. 22, 23.

*950 Tumbler
Probably New England
ca. 1850-1880
H. 10.6 cm

73.4.59

Colorless lead glass; pressed in
the form of a six-sided cylinder.
Gift of Mrs. Robert Brearey
Comments: Very thick glass; the
capacity of the tumbler is about

half of what it looks; its base also
has a cavity, although a somewhat smaller one. Donor stated
that when glass was turned up-
side down it was used as a salt dish.

951 Salt dish
United States
ca. 1840-1860
H. 6.9 cm; D. (rim) 7.1 cm

67.4.55

Colorless lead glass; hexagonal.
Gift of Mr. and Mrs. John F.
Staub

952 Tumbler
Probably Midwest
ca. 1850-1880
H. 9.25 cm; D. (rim) 8.8 cm

50.4.218

Cobalt blue glass.
Ex coll: George S. McKearin
Comments: These tumblers,
which are found in many sizes
and colors, are often attributed
to the Bakewell factory but were
probably made in nearly every
Midwestern glasshouse.
Parallels: Innes, Pittsburgh Glass,
pl. 325, pp. 301-304; *McKearin,*
American Glass, pl. 209, nos. 17,
20.

*953 Another

74.4.158

Bluish green glass.
Bequest of Mrs. Jason Westerfield

243

954 Salt dish
Harp pattern
Pittsburgh, Pennsylvania, probably McKee & Brothers
ca. 1850-1870
H. 4.9 cm; D. (top) 8.5 cm

68.4.92

Colorless lead glass; a harp on each of six panels around body.
Gift of Mr. and Mrs. Harry A. Snyder
Parallels: Lee, E..A.P.G., pl. 14.

955 Egg cup
Excelsior pattern
Pittsburgh, C. Ihmsen, or McKee & Brothers
ca. 1850-1870
H. 12 cm; D. (rim) 6 cm

50.4.389

Colorless lead glass.
Ex coll: George S. McKearin
Comments: This pattern was made by several different glass factories in Pittsburgh.
Parallels: Innes, Pittsburgh Glass, pp. 302, 303, 310, 311; *Lee, E.A.P.G.*, pls. 1, 4, 7, 34; *McKearin, American Glass,* pls. 206, 208, 209.

956 Candlestick
Excelsior pattern
H. 21 cm

50.4.424

Ex coll: George S. McKearin

957 Ale glass
Brooklyn pattern
United States, probably Midwest
ca. 1850-1870
H. 17 cm; D. (rim) 7.3 cm

50.4.418

Colorless lead glass.
Ex coll: George S. McKearin
Comments: This pattern is attributed to Bakewell, Pears & Company, Pittsburgh.
Parallels: Lee, E.A.P.G., pl. 154, pp. 63, 64; Bakewell, Pears & Co. catalog, ca. 1875, pg. 5.

958 **Toothpick holder
or small vase**
New England
ca. 1850-1870
H. 7.6 cm; D. (base) 4.3 cm

69.4.63

Yellow-green glass; pattern of
two rows of eight ovals around
sides.
Gift of Mr. and Mrs. Harry A.
Snyder
*Parallels: McKearin, American
Glass*, pl. 196, no. 3 (similar in
form).

959 **Candlestick**
Pittsburgh, M'Kee & Brothers
ca. 1855-1880
H. 20 cm

50.4.239

Dark, olive-green glass; hexagonal form with hollow hexagonal
foot.
Ex coll: George S. McKearin
Comments: This seems to be the
same as a "6 Flute candlestick"
illustrated in the M'Kee catalog
of 1860 in CMG collection and
the "French Candlestick" illustrated in their 1880 catalog.
Parallels: M'Kee and Brother,
*Prices of Glassware Manufactured
by M'Kee and Brother*, Pittsburgh,
1860, 20th plate; Stout, Sandra,
The Complete M'Kee Glass, 1972,
p. 84.

960 **Compote**
Midwest, probably Bakewell,
Pears & Co., Pittsburgh
Mid-19th century
H. 7.5 cm; D. (bowl) 24 cm

50.4.432

Fiery opalescent glass; pressed
in one piece, very short hexag-
onal stem with circular foot.
Ex coll: George S. McKearin
Parallels: Lee, E.A.P.G., pl. 17,
illustrating a catalog of
Bakewell, Pears & Company of
Pittsburgh, Broad Flute pattern.

*961 **Another**

58.4.62

Translucent greenish-blue.
Gift of Louise S. Esterly

962 Bowl
United States, East or Midwest
Mid-19th century,
ca. 1850-1870
H. 4.3 cm; D. (rim) 17 cm

50.4.434

Greenish yellow glass; sunburst
in base.
Ex coll: George S. McKearin
Parallels: Innes, Pittsburgh Glass,
pls. 369, 370; *Lee, E.A.P.G.,* pl.
10; *McKearin, American Glass,*
pls. 198, 203.
Comments: Ruth Webb Lee
seems to be the first to have
named this pattern Bigler.

963 Vase
Bigler pattern
H. 29 cm; D. (base) 8 cm sq.

50.4.242

Amethyst.
Ex coll: George S. McKearin

964 Goblet
Colonial pattern
United States, probably Mid-
west
ca. 1850-1870
H. 15.3 cm; D. (rim) 9.3 cm

50.4.435

Fiery opalescent glass; rough
pontil mark on foot.
Ex coll: George S. McKearin
Comments: Colonial is the modern collector's term for this pattern which was made in a
number of different glasshouses
in the Midwest and possibly in
New England, as well.
Parallels: Innes, Pittsburgh Glass,
pl. 328; *Lee, E.A.P.G.,* pls. 2,10.

965 Covered sugar bowl
United States
ca. 1850-1870
H. (with cover) 22.5 cm;
D. (rim) 13.3 cm

50.4.433

Brownish-amber glass; cover
with acorn knop.
Ex coll: George S. McKearin
Parallels: Innes, Pittsburgh Glass,
Fig. 399.

966 Perfume bottle
New England
ca. 1845-1865
H. (with stopper) 17.2 cm;
D. (base) 6.4 cm

68.4.503

Jade green glass; six panels
around body, three with a star
and a circle, alternating with
three with an oval containing a
star; stopper with six polished
flat sides and polished flat top.
Ex coll: Louise S. Esterly
*Parallels: McKearin, American
Glass,* pl. 196; Watkins, Lura
Woodside, "Positively
Sandwich," *Antiques,* 27, no. 4,
April 1935, p. 132, Fig. 2.

*967 Another

68.4.492

Amethyst glass.
Ex coll: Louise S. Esterly

*968 Another

68.4.523

Cobalt blue.
Ex coll: Louise S. Esterly

*969 Another

68.4.528

Vaseline glass.
Ex coll: Louise S. Esterly

970 Spillholder
Same pattern
H. 12.2 cm; D. (rim) 8 cm

68.4.504

Jade green.
Ex coll: Louise S. Esterly

971 Egg cup or salt cellar
United States
ca. 1845-1865
H. 8.8 cm; D. (rim) 10 cm

50.4.410

Gray-blue glass.
Ex coll: George S. McKearin
Comments: This pattern is copied
in several miniature spill holders.

972 Sugar bowl
New England
ca. 1840-1860
H. (with cover) 13.4 cm;
D. (rim) 12 cm

59.4.62

Colorless lead glass; octagonal;
sides filled with Gothic arch design in several varieties; round
foot; matching lid with eight-
sided knob.
Gift of Louise S. Esterly
Comments: Numerous fragments
of this pattern in several colors
have been found at the site of
the Sandwich factory.
However, the pattern was probably made over a long period of
time in more than one factory.
Parallels: Lee, Sandwich Glass,
pl. 158; *McKearin, American
Glass,* pl. 163, nos. 7, 9.

*973 **Another**

68.4.128

Turquoise.
Ex coll: Louise S. Esterly

†*974 **Another**

68.4.502

Amethyst.
Ex colls: Louise S. Esterly; Dr.
and Mrs. C. J. Baldridge

†*975 **Another**

68.4.544

Opaque light blue.
Ex coll: Louise S. Esterly

†*976 **Another**

68.4.549

Light yellow.
Ex colls: Louise S. Esterly;
George S. McKearin

†*977 **A variant**

68.4.475

Scalloped foot,
greenish blue.
Ex colls: Louise S. Esterly, Edward MacGowan

978 **Creamer and sugar bowl**
979 California pattern
Probably New England Glass
Company, Cambridge, Mas-
sachusetts; possibly Curling,
Robertson & Sons, Pittsburgh,
Pennsylvania
ca. 1850-1870
Sugar: H. (with cover) 14.8 cm;
D. (rim) 12 cm.
Creamer: H. 13 cm; W. (includ-
ing handles) 11 cm

50.4.206, 207

Colorless, lead glass; eight-sided
shape, each side with a stippled
or lined background and a different pattern of scrolls; diamond pattern on foot. Sugar
has octagonal cover with matching patterns.
Ex coll: George S. McKearin
Comments: This pattern is shown
in catalogs of both companies
mentioned above. The name is
probably a reference to the
California gold rush of 1849. Although both sugar and creamer
are shown in the New England
Glass Company catalog, their
patterns do not match exactly in
the catalog or on the actual objects.
Parallels: Innes, Pittsburgh Glass,
pl. 328; *Lee, Sandwich Glass,* pl.
148; *Watkins, Cambridge Glass,*
pl. 44; *Watkins, Pressed Glass,*
Fig. 14.

980 **Door knob**
United States
ca. 1850
D. 5.7 cm

51.4.76

Colorless glass with slight
purplish tinge; octagonal
mushroom-shaped knob with
flat ground top and threaded
metal shank.

981 **Door knob**
United States
ca. 1850
D. 5.6 cm

51.4.727

Light amethyst glass; octagonal
mushroom-shaped knob with
rounded top and threaded metal
shank.

982 **Footed Punchbowl**
Argus pattern
Midwest, probably Bakewell,
Pears & Company, Pittsburgh
ca. 1850-1870
H. 30.5 cm; D. (rim) 35.25 cm
50.4.363

983 **Covered bowl**
Argus pattern
50.4.364

984 **Cordial glass**
Argus pattern
50.4.365

*985 **Honey dish**
Argus pattern
50.4.366

986 **Sauce dish**
Argus pattern
50.4.367

*987 **Another**
50.4.368

988 **Tumbler**
Argus pattern
50.4.369

Colorless lead glass pressed in
two parts and joined by a wafer.
Ex coll: George S. McKearin
(982-988)
Comments: The Argus pattern
seems to have originated with
Bakewell in mid-century although it was certainly produced
by several other firms over a
period of twenty years or so.

This large size is very rare.
Parallels: Innes, Pittsburgh Glass,
pls. 357-360; *Lee, E.A.P.G.*, pls.
15, 18, 23, 24, 59; *McKearin,
American Glass*, pls. 207, 212,
213, pp. 403, 407f; McKearin,
George S. "Variations in Early
Thumbprint Glass," Parts I-III,
American Collector, Oct. 1938,
March and April 1939.

989 **Footed tumbler**
Argus pattern
H. 9.3 cm; D. 6.8 cm

50.4.370

Ex coll: George S. McKearin

990 **Paperweight**
Argus pattern
H. 8.5 cm; D. 8.5 cm

50.4.428

Ex coll: George S. McKearin

991 Compote
Pittsburgh, probably Bakewell,
Pears & Co. or M'Kee &
Brothers
ca. 1850-1870
H. 22.6 cm; D. (rim) 23.7 cm

67.4.101

Colorless glass pressed in two
parts and joined with a wafer.
Gift of Susanne G. Swift
Comments: This pattern resembles
both Bakewell's Argus and
M'Kee's Concave, as illustrated
in their catalogs; the standard is
identical to that on no. 1015.

992 Pitcher
Ashburton pattern
New England, probably New
England Glass Company, Cambridge, Massachusetts
ca. 1845-1875
H. 16.8 cm; D. (foot) 7.8 cm

50.4.392

Colorless lead glass; tooled lip
and applied tooled handle;
polished pontil mark on base.
Ex coll: George S. McKearin
Comments: This pattern was
made by several companies and
seems to have been inspired by
a cut glass design of the same
period. It may have been named
after Lord Ashburton who came
to this country in 1843 to settle a
boundary dispute.
*Published: McKearin, American
Glass,* pl. 207, no. 1.
Parallels: Innes, Pittsburgh Glass,
pls. 364, 365; *Lee, E.A.P.G.,* pls.
1, 3: *McKearin, American Glass,*
pls. 205, 207, 208, 211; *Watkins,
Cambridge Glass,* p. 99; *Watkins,
Pressed Glass,* Fig. 9.

993 Egg cup
Ashburton pattern
H. 9.5 cm; D. (rim) 6.4 cm

67.4.52

Gift of Mr. and Mrs. John F.
Staub

994 Bar bottle
Ashburton pattern
H. 26.5 cm; D. (base) 8.8 cm

67.4.147

Gift of the Hon. and Mrs.
Amory Houghton

995 Pitcher
New York Honeycomb pattern
United States, possibly New
England Glass Company, Cambridge, Massachusetts, or
Pittsburgh
ca. 1850-1870
H. 19 cm; D. (foot) 10.5 cm

50.4.422

996 Decanter
Honeycomb pattern
Ex coll: George S. McKearin

50.4.420

997 Another
Ex coll: George S. McKearin

50.4.421

998 Bitters bottle
Honeycomb pattern
Ex coll: George S. McKearin

50.4.423

*999 Wineglass
Honeycomb pattern
Gift of Mr. and Mrs. John F.
Staub

67.4.53

*1000 Celery vase
Honeycomb pattern
Gift of Suzanne G. Swift

67.4.100

Colorless non-lead glass; globular body with four rows of hexagonal facets; applied thick ear-shaped handle with tooled end.
Ex coll: George S. McKearin
Comments: This pattern was made by a number of different companies. It is illustrated in the 1869 catalog of the New England Glass Company in two variations as New York and Vernon pattern with only slight differences. It was also made by several Pittsburgh companies,

among them Bryce Brothers;
Curling, Robertson & Son;
George Duncan & Sons; James
B. Lyon; and M'Kee Brothers.
Another name for the pattern is
Cincinnati which was commonly
used in Pittsburgh.
*Published: McKearin, American
Glass,* pl. 205, no. 7
Parallels: Innes, Pittsburgh Glass,
pp. 341, 342, pl. 363; *Lee,
E.A.P.G.,* pl. 60; *McKearin,
American Glass,* pls. 206, 208;
Watkins, Pressed Glass, Fig. 4.

1001 Compote
Honeycomb pattern
H. 19.6 cm; D. (bowl) 23.7 cm

73.4.60

With engraved decoration.
Gift of Mrs. Robert Brearey

1002 Salver
Sharp Diamond pattern
New England Glass company,
Cambridge, Massachusetts
ca. 1850-1870
H. 18.8 cm; D. 37.25 cm

50.4.372

Colorless lead glass; tray attached by a wafer to hollow
standard and round foot.
Ex coll: George S. McKearin
Comments: This pattern is shown
in the New England Glass
Company catalog in the Museum collection and was exhibited at the New York Crystal
Palace in 1853.
Parallels: Lee, E..A.P.G., pls.
42-45; *Watkins, Cambridge Glass*,
94f; *Watkins, Pressed Glass*, Fig.
3; Goodrich, C. R. *Science and
Mechanism: Illustrated by Examples in the New York Exhibition,
1853-4, from Manufacturers of
Glass*, New York: G.P. Putnam,
1854, p. 220.

1003 Jelly glass
Sharp Diamond pattern
H. 13.8 cm; D. (rim) 5.8 cm

50.4.386

Ex coll: George S. McKearin

1004 Goblet
United States
ca. 1850-1870
H. 15.8 cm; D. (rim) 8.6 cm

50.4.416

Colorless lead glass pressed in
one piece.
Ex coll: George S. McKearin
Comments: This pattern is called
Smocking by collectors.
Parallels: Lee, Victorian Glass,
pl. 25.

1005 Covered nappy
Mitre Diamond pattern
New England Glass Company,
Cambridge, Massachussetts or
James B. Lyon & Co.,
Pittsburgh, Pennsylvania
ca. 1850-1870
OH. 12 cm; D. (rim) 14 cm

50.4.429

Opaque white glass; cover and
bowl fit together with a row of
interlocking diamonds, or saw
teeth.
Ex coll: George S. McKearin
Comments: This pattern is shown
as Mitre Diamond on plate 14 of
a New England Glass Company
catalog in the CMG collection,
and in a James B. Lyon catalog
of 1861.
Parallels: Lee, E.A.P.G., pl. 40;
Watkins, Pressed Glass, Fig. 7;
Innes, Pittsburgh Glass, p. 307.

1006 Covered compote
Mitre Diamond pattern
OH. 23.5 cm; D. (rim) 24.2 cm

66.4.40

Gift of Mrs. Jason Westerfield

1007 Covered salt
Mitre Diamond pattern
OH. 12.4 cm;
D. 17.5 cm

78.4.50

Ex coll: Mr. and Mrs. George
Lookup

1008 Salt
Mitre Diamond pattern
Probably New England
ca. 1850-1875
H. 7 cm; D. 7.6 cm

68.4.9

Colorless glass.
Gift of Mary Bowker
Parallels: Watkins, Pressed Glass,
p. 156, Fig. 7, No. 740.

1009 Spoon or spillholder
New England, probably Boston
& Sandwich Glass Company,
Sandwich, Massachusetts
ca. 1850-1870
H. 13 cm; D. (rim) 9.4 cm

64.4.69

Colorless lead glass; polished
pontil mark underneath foot.
Gift of Mrs. Jason Westerfield.
Comments: This pattern is called
Sandwich Star by collectors.
Parallels: Lee, E.A.P.G., pl. 14.

1010 Salt dish
United States
1850-1870
H. 3.5 cm; L. 6.7 cm

68.4.93

Colorless non-lead glass; four
ribbed feet.
Gift of Mr. and Mrs. Harry A.
Snyder

1011 Double lamp
Probably New England
ca. 1850-1870
H. 29.5 cm; D. (base) 16.3 cm

72.4.82

Colorless lead glass; cylindrical
font; two arms extended from
font ending in octagonal sections, each with a drop-in white
metal collar and burner; base of
font marked "PATENT APPLIED
FOR"; pressed hollow stem and
flat foot.
Gift of Preston R. Bassett
Comments: This form is very
rare; the pattern on foot is Diamond Thumbprint.
*Parallels: McKearin, American
Glass,* pl. 206 *Early Lighting, A
Pictorial Guide,* Boston:
Rushlight Club, 1972, p. 57,
nos. 5-31.

1012 Compote
United States
ca. 1850-1870
H. 12.3 cm; D. (rim) 18 cm

50.4.383

Colorless lead glass; standard
with spool stem on flat foot.
Ex coll: George S. McKearin
Comments: This pattern is called
Diamond Thumbprint by col-
lectors.
Parallels: Lee, E.A.P.G., pls. 3
and 25; *McKearin American
Glass,* pls. 205, 206, 208, 209.

1013 Spoon holder
In the same pattern
H. 16 cm; D. (rim) 7.8 cm

50.4.384.

Ex. coll: George S. McKearin

1014 Egg Cup
United States
ca. 1850-1870
H. 9.3 cm; D. (rim) 6 cm

50.4.440

Colorless lead glass; funnel-
shaped bowl, sides covered with
diamonds, each vertically
bisected by a line; flat circular
foot; slightly rough pontil mark.
Ex coll: George S. McKearin
Comments: This pattern is called
Divided Diamond by collectors.

1015   Compote
Midwest, probably Bakewell,
Pears, & Company or M'Kee &
Brothers
ca. 1850-1870
H. 17.1 cm; D. (rim) 19.1 cm

69.4.199

Colorless lead glass; bowl attached by a wafer to a hollow,
hexagonal baluster stem ending
in a round foot.
Gift of Mrs. Florence Bushee
Comments: See no. 991 for compote with same standard.

1016   Hand lamp
Union pattern
New England Glass Company,
Cambridge, Massachusetts
ca. 1850-1870
H. 10.3 cm; D. (base) 8.8 cm

50.4.373

Colorless lead glass; bell-shaped
with applied looped handle and
pattern of bull's-eye and diamond point; double-wicked
burner for burning fluid at top.
Ex coll: George S. McKearin
Comments: This pattern is shown
in the New England Glass
Company catalog of 1869 in the
Museum collection.
Parallels: Lee, E.A.P.G., pls. 27,
49; *McKearin, American Glass*,
pl. 208; *Watkins, Cambridge
Glass*, p. 103; *Watkins, Pressed
Glass*, Fig. 10.

1017   Tumbler
Midwest, possibly Bakewell,
Pears & Company, Pittsburgh
ca. 1850-1870
H. 11.5 cm; D. (rim) 9 cm

50.4.391

Colorless lead glass; round fun-
nel bowl with pattern of dia-
monds and arches around sides.
Ex coll: George S. McKearin
Comments: This pattern is called
Victoria by collectors.
Parallels: Lee, E.A.P.G., pls. 18,
23.

1018 Plate
Comet pattern
M'Kee & Brother, Pittsburgh,
Pennsylvania, or Boston &
Sandwich Glass Company,
Sandwich, Massachusetts
ca. 1850-1870
D. 16.5 cm; H. 1.9 cm

50.4.378

Colorless lead glass.
Ex coll: George S. McKearin
Comments: The pattern name
may be a reference to the mid-
19th century appearance of a
comet. This pattern is illustrated in the 1860 M'Kee catalog
in the Corning Museum Li-
brary. Molds for the pattern
were found at Sandwich, according to Ruth Webb Lee. The
Cape Cod Glass Company listed
a Comet pattern for sale in about
1863, although since it is not illustrated, it might not have been
the same. Collectors now refer
to the pattern as Horn of Plenty.
Parallels: Innes, Pittsburgh Glass,
pp. 310, 311; *Lee, E.A.P.G.,* pls.
32, 47; *McKearin, American
Glass,* pls. 205, 211, 213; *Revi,*
pp. 231, 237, 238.

1019 Compote
Comet pattern
H. 25.2 cm; D. (rim) 25.1 cm

79.4.143

Gift of Mrs. William C.
Steinhorst in memory of Theo-
dore R. Steinhorst

*1020 Footed bowl
Comet pattern
Ex coll: George S. McKearin
50.4.379

*1021 Lamp
Comet pattern
Ex coll: George S. McKearin
50.4.380

1022 Another
Ex. coll: Amy Chace
Gift of E.S. Chace
68.4.22

*1023 Sugar bowl
Comet pattern
79.4.98

1024 Celery vase
Comet pattern
Ex coll: Amy Chace
Gift of E.S. Chace
68.4.12

*1025 Plate
Comet pattern
Ex coll: Amy Chace
Gift of E.S. Chace
68.4.13

1026 Covered butter dish
Comet pattern
Finial in form of George
Washington's head
H. (with cover) 12.3 cm;
D. 15.5 cm
Ex coll: Amy Chace
Gift of E.S. Chace
68.4.14

*1027 Covered butter dish
Comet pattern
With a plain finial.
Ex coll: Amy Chace
Gift of E.S. Chace
68.4.15

1028 Mug
Comet pattern
Ex coll: Amy Chace
Gift of E.S. Chace
68.4.16

1029 Tumbler
Comet pattern
Ex coll: Amy Chace
Gift of E.S. Chace
68.4.17

1030 Champagne glass
Comet pattern
Ex coll: Amy Chace
Gift of E.S. Chace
68.4.18

1031 Wineglass
Comet pattern
Ex coll: Amy Chace
Gift of E.S. Chace
68.4.19

1032 Egg cup
Comet pattern
Ex coll: Amy Chace
Gift of E.S. Chace
68.4.20

1033 Decanter
Comet pattern
Ex coll: Amy Chace
Gift of E.S. Chace
68.4.21

1034 Cream pitcher
Comet pattern
Ex coll: Amy Chace
Gift of E.S. Chace
68.4.23

1035 Goblet
New England, possibly
Sandwich, Massachusetts, Boston & Sandwich Glass Com-
pany.
ca. 1850-1870
H. 16.1 cm; D. 8.7 cm

62.4.59

Colorless lead glass; polished
pontil mark on round base.
Comments: This pattern is called
Comet by collectors.
Parallels: Lee E.A.P.G. pls. 48,
49, pp. 157-158.

1036 Lamp, burning fluid
Palace pattern
New England Glass Company or
Curling Robertson & Sons,
Pittsburgh, or James B. Lyon &
Company, Pittsburgh
ca. 1850-1870
H. 25.8 cm;

50.4.427

Colorless lead glass; font lined
with a tinned receptacle for
burning fluid; hollow hexagonal
standard with hollow hexagonal
foot.
Ex coll: George S. McKearin
Comments: This pattern was advertised by all three of the companies listed above.
Parallels: Innes Pittsburgh Glass,
pl. 328, 329; *Lee E.A.P.G.,* pl. 10
McKearin, American Glass, pl.
206; *Watkins, Pressed Glass,* Fig. 12.

1037 Egg cup
Palace pattern

50.4.388.

Ex coll: George S. McKearin

1038 Covered sugar bowl
Possibly Somerville, Massachusetts, Union Glass Company
ca. 1850-1870
H. (overall) 22 cm; D. (bowl at rim) 11 cm

50.4.382

Colorless lead glass; cover, with acorn knop.
Ex coll: George S. McKearin
Comments: This pattern could have been made at more than one factory but can only be reliably attributed to the Union Glass Company on the basis of molds used there. It is called by collectors, Bull's-eye and Fleur-de-lis.
Parallels: E.A.P.G., pls. 48, 51; *McKearin American Glass,* p. 404; *Kamm, Book VIII,* pp. 46-47; *Metz, Book I,* pp. 12-13; *Revi,* p. 304; Watkins, Lura Woodside, "The Union Glass Company," *Antiques* 30, No. 5, Nov. 1936. pp. 222-225.

1039 Celery vase
In the same pattern
H. 14.5 cm; D. (rim) 13 cm

50.4.381

Ex coll: George S. McKearin

1040 Bowl
In the same pattern
H. 6 cm; D. (rim) 20.2 cm

69.4.49

Gift of Mrs. William Hampton

1041 Butter dish
In the same pattern
H. (with cover) 11.7 cm;
D. 16.2 cm

74.4.7

Gift of Ruth I. Roth

1042 Tumbler
Reeded pattern
Probably New England Glass
Company, Cambridge, Massachusetts or Pittsburgh, Pennsylvania, James B. Lyon &
Company
ca.1850-1870
H. 9.3 cm; D. (rim) 8 cm

50.4.439

Colorless lead glass.
Ex coll: George S. McKearin
Comments: This pattern was also
made by James B. Lyon & Company.
Parallels: Innes, Pittsburgh Glass,
pl. 330; *Lee, E.A.P.G.,* pls. 27,
36; *McKearin, American Glass,*
pl. 208; *Watkins, Pressed Glass,*
Fig. 5.

1043 Tumbler
United States, probably
Pittsburgh, possibly New England Glass Company, Cambridge, Masachusetts
ca. 1850-1870
H. 7 cm; D. (rim) 6.5 cm

50.4.376

Colorless lead glass; pressed.
Ex coll: George S. McKearin
Comments: This pattern seems
similar to many pressed in
Pittsburgh although its exact origin and name are not known. It
is called Ribbed Ivy by collectors.
Parallels: Lee, E.A.P.G., pls. 32,
33; *McKearin, American Glass,*
pl. 213.

1044 Sauce dish
In the same pattern
H. 3.1 cm; D. 10.5 cm

50.4.377

Ex coll: George S. McKearin

1045 Honey dish
United States
ca. 1850-1870
H. 2.5 cm; D (rim) 8.6 cm

50.4.442

Colorless lead glass.
Ex coll: George S. McKearin
Comments: This pattern is called
Inverted Fern by collectors.
Parallels: Lee, E.A.P.G., pl. 33.

1046 Pitcher
R.L. (Ribbed Leaf) pattern
M'Kee & Brothers, Pittsburgh,
Pennsylvania
ca. 1850-1870
H. 20.3 cm; D. (base) 10.5 cm

50.4.371

1047 Castor set
R.L. pattern, with pewter
holder
Ex coll: George S. McKearin

50.4.425

1048 Spillholder or spooner
R.L. pattern
Ex coll: George S. McKearin

50.4.419

Colorless lead glass; cylindrical
body with pattern of double row
of bellflowers on background of
fine vertical ribbing; applied
strap handle; ground and
polished pontil mark.
Ex coll: George S. McKearin
Comments: This pattern is fea-
tured in the M'Kee catalog of
1864 but it is possible that it was
made in the East as well.
Parallels: Lee, Pittsburgh Glass,
pp. 310, 311; *Lee, E.A.P.G.*, pls.
30-35; *McKearin, American
Glass,* pp. 385, 402, 406; *Prices
of Glassware Manufactured by
M'Kee and Brothers* Pittsburgh,
Pennsylvania, April 1, 1868.

**1049 Champagne or large
wineglass**
Stedman pattern
Pittsburgh, probably M'Kee &
Brothers
ca. 1850-1870
H. 13.3 cm; D. (rim) 9.1 cm

50.4.436

Colorless lead glass; deep ovoid
bowl with pattern of vertical
blazes around sides; circular
foot.
Ex coll: George S. McKearin
Parallels: Innes, Pittsburgh Glass,
pp. 310, 311; *Lee, E.A.P.G.*, pl.
13; *McKearin, American Glass,*
pl. 208.

1050 Covered butter dish
Prism pattern
Pittsburgh, Pennsylvania;
McKee & Brothers, King, Son
& Company
ca. 1850-1870
H. (with cover) 13.1 cm;
D. 15.4 cm

74.4.9

Colorless lead glass with continuous vertical ribbing on base and cover; acorn knob.
Gift of Ruth I. Roth
Comments: This pattern appears as Prism in the McKee catalog of 1860 in the Corning Museum, as well as in the King, Son & Company catalog.
Parallels: Innes, Pittsburgh Glass, pp. 325, 337, 357; *Lee, E.A.P.G.*, pls. 13, 17; *Revi*, pp. 230-244.

1051 Salt Dish
Probably United States
ca. 1850-1870
H. 3.7. cm; L. 8 cm

68.4.353

Pale opaque lavender glass; sunburst on base.
Ex coll: Louise S. Esterly

1052 Salt dish
United States
ca. 1840-1860
H.3.4.cm; D. 7.9 cm

68.4.356

Amethyst glass.
Ex coll: Louise S. Esterly

1053 Wineglass
New England
ca. 1850-1870
H. 13.1 cm; D. (rim) 6.5 cm

50.4.385

Colorless lead glass; hexagonal stem; flat circular foot.
Ex-coll: George S. McKearin
Comments: This is called New England Pineapple by collectors.
Parallels: Lee, E.A.P.G., pls. 42, 52, 53, 167; *McKearin, American Glass,* pls. 207, 209.

1054 Wineglass
United States
ca. 1850-1870
H. 10 cm; D. (rim) 5 cm

50.4.374

Colorless lead glass; octagonal stem.
Ex coll: George S. McKearin
Comments: This pattern is called Frosted Leaf by collectors.
Parallels: Lee, E.A.P.G., p. 223; *McKearin, American Glass,* pl. 209.

1055 Goblet
United States
ca. 1850-1870
H. 16.8 cm; D. (rim) 9 cm

50.4.417

Colorless lead glass.
Ex coll: George S. McKearin
Comments: This pattern is called Magnet and Grape by collectors.
Parallels: Lee, E.A.P.G., pls, 62, 63; *McKearin, American Glass,* pl. 206.

1056 Spillholder
New England, probably Boston
& Sandwich Glass Company,
Sandwich, Massachusetts
ca. 1850-1870
H. 11.5 cm; D. (rim) 8.1 cm

72.4.175

Grayish clambroth glass; flat
foot with polished pontil mark.
Gift of Mr. and Mrs. Harry A.
Snyder
Parallels: Lee, Sandwich Glass,
pl. 210.

1057 Goblet
Probably Midwest; possibly
Bryce, Walker & Company
ca. 1850-1865
H. 16.8 cm; D. (rim) 8.5 cm

50.4.438

Colorless non-lead glass.
Ex coll: George S. McKearin
Comments: This pattern is called
Tulip by collectors.
Parallels: Lee, E.A.P.G., pls. 37,
42, 53, 54.

1058 Curtain tieback
New England
ca. 1850
D. 6.4 cm

61.4.155

Opalescent glass; flat circular
plate with six-petaled rosette in
relief on top; metal shank.
Ex coll: George S. McKearin
Parallels: Lee, Sandwich Glass,
pl. 19, top left.

*1059 Another
D. 14.4 cm

68.4.378

Opalescent.
Ex coll: Louise S. Esterly

*1060 Another
D. 12.1 cm

68.4.383

Opalescent.
Ex coll: Louise S. Esterly

1061 **Pair of curtain tiebacks**
Probably New England
ca. 1850
D. 8.5 cm

59.4.77 A,B

Opalescent glass with silver-stained and gilt decoration; six-petaled rosette with metal shank.
Gift of Louise S. Esterly
Parallels: Lee, Sandwich Glass, pl. 19, top and lower center.

*1062 **Another**

60.4.817

Yellow.
Gift of Louise S. Esterly

1063A **Curtain tieback**
New England
ca. 1850
D. 13.3 cm

68.4.497

Opalescent glass; circular with scalloped design in high relief, metal shank.
Ex coll: Louise S. Esterly

1063B **Another**
As above
68.4.498

1064 **Paperweight**
New England Glass Company,
Cambridge, Massachusetts
1851
W. 7.8 cm; H.9.1 cm

78.4.178

Colorless hexagonal weight with impressed portraits of Victoria and Albert and the inscription VICTORIA D.G. BRIT. REG F.D. ALBERTUS PRINCEPS CON-JUX/MDCCCLI ROYAL MINT.
Comments: This design is taken from a medal struck by the Royal Mint at the time of the Great Exhibition at the Crystal Palace in London.
Parallels; Watkins, Cambridge Glass, pp. 133, 134.

1065 **Pane**
United States
ca. 1850-1890
14.6 cm x 14.5 cm

63.4.74

Amber with a floral pattern in heavy relief.
Gift of Louise S. Esterly

1066 Set of glassware
Two covered bowls, covered
nappy, creamer, two goblets,
sugar bowl base, spooner, Floral
Ware pattern
Pittsburgh, Pennsylvania, King,
Son & Company or Wheeling,
West Virginia, Central Glass
Company
ca: 1869-1880
H. (tallest bowl) 25 cm;
D. (rim) 21.1 cm

63.4.17A-H

All pieces are pressed of colorless non-lead glass.
Gift of Mrs. M. L. Baldwin
Comments: Floral Ware appears
in a King, Son & Company
catalog in The Corning Museum
of Glass Library; it was also
made by Central. It is now
called Bleeding Heart by collectors.

Parallels: Innes, Pittsburgh Glass,
pls. 387-389; *Revi,* pp. 210 and 213.

1067 Toothpick holder, or egg cup
Possibly Portland, Maine,
Portland Glass Company, or a
Pittsburgh factory
ca. 1865-1885
H. 7.9 cm; D. 5.5 cm

74.4.161

Light greenish glass.
Bequest of Mrs. Jason Wester-
field
Comments: This pattern, called
Tree-of-Life by collectors, was
made in the Portland Glass
Company, possibly at Sandwich,
and in several Pittsburgh fac-
tories. Some pieces in this pat-
tern are marked "P.G. Co." for
Portland Glass Company.
Parallels: Metz, Book II, p. 121;
Swan, Frank H. *Portland Glass,*
Des Moines, Wallace-
Homestead Book Co., 1969, pp.
36-43, illus. p. 43.

1068 Wineglass
United States
ca. 1865-1885
H. 12.5 cm; D. (rim) 5.7 cm

50.4.387

Colorless non-lead glass;
pressed in one piece.
Ex coll: George S. McKearin

1069 Small plate
United States, possibly Port-
land, Maine, Portland Glass
Company
ca. 1865-1875
D. 7.8 cm

65.4.83

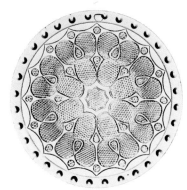

Colorless non-lead glass.
Gift of Mrs. Leon S. Bard
Comments: This pattern was
produced by the Portland Glass
Company as well as other firms.
It is called Loop and Dart with
Round Ornament by collectors.
Parallels: Lee and Rose, p. 501,
no. 891.

1070 Covered butter dish
Probably Midwest
ca. 1865-1875
H. (with cover) 11.4 cm;
D. 16.1 cm

74.4.33

Colorless non-lead glass.
Gift of Ruth I. Roth
Comments: This pattern is called
Stippled Double Loop by col-
lectors.
Parallels: Lee, E.A.P.G., pl. 101.

1071 Covered butter dish
Cambridge, Massachusetts,
Boston Silver-Glass Company
ca. 1869-1871
H. (with cover) 10.2 cm;
D. 14.6 cm

74.4.8

Colorless lead glass.
Gift of Ruth I. Roth
Comments: Mold was patented
May 11, 1869, by Alonzo C.
Young for the Boston Silver-
Glass Company. This pattern is
called Beaded Mirror by collec-
tors.
Parallels: Lee, Victorian Glass, pl.
56; *Metz, Book I*, pp. 180-181;
Revi, pp. 76-78.

1072 Covered butter dish
Cambridge, Massachusetts,
Boston Silver-Glass Company
ca. 1869-1871
H. (with cover) 10.7 cm;
D. 15.3 cm

74.4.4

Colorless non-lead glass.
Gift of Ruth I. Roth
Comments: The mold for this
pattern was patented in 1869 by
Alonzo C. Young for the Boston
Silver-Glass Company.
Parallels: Lee, E.A.P.G., pl. 66;
Metz, Book 2, pp. 76, 77; *Revi,*
pp. 76-78.

1073 Covered butter dish
Cambridge, Massachusetts,
Boston Silver-Glass Company;
and probably Midwest
ca. 1869-1871; base, 1890's
H. (with cover) 11.4 cm;
D. 17.6 cm

74.4.5

Colorless non-lead glass.
Gift of Ruth I. Roth
Comments: This is obviously a
marriage; the cover was made at
the Boston Silver-Glass Company, and the base is probably
Midwestern.
Parallels: Lee, Victorian Glass, pl.
55; *Revi,* p. 112; *Metz, Book 1,* p.
135.

1074 Bowl
New England, probably Union
Glass Company, Somerville,
Massachusetts
ca. 1865
H. 2.8 cm; D. 10.6 cm

69.4.43

Colorless, non-lead glass; circular shape, diamond pattern around sides, pinwheel in center of base.
Gift of Mrs. William Hampton who inherited the bowl from her great-grandmother, Nancy Houghton Lawrence (1817-1895).
Published: Wilson, p. 312, Fig. 257.

1075 Berry bowl
As above.
H. 3.4 cm; D. (rim) 18.4 cm

69.4.47

Gift of Mrs. William Hampton

1076 Three goblets
As above.
H. 16.7 cm; D. (base) 8.5 cm

69.4.48 A,B,C

Gift of Mrs. William Hampton

1077 Egg cup
United States
ca. 1865-1875
H. 9 cm; D. 6.3 cm

50.4.443

Colorless non-lead glass.
Ex coll: George S. McKearin
Comments: This pattern is called Hamilton by collectors.
Parallels: Lee, E.A.P.G., pl. 56; *McKearin, American Glass*, pls. 207, 209.

1078 Wineglass
United States
ca. 1865-1875
H. 10.3 cm; D. (rim) 5.3 cm

50.4.444

Colorless non-lead glass.
Ex coll: George S. McKearin
Parallels: Lee, E.A.P.G., pl. 154;
McKearin, American Glass, pl. 210.

1079 Bowl on stand
United States
ca. 1860-1870
H. 15.5 cm; D. (rim) 19 cm

50.4.437

Colorless glass.
Ex coll: George S. McKearin
Comments: This pattern is said to
have been created at the time of
Lincoln's assassination or shortly
afterward. However, no proof of
that has been found. Pattern is
called Lincoln Drape by collectors.
Parallels: Lee, E.A.P.G., pls. 26,
46; *McKearin, American Glass*,
pl. 210.

1080 Goblet
In the same pattern
H. 15 cm; D. (rim) 8.5 cm

62.4.6.

1081 Salt dish
United States
ca. 1860-1870
H. 8.5 cm; D. (rim) 7.5 cm

50.4.390

Colorless lead glass.
Ex coll: George S. McKearin
Comments: This pattern is said to commemorate the successful laying of the Atlantic cable by Cyrus W. Field in 1858.
Parallels: Lee, E.A.P.G., pls. 32, 36; *McKearin, American Glass,* pls. 205, 207.

1082 Covered sugar bowl
United States
ca. 1860-1890
H. (with cover) 12.2 cm;
D. (rim) 14.2 cm

67.4.106

Colorless lead glass.
Bequest of Frances Craig Hawkes McAllister

1083 Ointment jar
Cambridge, Massachusetts,
New England Glass Company
ca. 1870-1888
H. 2.5 cm; D. 6.3 cm

63.4.84

Opalescent glass and white metal.
Gift of Louise S. Esterly
Parallels: Watkins, Pressed Glass, fig. 15.

1084 Covered powder box
Cambridge, Massachusetts,
New England Glass Company
ca. 1869
H. (with cover) 9 cm; D. 10 cm

73.4.39

Grayish-white glass; fourteen vertical panels around sides.
Gift of Marion Pike
Comments: This piece is illustrated on plate 25 of the New England Glass Company catalog owned by The Corning Museum of Glass Library.
Published: Watkins, Cambridge Glass, pl. 38; The Toledo Museum of Art. *The New England Glass Company, 1818-1888,* Toledo, Ohio: museum, 1963, no. 205, p. 75.
Parallels: Watkins, Pressed Glass, pp. 149-164.

1085 Perfume bottle
Cambridge, Massachusetts,
New England Glass Company
ca. 1869-1875
H. 12.2 cm

72.4.174

Opaque white hexagonal bottle; with a diamond pattern on each side; pressed from the bottom and tooled shut.
Gift of Mr. and Mrs. Harry A. Snyder
Comments: This bottle appears in an 1869 catalog of the New England Glass Company, and was patented by Henry Whitney, July 2, 1868.
Parallels: Watkins, Pressed Glass, Fig. 15.

1086 Plate

Pittsburgh, Pennsylvania;
Campbell, Jones & Company
ca. 1877-1895
D. (rim) 18.8

50.4.375

Colorless, non-lead glass; overall
pattern of circular depressions
with star in center.
Ex coll: George S. McKearin
Comments: Patented by Jenkin
Jones, July 17, 1877, the pattern
is now called Dewdrop with Star
by collectors.
Parallels: Lee, E.A.P.G., pl. 73;
Innes, Pittsburgh Glass, figs. 374,
375.

1087 Goblet

Pittsburgh, Pennsylvania; probably George Duncan & Sons
ca. 1870-1885
H. 16.7 cm; D. (rim) 8.2 cm

67.4.105

Colorless non-lead glass with
acid-frosted vertical ribs.
Bequest of Frances Craig
Hawkes McAllister
Parallels: Lee, E.A.P.G., pl. 68.

1088 Covered butter dish

Bryce pattern
Pittsburgh, Pennsylvania,
Bryce, Walker & Co.; United
States Glass Company
ca. 1875-1895
H. (with cover) 13.5 cm;
D. 16.2 cm

74.4.20

Colorless non-lead glass with
double bands of ribbon candy-
like loops around bowl and
cover.
Gift of Ruth I. Roth
Comments: Pattern reissued as
No. 15,010 by United States
Glass Company after 1891.
Parallels: Lee, Victorian Glass, pl.
32; *Revi,* pp. 86, 89.

1089 Salt Dish
Eastern United States
ca. 1870-1880
H. 4 cm; L. 8.5 cm

68.4.94

Colorless, non-lead glass; oval-shaped, series of circles around body with smaller circle in center.
Gift of Mr. and Mrs. Harry A. Snyder
Comments: This pattern is called Banded Buckle by collectors.
Parallels: Lee, E..A.P.G., pl. 102, pp. 328 and 335.

1090 Covered butter dish
Crystal Wedding pattern
Pittsburgh, Pennsylvania;
O'Hara Glass Company
ca. 1875-1885
H. (with cover) 14.8 cm;
D. 16.1 cm

74.4.86

Colorless non-lead glass; spherical form with multi-sided knob on half-spherical cover; base with four feet and vertically scalloped flange.
Gift of Ruth I. Roth
Comments: This pattern was introduced July 6, 1875.
Parallels: Kamm, Book VIII, pls. 12, 13.

1091 Lamp
United States, probably Somerville, Massachusetts, Union Glass Company
ca. 1870-1888
H. 9.8 cm; D. 11.4 cm

70.4.40

Colorless non-lead glass; pressed and tooled. Mold seams down each side; pressed inscription under foot "OIL GUARD LAMP/PAT[d], SEP. 20, 1870."
Comments: This patent date refers to pat. no. 107,514 granted to George Henry Lomax of Somerville, Massachusetts.
Parallels: Russell, Fig. 116.

1092 Covered butter dish
Probably Midwest
ca. 1875-1885
H. (with cover) 12.7 cm; D. 16.3 cm

74.4.87

Colorless non-lead glass.
Gift of Ruth I. Roth

1093 Covered butter dish
Probably Midwest
ca. 1875-1890
H. (with cover) 13.1 cm;
D. 16 cm

74.4.83

Colorless non-lead glass.
Gift of Ruth I. Roth

1094 Covered butter dish
Wheeling, West Virginia;
Central Glass Company
ca. 1875-1891
H. (with cover) 11.2 cm;
D. 16.2 cm

74.4.22

Colorless non-lead glass.
Gift of Ruth I. Roth
Comments: This pattern is called
Prism and Diamond Band by
collectors.
Parallels: Metz, Book I, pp. 192,
193; *Revi*, p. 119.

1095 Covered butter dish
Amazon pattern
Pittsburgh, Pennsylvania;
Bryce, Walker & Company and
United States Glass Company
ca. 1875-1900
H. (with cover) 14.9 cm;
D. 18.1 cm

74.4.27

Colorless non-lead glass.
Gift of Ruth I. Roth
Parallels: Kamm, Book III, p. 10;
Lee, Victorian Glass, pl. 42; *Metz*,
Book I, pp. 34, 37; *Revi*, pp. 86,
310

1096 Bowl
Midwest
ca. 1870-1900
H. 10.6 cm; D. (rim) 10.6 cm

71.4.168

Colorless non-lead glass.
Gift of Mr. and Mrs. Vincent M. Anderson
Comments: This pattern is called Nailhead by Lee. This is probably a sugar bowl base, but no ledge to hold a cover is evident. It may be a spoonholder.
Parallels: Lee, E.A.P.G. pp. 559-560.

1097 Covered butter dish
Fan with Diamond pattern
Jeannette, Pennsylvania,
McKee & Brothers
ca. 1870-1890
H. (with cover) 10.5 cm;
D. 15.6 cm

74.4.6

Colorless non-lead glass.
Gift of Ruth I. Roth
Comments: This pattern is illustrated in McKee's 1880 catalog but probably originated earlier.
Parallels: Lee, E.A.P.G., pl. 76; *Metz, Book I*, pp. 154-155; Stout, Sandra McPhee. *The Complete Book of McKee Glass*, North Kansas City: Trojan Press, 1972, pp. 67-73.

1098 Covered bowl
Wheeling, West Virginia;
Hobbs, Brockunier & Company
ca. 1876-1890
H. (with cover) 22.5 cm;
D. (rim) 20.7 cm

71.4.172

Colorless non-lead glass; domed
lid with a double-faced Viking's
head for knob, and a scalloped
flange; base has three feet, each
a Viking's head.
Gift of Iva Irene Swift
Comments: Design patent no.
9,647, issued to John L. Hobbs
on November 21, 1876, covered
this design.
Parallels: Peterson, Arthur G.
Glass Patents and Patterns, Sanford, Florida, author, 1973, pp.
198-199; *Revi*, p. 187.

1099 Pitcher
Classic pattern
Philadelphia, Pennsylvania;
Gillinder & Sons
ca. 1876-1890
H. 25.1 cm; (with handle)
21.8 cm

62.4.11

Colorless non-lead glass;
pressed in hexagonal shape with
pointed arches on each side; alternating arches are filled with
daisy and button design or have
a female figure; fixed tree-bark
feet; tree-bark handle.
Gift of Mrs. Charles Oliver
Parallels: Lee, E.A.P.G. pl. 97;
Revi, p. 169.

1100 Set of glassware
Three Face pattern
Pittsburgh, Pennsylvania;
George Duncan & Sons
ca. 1878-1890
H. salver, 20.4 cm; D. salver
(rim) 26.8 cm

64.4.3 A-D

1101 Cordial glass
Three Face pattern

78.4.32

Engraved "Florence" and
"Saratoga/1880"
Gift of Grace Milnor

Colorless non-lead glass; salver,
covered butter dish, creamer
and sugar bowl, all plain except
that each has an acid-etched
stem in the form of three wom-
en's faces above a flat, circular
foot.
Ex coll: Mrs. Walter Wood.

Comments: Design patented
June 18, 1878, by John Ernest
Miller; the faces are said to be
Mrs. Miller's.
Parallels: Innes, Pittsburgh Glass,
pl. 391; *Revi*, p. 142-143.

1102 Covered butter dish
Pioneer pattern
Philadelphia, Pennsylvania;
Gillinder & Sons
ca. 1876-1886
H. (with cover) 22.75 cm;
D. (rim) 15.7 cm

50.4.426

Colorless non-lead glass; cylindrical shape with kneeling Indian on a knob on top of a cover; pattern of buffaloes, log cabin, and trees around.
Ex coll: George S. McKearin
Comments: This was presumably designed around the time of the Centennial but was probably carried for some time afterward. The original name of the pattern was Pioneer, but it is now called Westward Ho by collectors.
Parallels: Lee, E.A.P.G., pls. 89-92; *McKearin, American Glass,* pl. 209; *Revi,* pp. 163, 170.

1103 Sauce dish
Pioneer pattern
H. 6.5 cm; D. (rim) 8.9 cm

50.4.441

Ex coll: George S. McKearin

1104 Compote
United States, Pittsburgh,
Pennsylvania, probably Atterbury & Company
ca. 1870-1890
H. 20.7 cm; D (rim), 23.2 cm

79.4.164

Opaque white glass; circular top with open scalloped rim supported by a male figure kneeling on a circular base.
Gift of Mr. and Mrs. William Gelabert
Comments: This is called Atlas pattern by modern collectors.
Parallels: Belknap, Fig. 104.

1105 Match safe
Probably Pittsburgh,
Pennsylvania
ca. 1876-1880
H. 11.3 cm; W. (max) 7 cm

75.4.8

Colorless non-lead glass; shaped like a woman's head with classical headdress; hollow behind face for matches; flat back inscribed, "PATᵈ JUNE 13, 1876"; hole in top of back for hanging. *Comments:* Patented by Washington Beck, June 13, 1876. He was associated with several glass factories in the Pittsburgh area and designed a variety of novelties *Parallels: Revi*, pp. 338, 340, and 342.

1106 Tumbler
United States, probably
Midwest
ca. 1880
H. 9 cm; W. 8 cm

79.4.285

Colorless non-lead glass; cylindrical shape with impression of a coin in base which shows Columbia head facing left with "E PLURIBUS UNUM" above and "1879" below.
Gift of Mrs. Fred C. Archer
Comments: This is not the later Silver Age or Coin pattern made in Wheeling, West Virginia.
Parallels: Lee, Victorian Glass, pl. 15, p. 35.
Lindsay, Bessie M. *American Historical Glass*, Rutland, Vermont, Charles E. Tuttle Co., 1967, p. 85.

1107 Caryatid candlestick
Cambridge, Massachusetts,
New England Glass Company
ca. 1870-1880
H. 25.8 cm

50.4.244

Fiery opalescent glass in the shape of a woman in classical dress.
Ex coll: George S. McKearin
Comments: Designed by Henry Whitney and patented by him for the New England Glass Company, May 10, 1870.
Parallels: Revi, p. 256.

1108   Candlestick
Cambridge, Massachusetts;
New England Glass Company
ca. 1865-1880
H. 25.1 cm; D. (base) 19 cm

59.4.77

Opaque blue glass in the shape
of a crucifix with the figure of
Christ; hexagonal base.
Gift of Louise S. Esterly
Comments: Several companies
made crucifix candlesticks as
late as 1898, but these match
those advertised in the New
England Glass Company catalog
in the Corning collection
Parallels: Watkins, Pressed Glass,
Fig. 15

1109   Candlesticks
In the same pattern

67.4.21 A,B

A pair, bluish-green.
Gift of Mr. and Mrs. Harry A.
Snyder

1110   Baptismal font candelabrum
Pittsburgh, Pennsylvania,
Ripley & Company
ca. 1870
H. 34.6 cm; D. (at base) 13.9 cm

68.4.631

Grayish white glass and white
metal; bowl with "I.H.S." in an
oval on each side; two branches
extend from outer sides of bowl
and end in metal candle sockets;
metal collar underneath bowl;
glass standard with a cross impressed on each side, ending in
a circular domed base with
"PATENT PENDING" on one side.
Gift of Maude B. Feld
Comments: The patent referred
to is design patent no. 3954 of
February 1870. The Henry Ford
Museum has an example with a
cover on the bowl.
Parallels: Innes, Pittsburgh Glass,
Figs. 21, 22; *Revi,* p. 290;
Palmer, Arlene, "Religion in
Clay and Glass," *American Art
and Antiques,* 2, no. 1, July-Aug.
1971, p.85.

1111 Covered butter dish
Pittsburgh, or Bridgeport,
Pennsylvania, Crystal Glass
Company
ca. 1870-1890
H. (with cover) 18.3 cm;
D. 19.9 cm

74.4.12

Colorless non-lead glass; surmounted by an eagle with upraised wings having an acid finish; plain bowl with two handles.
Gift of Ruth I. Roth
Comments: This pattern was named Frosted Eagle by Kamm.
Parallels: Kamm, Book VI, p. 62; *Metz, Book I,* pp. 94-95; *Revi,* p. 132.

1112 Cream pitcher
Probably Midwest
1870-1890
H. 17 cm

73.4.72

Colorless non-lead glass; cylindrical body with a simple quatrefoil design pressed into the lip and squared-off handle; two dolphins, frosted, tail to tail, form the stem.
Gift of Mrs. F. A. Keyser
Parallels: Lee, Victorian Glass, pl. 68; *Kamm, Book III,* pp. 7-8.

1113 Pair of celery vases
Lion pattern
Philadelphia, Pennsylvania,
Gillinder & Sons
ca. 1876-1886
H. 22.5 cm; D. (rim) 11 cm

50.4.445

Colorless non-lead glass; pressed in one piece; cylindrical bowl with three lions-heads back to back forming stem; circular foot.
Ex colls: George S, McKearin; W. Griffith Gribbel
Comments: This is believed to be a Centennial souvenir.
Parallels: Lee, E..A.P.G., pls. 91-93; *McKearin, American* Glass, pls. 209-211.

1114 Pickle dish
United States, Pittsburgh,
Pennsylvania, Atterbury &
Company
ca. 1872-1891
L. 28.5 cm; W. 11.9 cm

79.4.163

Opaque white glass; in the form of two fish ornamented with scales; underneath is "PAT JUNE 4, '72."
Gift of Mr. and Mrs. William Gelabert, Washington D.C.
Parallels: Belknap, p. 225.
Innes, Pittsburgh Glass, pp. 399, 404; *Revi,* p. 29.

1115 Covered jar
Probably Sandwich, Massachusetts, Boston & Sandwich Glass Company
ca. 1870-1885
H. (with cover) 9.4 cm

60.4.813

Light opaque blue glass; pressed in the form of a bear sitting on his haunches with a harness on his head; the head is removable and forms a lid. Marked on base "X. BASIN PHILADA."
Gift of Louise S. Esterly
Comments: This is an ointment jar, probably for bear grease. The name on the base is presumably that of the retailer. Fragments of this pattern, including the head, 73.4.134 (see below), have been excavated at the site of the Sandwich factory.
Parallels: Lee, Sandwich Glass, pl. 207; *S.H.G.,* pp. 24-25.

*1116 Another

60.4.814

Opaque amethyst.
Gift of Louise S. Esterly
Marked on base "PHALEN & SON NY,"

*1117 Another

60.4.816

Opaque white.
Gift of Louise S. Esterly

*1118 Head
From another bear

73.4.134

Opaque light blue.
Gift of Mrs. Betty Greune

1119 Plymouth Rock paperweight
United States, Providence, Rhode Island, Providence Inkstand Company 1876
L. 10.3 cm, W. 7.4 cm, H. 4.3 cm

78.4.75

Colorless non-lead glass with a frosted surface; in the shape of Plymouth Rock; inscribed on surface "1620"; on base "A ROCK IN THE WILDERNESS WELCOMED OUR SIRES FROM BONDAGE FAR OVER THE DARK ROLLING SEA. ON THAT HOLY ALTAR THEY KINDLED THE FIRES JEHOVAH! WHICH GLOW IN OUR BOSOMS FOR THEE"; around base "MARY CHILTON WAS THE FIRST TO LAND UPON THE ROCK DEC. 21 1620. IN ATTEMPTING TO RAISE UP THE ROCK IN 1778 IT WAS SPLIT ASUNDER. THIS IS A FACSIMILE OF THE UPPER PART." and "INKSTAND CO PROV RI/PILGRIM ROCK TRADEMARK 1876."
Gift of the Hon. and Mrs. Amory Houghton
Parallels: Bergstrom, Ill. 80, p. 116; *Lindsey,* pp. 19-21.

1120 Creamer
Wheeling, West Virginia,
Hobbs, Brockunier & Company
ca. 1870-1880
H. (lip) 11.3 cm; D. (rim) 10.3
cm

50.4.430

Opaque white glass.
Ex coll: George S. McKearin
Comments: This pattern was patented by William Leighton for Hobbs, Brockunier & Company February 1, 1870; called Blackberry by collectors.
Parallels: Lee, E.A.P.G., pl. 150; *McKearin, American Glass*, pls. 210, 211; *Revi*, p. 186.

1121 Matching sugar bowl
H. (with cover) 17.5 cm;
D. (rim) 11.3 cm

50.4.431

1122 Salt dish
Midwest
ca. 1870
H. 6.6 cm; D. (rim) 6 cm

68.4.95

Colorless non-lead glass.
Gift of Mr. and Mrs. Harry A. Snyder
Parallels: Lee, E.A.P.G. pl. 139.

1123 Covered butter dish
Strawberry pattern
Pittsburgh, Pennsylvania;
Bryce, Walker & Company
ca. 1870-1895
H. (with cover) 13.3 cm;
D. 17.6 cm

74.4.14

Colorless lead glass; with band
of strawberries and leaves
around the cover; strawberry
finial.
Gift of Ruth I. Roth
Comments: This pattern was patented by John Bryce, February
22, 1870. This differs slightly
from the patent illustration and
may be a later reissue by the
United States Glass Company
after 1891.
Parallels: Kamm, Book V, p. 7;
Lee, E.A.P.G., pls. 142, 151, 152;
Revi, p. 82.

1124 Covered butter dish
Thistle pattern
Pittsburgh, Pennsylvania;
Bryce, Walker & Company
ca. 1872-1895
H. (with cover) 13.6 cm;
D. 17.8 cm

74.4.23

Colorless non-lead glass; thistle
finial and band of thistles and
leaves around cover and flange
of bowl.
Gift of Ruth I. Roth
Comments: Pattern patented by
John Bryce, April 2, 1872. This
differs slightly from the patent illustration and may be a reissue
of the United States Glass
Company after 1891.
Parallels: Lee, E.A.P.G., pl. 140;
Metz, Book I, pp. 68, 71; *Revi*, p.82.

1125 Covered butter dish
Gypsy pattern
Pittsburgh, Pennsylvania,
Adams & Company and United
States Glass Company
ca. 1874-80 and 1898-1900
H. (with cover) 12.0 cm;
D. 16.1 cm

74.4.54

Colorless non-lead glass; pears
and leaves in three places on
cover and on base.
Gift of Ruth I. Roth
Comments: This pattern is called
Baltimore Pear by collectors
today and has been extensively
reproduced since the 1930's. It
was reissued by the United
States Glass Company after 1891.
Parallels: Kamm, Book I, p. 31;
Lee, E.A.P.G., pls. 66, 154;
Metz, Book I, pp. 84, 85; *Revi*,
p. 20.

1126 Covered butter dish
Probably Midwest
ca. 1875-1890
H. (with cover) 10.2 cm;
D. 15.7 cm

74.4.11

Colorless non-lead glass; a band
of oak leaves and acorns around
both bowl and cover; small scallops around rim of bowl; acorn
knob.
Gift of Ruth I. Roth
Comments: This pattern was
named Acorn by Ruth Webb
Lee.
Parallels: Lee, E.A.P.G., pl. 125;
Metz, Book I, p. 72.

1127 Sugar and creamer

United States, Pittsburgh area,
possibly Challinor, Taylor &
Company
ca. 1870-1890
H. (A) 13 cm, (B) 13.9 cm; W.
(A) 10.5 cm, (B) 15.3 cm

79.4.168

Opaque white glass; oval shape
with flat oval sides enameled
with fruit and leaves.
Gift of Mr. and Mrs. William
Gelabert
Comments: This set also appears
in "marble" or "mosaic" glass, a
specialty of Challinor, Taylor &
Company.
Parallels: Belknap, fig. 208a.

1128 Goblet

Possibly Sandwich, Mas-
sachusetts, Boston & Sandwich
Glass Company
ca. 1870-1880
H. 15.1 cm; D. ca. 8.3 cm

60.4.691

Colorless non-lead glass.
Gift of Henry H. Phillips
Comments: This pattern is called
Morning Glory by modern col-
lectors and is said to have been
made only at Sandwich.
Parallels: Lee, Sandwich Glass,
pl. 197.

1129 Bowl

In the same pattern

67.4.26

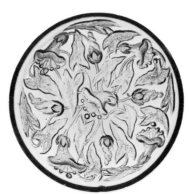

Gift of Mr. and Mrs. Harry A.
Snyder

1130   Covered butter dish
Centennial pattern
Pittsburgh, Pennsylvania; King,
Son & Company
ca. 1876-1891
H. (with cover) 12.4 cm;
D. 16 cm

74.4.18

Colorless non-lead glass; shell
knob and three shell feet; no
other ornamentation.
Gift of Ruth I. Roth
Comments: This pattern was pat-
ented by William C. King and
August Sperber for King, Son &
Company, April 27, 1875.
Parallels: Innes, Pittsburgh Glass,
Fig. 496; *Revi*, p. 218.

1131   Goblet
Probably Philadelphia, Pennsylvania, Gillinder & Sons
1876
H. 16 cm; D. (rim) 8 cm

59.4.17

Colorless non-lead glass;
bucket-shaped bowl; lower por-
tion is decorated with an inscription, "CENTENNIAL 1876" underneath festoons of cords
Gift of Mr. Lou Crandall
Parallels: Lee, E.A.P.G., pl. 164,
no. 5; *Metz, Book 1*, no. 1292,
pp. 112-113.

1132   Covered butter dish
Centennial pattern
Philadelphia, Pennsylvania;
Gillinder & Sons
ca. 1876-1880
H. (with cover) 11.5 cm;
D. 18.8 cm

74.4.17

Colorless non-lead glass;
pointed cover with Liberty Bell;
flat base with Liberty Bell and
wide scalloped flange; both
bells are surrounded by "100
YEARS AGO 1776 1876 DECLARA-
TION OF INDEPENDENCE."
Gift of Ruth I. Roth
Comments: This pattern was patented by James C. Gill for Gillinder & Sons, September 28,
1875.
Parallels: Lee, E.A.P.G., pls. 58,
113, 117; *Revi*, pp. 167-168;
Lindsey, Book 1, pp. 42-43.

1133 **Plate and Goblet**
Centennial pattern
D. (plate) 21.7 cm
H. (goblet) 15.5 cm

55.4.1. A,B

1134 **Mug**
United States
ca. 1876
H. 8.4 cm; D. (rim) 7.4 cm

66.4.66

Colorless non-lead glass; circular base with a view of Independence Hall, Philadelphia, with "INDEPENDENCE HALL" below and "1876" above. Engraved wreath enclosing "SANDFORD" on one side; engraved "1876" on other side.
Gift of Fred Sturm
Comments: This does not seem to be a patented souvenir but it was undoubtedly produced for the United States Centennial in Philadelphia in 1876.

1135 **Pilsner glass**
Wheeling, West Virginia, Central Glass Company
ca. 1876-1881
H. 18 cm; D. (foot) 7.4 cm

76.4.38

Colorless non-lead glass; "1776" and "1876" within a star on opposite sides.
Gift of Mrs. Ben Schirmer
Comments: Patented by John Oesterling and Julius Palme of the Central Glass Company, April 11, 1876, as a Centennial souvenir.
Parallels: Revi, p. 111.

1136 Portrait bust
Abraham Lincoln
Philadelphia, Pennsylvania;
Gillinder & Sons
1876
H. 14.9 cm

56.4.4

Opaque white glass; in the form of a portrait bust of President Abraham Lincoln; inscribed on back, "CENTENNIAL EXHIBITION GILLINDER & SONS." *Parallels: McKearin, American Glass*, pl. 610; *Revi*, p. 169.

1137 Portrait bust
George Washington
United States probably
Bakewell, Pears & Company
ca. 1876
H. 27.3 cm

56.4.5

Translucent white glass with acid-finished surface in the form of a bust of George Washington. *Parallels: Innes, Pittsburgh Glass*. p. 441.

1138 Figurine of Ruth
Philadelphia, Pennsylvania;
Gillinder & Sons
1876
H. 10.3 cm; D. (base) 6.2 cm

54.4.7

Colorless, transparent glass with an acid-frosted surface; pressed in the form of a kneeling girl in Biblical costume gleaning grain; inscription on base, "GILLINDER & SONS CENTENNIAL EXHIBITION."
Bequest of Ellen D. Sharpe
Parallels: Lindsey, Book I, pp. 231, 232.

1139 Paperweight
Probably Philadelphia, Pennsylvania, Gillinder & Sons
1876
H. 6 cm; (base) 11.3 x 15.5 cm

50.4.219

Dark amethyst and translucent glass; replica of Memorial Hall in Philadelphia on oval plinth, inscribed in front "1776 MEMORIAL HALL 1876."
Ex coll: George S. McKearin
Parallels: Lindsey, Book II, pp. 497, 502.

1140 Lion paperweight
United States, Philadelphia, Pennsylvania, Gillinder & Sons
ca. 1876
L. 14.3 cm; W. 7.2 cm; H. 6.6 cm

78.4.69

Colorless non-lead glass; reclining lion on an oval base with scalloped sides; impressed on base "GILLINDER & SONS/ CENTENNIAL EXHIBITION"; acid-etched.
Gift of the Hon. Amory Houghton
Parallels: Revi, p. 170.

1141 Vase
United States
ca. 1876
H. 18 cm; W. 4.8 cm

80.4.49

Colorless non-lead glass in the shape of a hand holding a torch; "CENTENNIAL/1876" on plinth.
Gift of Mr. and Mrs. Marvin Ashburn
Comments: This probably represents the hand of the Statue of Liberty which was exhibited at the Centennial.
Parallels: Lindsay, pp. 529-531.

1142 Shoe
Philadelphia, Pennsylvania, Gillinder & Sons
1876
H. 6.5 cm; L. 14 cm

62.4.23

Colorless non-lead glass; inscription inside shoe, "GILLINDER & SONS/CENTENNIAL EXHIBITION."
Gift of Herbert Weissberger
Comments: These slippers are supposed to have been made at Gillinder's glasshouse on the exhibition grounds at the Centennial.
Parallels: Revi, p. 164.

1143 Shoe
Pittsburgh, Pennsylvania;
George Duncan & Son or Bryce
Brothers
1886
H. 7.5 cm; L. 15.1 cm

65.4.24

Colorless non-lead glass;
marked on sole "PATD/OCT.
19/86" and ". . . T A L SLIPPER/
. . . STONTHEATRE."
Gift of Herbert Weissberger
Comments: This is the Daisy Miller slipper designed by John T.
Miller of Pittsburgh; the patent
was assigned to both Duncan &
Miller and Bryce Brothers. The
inscription on the base should
read, if it were legible, "CRYS-
TAL SLIPPER-BOSTON
THEATRE." The item was given
as a souvenir for a performance
by the Chicago Opera House
Company in 1888.
Parallels: Revi, pp. 84-85, 146-
147; Lenthall, Franklyn.
"Three Dimensional Theatrical
Souvenirs," *Spinning Wheel*, 34,
No. 3, April 1978, p. 21.

1144 Bread plate
Findlay, Ohio, or New Albany,
Ohio; Model Flint Glass Company
ca. 1888-1902 (the company
moved from Findlay to New
Albany in 1894)
L. 27.9 cm; W. 17.3 cm

71.4.174

Colorless non-lead glass.
Gift of Randall P. Marshman
Published: Palmer, Arlene. "Religion in Clay and Glass," *American Art and Antiques*, 2, no. 1,
July-August, 1979, p. 84.
Parallels: Revi, p. 243.

1145 Celery vase
Pittsburgh, Pennsylvania,
Daniel C. Ripley Company
ca. 1882-1890
H. 24.7 cm; W. 8.8 x 8.6 cm

75.4.19

Colorless non-lead glass; rectangular bowl and stem and square
foot; stem and base are hollow
and inside stem is a paper flower
with a wooden base bearing a
paper label "PATENTED/
NOVEMBER 81/JULY 26, 1882."
Comments: According to Russell
(see bibliography), the illegible
date should be November 15,
1881; the November '81 patent
was granted to Adams and Vogeley, the July '82 patent to Ripley. Both covered enclosed ornamentation.
Parallels: Revi, p. 294; *Russell*,
pp. 212, 213.

1146 Lamp
In the same pattern with identical stem
H. 24.6 cm;
W. (top) 11.8 x 12 cm

75.4.20

1147 Shingle
United States
ca. 1881
L. 30 cm

66.4.78

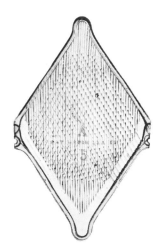

Greenish glass; pressed in a diamond shape with a ribbed surface marked on reverse: "A/PAT MARCH 22 1881/5."
Gift of John Debrucque
Comments: Came from the donor's grandfather's house in Canastota, New York.

1148 Sash guide blocks
United States
ca. 1868-1900
L. 9.3 cm overall;
W. 4.7 cm

80.4.44

Colorless glass and wood.
Marked on one side "PAT NOV 3/68" and on other "NO 2."
Gift of C. R. Jones
Comments: Ropes leading to the sash weights rode over the groove in the glass of this device to reduce fraying of the rope.

1149 Covered butter dish
Probably Midwest, probably United States Glass Company
ca. 1880's
H. (with cover) 10.2 cm;
L. 22.3 cm

74.4.49

Colorless non-lead glass in the shape of a flatiron.
Gift of Ruth I. Roth
Parallels: Metz, Book II, pp. 220, 221.

1150 A   Paperweight
United States
ca. 1880-1900
H. 11.4 cm, W. 7.6 cm

78.4.72

Colorless glass; oval with profile of Lincoln impressed underneath and "Saratoga" in script engraved on front.
Gift of The Hon. Amory Houghton
Comments: Although the paperweight was probably a souvenir of the spa at Saratoga, New York, its manufacturer is unknown.

1150 B   Paperweight
United States
ca. 1882
D. 7.8 cm; H. 4.4 cm

78.4.73

Colorless weight with impressed portrait of Ulysses S. Grant.

1150 C   Paperweight
United States
ca. 1875-1890
D. 8.1 cm; H. 2.8 cm

78.4.70

Colorless weight with impressed portrait of George Washington.

1150 D   Paperweight
United States
ca. 1875-1890
D. 7.9 cm; H. 2.8 cm

78.4.71

Colorless weight with impressed portrait of Abraham Lincoln.

1151 **Covered compote**
Jumbo pattern
Bellaire, Ohio, Aetna Glass and
Manufacturing Company, or
Canton, Ohio, Canton Glass
Company
ca. 1883-1885
H. (with cover) 33.1 cm;
D. (rim) 20.5 cm

75.4.44

Colorless non-lead glass.
Comments: Aetna advertised a
Jumbo covered compote mod-
eled after P. T. Barnum's cele-
brated elephant which was
killed by a train in 1883; the
Canton Glass Company pro-
duced several Jumbo pieces.
Gift of The Honorable and Mrs.
Amory Houghton
Parallels: Revi, pp. 23, 24, 103,
104.

1152 **Covered butter dish**
Probably Midwest
ca. 1880's
H. (with cover) 13.6 cm;
L. 16.4 cm

74.4.13

Colorless lead glass; squirrel
finial.
Gift of Ruth I. Roth
Comments: This pattern was
named Zigzag Band by Kamm.
Parallels: Kamm, Book IV, p. 10.

1153 **Covered butter dish**
Pittsburgh, Pennsylvania,
George Duncan & Sons
1880's
H. (with cover) 16.6 cm;
D. 19.4 cm

74.4.15

Colorless non-lead glass; knob
in form of a dog.
Gift of Ruth I. Roth
Comments: A variant of this pat-
tern was patented in 1881 by
Augustus Heisey for Duncan;
Ruth Webb Lee was the source
of its present name, Shell and
Tassel.
Parallels: Kamm, Book III, p. 59;
Lee, E.A.P.G., pl. 157, no. 2;
Metz, Book I, pp. 138-139; *Revi,*
p. 144.

1154 **Covered butter dish**
Tarentum, Pennsylvania;
United States Glass Company,
or Challinor, Taylor & Company
ca. 1885-1905
H. (with cover) 16.8 cm;
L. 22.2 cm

74.4.71

Colorless non-lead glass; sitting
rooster is the cover and basket is
the bowl.
Gift of Ruth I. Roth
Comments: See also the duck,
following. Rooster Butter &
Cover was advertised by the
United States Glass Company
and by Challinor, Taylor &
Company, which had a barnyard
assortment.
Parallels: Lee, Victorian Glass,
pls. 107, 109; *Revi,* p. 317.

1155 Covered butter dish
Midwest, United States Glass
Company or Challinor, Taylor &
Company, Tarentum, Pennsyl-
vania
ca. 1885-1905
H. (with cover) 12.3 cm;
L. 22 cm

74.4.72

Colorless non-lead glass with
slight bluish tinge; base flange
has wave-like lines to indicate
water; eyes show traces of paint.
Gift of Ruth I. Roth
Comments: See also the preceding, a rooster. The Duck Butter
was advertised by the United
States Glass Company and by
Challinor, Taylor & Company,
which had a barnyard assortment.
Parallels: Lee, Victorian Glass,
pls. 107, 114, 115.

1156 Covered dish
Pittsburgh, Pennsylvania;
Atterbury & Company
ca. 1887-1890
H. 12.6 cm; L. 27.8 cm

62.4.25

Opaque white glass; an opaque
white body and a purple head
and neck; applied yellow glass
eyes; lid of dish is formed by the
upper half of the duck's body;
marked in base, "PAT. MAR.
1887."
Parallels: Innes, Pittsburgh Glass,
p. 404; *Revi*, p. 31.

1157 Covered bowl
United States, Pittsburgh,
Pennsylvania; Atterbury &
Company
ca. 1889-1895
H. 16.6 cm, D. 18 cm

79.4.167

Opaque white glass; cover with
two entwined fish, each with a
red glass eye glued in; marked
inside cover "PAT. AUG 1889";
circular base.
Gift of Mr. and Mrs. William
Gelabert
Parallels: Belknap, p. 163a.
Revi, p. 32.

1158 Covered butter dish or nappy
Probably Midwest
ca. 1885-1905
H. (with cover) 11.1 cm;
L. 17.9 cm

74.4.77

Colorless non-lead glass; four
shell feet and shell finial.
Gift of Ruth I. Roth

1159 Toothpick holders
Probably Tiffin, Ohio; Tiffin
Glass Company
ca. 1890-1900
H. 5.1 cm; L. 12.1 cm

65.4.86 A, B

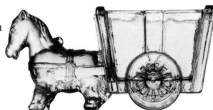

Colorless non-lead glass.
Gift of Miss Ruth Friedman
Comments: This is one of a line
of animal and cart containers
patented by Jonathan Haley on
October 7, 1890, assigned to the
Tiffin Glass Company.
Parallels: Revi, p. 332.

1160 Spoonholder
Grace pattern
Tarentum, Pennsylvania;
Richards & Hartley Glass Com-
pany
H. 15.6 cm; D. 8.8 cm

73.4.63

Colorless non-lead glass; cylin-
drical bowl with pseudo-
Japanese motifs.
Gift of Mrs. Robert Brearey
Parallels: Kamm, Book II, p. 16.
Lee, Victorian Glass, pl. 32; *Revi*,
p. 287.

1161 Covered butter dish
Probably Midwest
ca. 1880's
H. (with cover) 16.5 cm;
D. 15.8 cm

74.4.24

Colorless non-lead glass.
Gift of Ruth I. Roth
Comments: This pattern is called
Grasshopper by Ruth Webb Lee
as some pieces have a grass-
hopper as part of the pattern.
This butter dish does not.
Parallels: Kamm, Book I, p. 89;
Lee, Victorian Glass, pl. 34; *Metz,
Book I*, pp. 94, 95; *Metz, Book
II*, pp. 82, 83.

1162   Covered butter dish
Probably Midwest
ca. 1880's
H. (with cover) 12.8 cm;
D. 15.3 cm

74.4.63

Colorless lead glass; knob
formed of two stylized sea-
horses.
Gift of Ruth I. Roth

1163   Jar
Probably Midwest
ca. 1880
H. (with cover) 17 cm;
D. (base) 8 cm

67.4.111

Colorless non-lead glass; three
storks or herons in a marsh
around sides.
Bequest of Frances Craig
Hawkes McAllister
Parallels: Metz, Book 2, pp.
86-87.

Regal pattern
United States, probably
Pittsburgh, Pennsylvania,
Bryce, Walker & Company or
Doyle & Company
ca. 1875-1885

Colorless non-lead glass;
Gifts of Mr. and Mrs. William
Gelabert (1164-1172)

Comments: Doyle's pattern #29
also issued by Bryce, Walker &
Company as Regal; reissued by
the United States Glass Company after 1891 as Regal.
Parallels: Revi, pp. 88, 89, & 139.

1164 Compote
Regal pattern
Circular top with alternating
plain, geometric, and floral
panels; stem and paneled foot.
H. 18.1 cm; D. 18.8 cm

79.4.150

1165 Butter dish base
Regal pattern

79.4.154

1166 Celery vase
Regal pattern

79.4.151

1167 Sugar bowl base
Regal pattern

79.4.152

1168 Pair of goblets
Regal pattern

79.4.153 A,B

1169 Pair of bowls
Regal pattern

79.4.156 A,B

1170 Pair of dessert dishes
Regal pattern

79.4.158 A,B

1171 Two serving dishes
Regal pattern

79.4.157 A,B

1172 Platter
Regal pattern

79.4.155

1173 Covered butter dish
Pittsburgh, Pennsylvania; Bryce
Brothers
After 1882
H. (with cover) 12.3 cm;
W. 16.5 cm

74.4.81

Colorless non-lead glass; base
and cover pressed in two separate patterns.
Gift of Ruth I. Roth
Comments: The bowl is Bryce
Brothers' Wreath pattern; the lid
is Bryce Brothers' Regal pattern.
Parallels: Kamm, Book I, p. 36;
Lee, E.A.P.G., pls. 45, 129, 159,
78, 130, 133; *Metz, Book I*, pp.
62, 63; *Revi*, p. 90.

1174 Covered butter dish
Probably Midwest
ca. 1885
H. (with cover) 13.7 cm;
D. 16.6 cm

74.4.80

Colorless non-lead glass.
Gift of Ruth I. Roth
Comments: M. W. Kamm (see
bibliography) found this pattern
in a premium catalog dated
1885.
Parallels: Kamm, Book II, p. 82;
Book IV, pp. 136, 137.

1175 Covered butter dish
Midwest
ca. 1880's
H. (with cover) 11.5 cm; D. (including handles) 18.1 cm

74.4.75

Colorless non-lead glass.
Gift of Ruth I. Roth
Parallels: Lee, E.A.P.G., pl. 140.

1176 Bowl
United States, Pittsburgh,
Pennsylvania, Challinor, Taylor
& Company
ca. 1885
H. 9.8 cm, D. 20.6 cm

79.4.166

Opaque white glass; circular
shape; raised pattern of flowers
and leaves on outside surface;
single blossom and leaves in
center of base; fluted rim.
Gift of Mr. and Mrs. William
Gelabert
Comments: This is Challinor,
Taylor's pattern #313.
Parallels: Belknap, Fig. 106 C.
Innes, Pittsburgh Glass, p. 409.

1177 Covered butter dish
Probably Midwest
ca. 1880's
H. (with cover) 10.6 cm;
L. 19.9 cm

74.4.88

Colorless non-lead glass; handle
at each end with crossed willow
leaves.
Gift of Ruth I. Roth

1178 Covered butter dish
Barley pattern
Pittsburgh, Pennsylvania,
Campbell, Jones & Company
ca.1880's
H. (with cover) 11.5 cm;
D. 16.1 cm

74.4.19

Colorless non-lead glass.
Gift of Ruth I. Roth
Parallels: Kamm, Book I, p. 34;
Lee, E.A.P.G., pls. 113, 116;
Metz, Book I, pp. 84, 85; *Revi*,
p. 100.

†1179 Plate
Pittsburgh, Pennsylva-
nia, probably Adams &
Company
ca. 1885
D. 26.6 cm

61.4.120

Pale green glass; rim of overlapping maple leaves with inscription, "LET US HAVE PEACE"
above "U.S. GRANT." Bust of
Grant in center with "BORN
APRIL 22, 1822 — DIED JULY 23,
1885" above.
Comments: Although the Grant
plate was undoubtedly introduced immediately after his
death, the serving bowl set (see
below) could have been made at
any time in the 1870's or 1880's.
Parallels: Keyes, Eugene. "Presidential Portraits in Late Glass,"
Antiques, 34, no. 5, November
1938, pp. 240-245, Fig. 3; *Lee,
E.A.P.G.*, pl. 143.

**1180 Oval serving bowl, tray, and
three leaf-shaped bowls**
H. (bowl) 11.5 cm; L. 27.7 cm;
L. (tray) 33.7 cm

71.4.171 A-E

Same pattern, without bust and
inscription; vaseline glass,
Gift of Iva Irene Swift

1181 Set of glassware
Plate, 2 pitchers, 5 nappies
Midwest
ca. 1881-1890
(A) D. 29.6 cm

63.4.15 A-H

Colorless non-lead glass; plate
with a bust of President Garfield
in center with inscription around
bust "WE MOURN OUR NATION'S
LOSS/BORN NOVEMBER 18,
1831/SHOT JULY 2, 1881/DIED
SEPTEMBER 19, 1881."
Gift of Miss Ina M. LeRoy
Comments: The plate was obviously produced soon after Garfield's death and probably only
for a short time. The remainder
of the set, without bust and inscription, may have been a standard pattern, popular over a
period of years.
Parallels: Keyes, H. E. "Presidential Portraits in Late Glass"
Antiques, 34, no. 5, November
1938, p. 240, Fig. 7; *Kamm,
Book I*, p. 283; *Metz, Book 2*, pp.
182-183.

1182 **Covered butter dish**
Bridgeport, Ohio, probably
LaBelle Glass Company
ca. 1880-1887
H. (with cover) 17.1 cm;
L. 19.1 cm

74.4.45

Colorless non-lead glass; lacy
pattern on the rounded ends of
the cover and on the underside
of the wide flange.
Gift of Ruth I. Roth
Comments: Attribution based on
similarity to a group of patterns
made at the LaBelle factory.
Parallels: Kamm, Book II, p. 34;
Book V, p. 21; *Metz, Book II,* pp.
70, 71.

1183 **Covered butter dish**
Albion pattern
Pittsburgh, Pennsylvania; Bryce
Brothers
ca. 1882-1891
H. (with cover) 9.6 cm;
W. 17.2 cm

74.4.46

Colorless non-lead glass; octagonal flat rim on cover.
Gift of Ruth I. Roth
Parallels: Lee, Victorian Glass, pl.
77.

1184 **Covered butter dish**
No. 80 pattern
Pittsburgh, Pennsylvania; Bryce
Brothers
ca. 1880's
H. (with cover) 13.7 cm;
D. 17.5 cm

74.4.73

Colorless non-lead glass.
Gift of Ruth I. Roth
Comments: Bryce Brothers adver-
tised this in the 1880's as No. 80
Flanged Butter.
Parallels: Kamm, Book VIII, pl. 39.

1185 **Covered butter dish**
Probably Midwest; possibly
LaBelle Glass Company,
Bridgeport, Ohio
ca. 1880's
H. (with cover) 15.3 cm; D. (in-
cluding handles) 19.9 cm

74.4.64

Colorless non-lead glass.
Gift of Ruth I. Roth
Comments: Attribution is based
on likeness to LaBelle's Queen
Anne pattern.
Parallels: Kamm, Book I, pp. 64,
90; *Metz, Book II,* pp. 168, 169,
208, 209.

1186 Covered butter dish
Coral pattern
Pittsburgh, Pennsylvania; Bryce
Brothers and the United States
Glass Company (United States
Glass Company after 1891)
ca. 1888-1900
H. (with cover) 13.1 cm;
W. 15 cm

74.4.25

Colorless non-lead glass.
Gift of Ruth I. Roth
Comments: This pattern appears
in a United States Glass Company Catalog of 1898.
Parallels: Lee, E.A.P.G., pls. 120,
156; *Metz, Book I*, p. 141; *Revi,*
pp. 86, 87.

1187 Covered butter dish
No. 79 pattern
Pittsburgh, Pennsylvania; Bryce
Brothers
ca. 1885-1903
H. (with cover) 11.3 cm;
D. 15.3 cm

74.4.34

Colorless non-lead glass.
Gift of Ruth I. Roth
Comments: This is Bryce
Brothers pattern no. 79 called
Chain with Star by modern col-
lectors.
Parallels: Kamm, Book VIII, p.
12; *Lee, E.A.P.G.*, pp. 572, 573;
Metz, Book I, p. 117; *Revi,* p. 87.

1188 Plate
United States
ca. 1850-1890
D. 8.8 cm

65.4.75

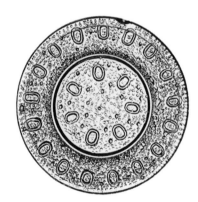

Colorless non-lead glass.
Gift of Mrs. Leon S. Bard
Parallels: Lee and Rose, p. 401,
no. 890.

1189 Celery vase
Mikado pattern
Tarentum, Pennsylvania,
Richards & Hartley Glass Com-
pany
ca. 1885-1900
H. 18.8 cm; D. (rim) 10.8 cm

75.4.46

Amber glass.
Gift of Mrs. Mary Kelly, in
memory of James H. and
Catherine M. Holleran
Comments: Richards & Hartley
also called this pattern No. 99.
Lee named it Daisy & Button
with Crossbars.
Parallels: Lee, E.A.P.G., pp.
592-594.

1190 Vase
Probably Midwest, possibly
Duncan & Miller Glass Com-
pany
ca. 1900
H. 17.9 cm; W. 9.1 cm x 9.1 cm

75.4.83

Amber glass.
Gift of Otto W. Hilbert
Comments: Kamm called this
Column Block.
Parallels: Kamm, Book 3, p. 75.

1191 Covered butter dish
Banner design
Pittsburgh, Pennsylvania; Bryce
Brothers Glass Company
ca. 1882-1891
H. 9.5 cm; L. 19.5 cm

74.4.37

Colorless non-lead glass;
shield-shaped with a design of
stars and stripes.
Gift of Ruth I. Roth
Comments: This is the Banner
Butter, one of a series produced
by Bryce in 1882.
Parallels: Lee, Victorian Glass, pl.
76; *Metz, Book I,* pp. 156, 157.

1192 Lamp
Pittsburgh, Pennsylvania,
George Duncan & Sons; Brilliant, Ohio, Dalzell Brothers &
Gilmore; Steubenville, Ohio,
Alexander J. Beatty & Sons
ca. 1886-1891
H. 25 cm; D. (base) 10.1 cm

58.4.79

Colorless non-lead glass; with
three panels around top of font
silver-stained yellow.
Gift of Louise S. Esterly
Comments: This pattern was patented by G. W. Blair, May 25,
1886, and again by August
Lang, June 29, 1886. Lang assigned the patent to George
Duncan & Sons and they issued
it both as Daisy and Button,
Single Panel and Amberette.
The two Ohio firms made it
slightly later.
Parallels: Innes, Pittsburgh Glass,
fig. 416.

1193 Covered butter dish
Westmoreland pattern
Greensburg, Pennsylvania; Gillinder & Sons, United States
Glass Company
ca. 1889-1907
H. (with cover) 13.5 cm;
D. 19 cm

74.4.3

Colorless non-lead glass.
Gift of Ruth I. Roth
Comments: This pattern was reissued by the United States Glass
Company after 1891 as no. 420.
The patent is dated July 6, 1889
and was registered by Thomas
Mellor for Gillinder & Sons, a
Philadelphia glass company
which built the Greensburg
plant in 1889 for pressed tablewares but sold it to the United
States Glass Company in 1891.
Parallels: Kamm, Book I, p. 116;
Lee, Victorian Glass, pl. 49; *Revi*
pp. 164, 168.

1194 Pair of napkin rings
United States, probably Midwest
ca. 1890-1910
H. (A) 8.1 cm, (B) 8.2 cm;
D. (A) 6.5 cm, (B) 6.5 cm

79.4.161 A, B

Colorless non-lead glass;
pressed in the form of an open
octagon set at right angles to a
ribbed octagonal base, hollow
underneath.
Gift of Mr. and Mrs. William
Gelabert

1195 Bowl
Hobnail Diamond pattern
Probably Hobbs, Brockunier &
Co., Wheeling, West Virginia
ca. 1886-1890
H. 5.6 cm; L. 26.4 cm

63.4.117

Amber glass shading to red at
the top edge.
Ex coll: Lola Kincaid Ford; gift
of Fletcher Ford and Sally
Recker in memory of Lola Kincaid Ford
Comments: Hobbs, Brockunier
produced pressed Amberina
under license from the New
England Glass Company in this
pattern, called by them both
Hobnail Diamond and No. 101.
Modern collectors call it Daisy
and Button.
Parallels: Revi, Albert C.
*Nineteenth Century Glass, Its
Genesis and Development*, (rev.
ed.), New York: Thomas Nelson
and Sons, 1967, p. 23.

*1196 Another
Hobnail Diamond pattern,
square
W. 22.2 cm

63.4.158

Ex coll: Lola Kincaid Ford
Gift of Fletcher Ford and Sally
Recker in memory of Lola Kin-
caid Ford

1197 Another
Hobnail Diamond pattern,
boat-shaped
L. 35.5 cm

79.4.33

Gift, in part, of William Hammond

1198 Covered butter dish
Clio pattern
Tarentum, Pennsylvania; Chal-
linor, Taylor & Company, or
United States Glass Company
ca. 1884-1891, or ca. 1900
H. (with cover) 14.3 cm;
D. 19.8 cm

74.4.70

Colorless non-lead glass.
Gift of Ruth I. Roth
Comments: This piece is heavy
and characteristic of the wares
made at the United States Glass
Company around 1900 rather
than earlier. No evidence exists
to indicate that the United
States Glass Company reissued
Challinor, Taylor's pattern after
the merger, but it seems likely.
Parallels: Lee, Victorian Glass, pl.
46; *Metz, Book III*, pp. 156, 157;
Revi, p. 122.

1199 Covered butter dish
No. 76 pattern
Pittsburgh, Pennsylvania; Doyle
& Company; United States
Glass Company
ca. 1885-1900
H. (with cover) 13.1 cm; D. (including handles) 20.5 cm

74.4.57

Colorless non-lead glass.
Gift of Ruth I. Roth
Parallels: Kamm, Book VIII, pls.
6, 7, 73; *Revi*, p. 139.

1200 Covered butter dish
Probably Midwest
ca. 1880's
H. (with cover) 13.7 cm;
D. 15.4 cm

74.4.38

Colorless non-lead glass; cover
and base decorated with arches
and diamonds; flat octagonal
knob.
Gift of Ruth I. Roth
Comments: Pattern named Curtain Tie Back by Kamm.
Parallels: Kamm, Book III, p.
118; *Metz, Book I*, pp. 130, 131.

1201 Covered butter dish
Pittsburgh, Pennsylvania; Bryce
Brothers and United States
Glass Company
ca. 1880-1900
H. (with cover) 13.2 cm;
D. 17.9 cm

74.4.29

Colorless non-lead glass.
Gift of Ruth I. Roth
Comments: The cover of this dish
fits on the rim, not over the rim
as is usual; cover is notched to
keep it from slipping.
Parallels: Kamm, Book I, p. 21;
Lee, E.A.P.G., pp. 516, 517;
Metz, Book I, p. 159; *Revi*, pp.
88, 310.

1202 Bowl
Palace pattern
United States, Pittsburgh area,
probably Wilson Glass Company
or Co-Operative Flint Glass
Company, possibly Phoenix
Glass Company
Probably ca. 1890-1910, possibly
ca. 1937-1940
H. 4.3 cm; D. 18.7 cm

79.4.169

Colorless non-lead glass; half-spherical with concentric rings of
bull's eyes and stars around
sides; star in base.
Gift of Mr. and Mrs. William
Gelabert
Comments: This pattern was originally issued as "Palace" by
Adams & Co. in the 1870's but
it has been reissued many times.
Modern collectors call it "Moon
and Star.
Parallels: Revi, p. 21.

1203 **Goblet**
Probably Midwest
ca.1880-1900
H. 15 cm

73.4.62

Colorless non-lead glass;
roughly engraved with a leaf
spray.
Gift of Mrs. Robert Brearey.

*1204 **Another**
H. 11.7 cm

71.4.99

Engraved "Saratoga 1889/
Hallenbeck."
Gift of Edna and Harold
St. John

1205 **Covered butter dish**
Probably Midwest
ca. 1880-1890
H. (with cover) 14.4 cm;
D. 16.1 cm

74.4.43

Colorless non-lead glass; two
leaf sprays very crudely en-
graved on bowl.
Gift of Ruth I. Roth
Comments: Mrs. Kamm named
this pattern Sunken Teardrop.
Parallels: Kamm, Book IV, p. 26;
Metz, Book II, pp. 136, 137.

1206 **Covered butter dish**
Midwest, possibly Central Glass
Company, Wheeling West Vir-
ginia,
ca. 1880-1900
H. (with cover) 16.3 cm;
D. (including handles) 19.9 cm

74.4.62

Colorless non-lead glass; upcurving floral spray engraved on
plain lid.
Gift of Ruth I. Roth
Parallels: Revi, p. 114.

1207 **Footed bowl**
United States, Midwest
ca. 1880-1900
H. 10 cm; D. (rim) 19.5 cm

67.4.103

Colorless non-lead glass; circular
shape with a medallion containing a woman's head with classical hair arrangement on each side.
Bequest of Frances Craig
Hawkes McAllister.
Comments: This pattern was
named Cameo by Lee and Classic Medallion by Kamm.
Parallels: Kamm, Book I, 24;
Lee, Victorian Glass, pl. 36, p.
102; *Metz, Book I,* pp. 102-103.

1208 Covered butter dish
Banded Star pattern
Pittsburgh, Pennsylvania; King,
Son & Company
ca. 1880-1891
H. (with cover) 15.6 cm;
D. 13.5 cm

74.4.21

Colorless non-lead glass.
Gift of Ruth I. Roth
Comments: This pattern was patented by G.B. Swift and W.C. King, December 20, 1880.
Parallels: Kamm, Book IV, p. 110; *Lee, Victorian Glass*, pl. 67; *Metz, Book I*, pp. 120, 121; *Revi*, p. 211.

1209 Covered butter dish
Dakota pattern
Pittsburgh, Pennsylvania; Doyle
& Company, United States
Glass Company Factory F or
Ripley & Company
ca. 1885-1900
H. (with cover) 14.4 cm;
D. 19.6 cm

74.4.2

Colorless non-lead glass; cover with lightly engraved design of leaves and flowers; circular plate with sheared and fluted rim.
Gift of Ruth I. Roth
Comments: This is the hotel model. See entry following for a home model. The covers on the two are identical.
Parallels: Innes Pittsburgh Glass, pls. 417-421; *Kamm, Book I*, p. 194; *Victorian Glass*, pl. 67; *Revi*, pp. 138, 293.

1210 Covered butter dish
Dakota pattern
Pittsburgh, Pennsylvania; Doyle
& Company, United States
Glass Company Factory F or
Ripley & Company
ca. 1885-1900
H. (with cover) 15 cm;
D. 19.7 cm

74.4.1

Colorless, non-lead glass; cover with lightly engraved design of leaves and flowers.
Gift of Ruth I. Roth
Comments: This is the home version of the butter dish and differs from the hotel model, preceding, in having a heavier base.
Parallels: Innes Pittsburgh Glass, pls. 417-421; *Kamm, Book I*, p. 194; *Lee, Victorian Glass*, pl. 67; *Revi*, pp. 138, 293.

1211 Covered butter dish
No. 15021 pattern
Tarentum, Pennsylvania,
Richards & Hartley Glass Com-
pany, United States Company,
Columbia Glass Company
(United States Glass Company
after 1891)
ca. 1885-1893
H. (with cover) 15.4 cm;
D. 18.7 cm

74.4.16

Colorless and ruby stained non-
lead glass; ovals on the cover are
ruby stained.
Gift of Ruth I. Roth
Comments: This is United States
Glass Company pattern no.
15021, issued in 1891 and now
called Broken Column.
Richards & Hartley's original
name is not known. This is
probably a marriage; the bowl is
not stained.
Parallels: Kamm, Book IV, p. 116;
Lee, Victorian Glass, pl. 71; *Metz,
Book I,* pp. 140-141; *Revi,* pp.
125, 126, 286, 310; *Innes,
Pittsburgh Glass,* Fig. 415.

1212 Berry bowl
Pioneer or No. 15 pattern
Pittsburgh, Pennsylvania,
Pioneer Glass Company
ca. 1885-1890
H. 7.4 cm, D. 14.9 cm

51.4.722

Colorless non-lead glass; rows of
vertical columns with indenta-
tions.
Gift of Mrs. Robert C. Woods
Parallels: Kamm, Book 3, p. 94.

1213 Covered butter dish
Cobb pattern
Tarentum, Pennsylvania,
Richards & Hartley Glass Com-
pany, or possibly United States
Glass Company
ca. 1880's-1890's
H. (with cover) 18.3 cm;
D. 17.9 cm

74.4.50

Colorless non-lead glass with
vertical zipper pattern; footed
base with same zippers and wide
flange.
Gift of Ruth I. Roth
Parallels: Lee, Victorian Glass, pl.
36; *Revi,* p. 286.

1214 Covered butter dish
Probably Midwest
ca. 1890-1900
H. (with cover) 11.1 cm;
D. 15.9 cm

74.4.10

Colorless non-lead glass.
Gift of Ruth I. Roth
Comments: There are many variations of the honeycomb pattern
by almost every company making pressed tableware. This appears to be a late one.

1215 Lamp
In a similar pattern
H. 17.1 cm; D. (base) 12.4 cm

74.4.163

Colorless non-lead glass.
Bequest of Mrs. Jason Westerfield
Comments: There are many variations of the honeycomb pattern
by almost every company making pressed tableware. This appears to be a late one.

1216 Covered butter dish
Probably Midwest
ca. 1880's-1890's
H. (with cover) 13.7 cm;
D. 20 cm

74.4.66

Colorless non-lead glass.
Gift of Ruth I. Roth
Parallels: Kamm Book I, p. 30;
Metz, Book I, pp. 162, 163.

1217A Vase
Opalescent Dewdrop
Wheeling, West Virginia,
Hobbs, Brockunier & Company
ca. 1886-1891
H. 16.8 cm; D. (rim) 9.3 cm

50.4.331

Deep cranberry glass; pressed in
a cylindrical form, the surface
completely studded with (opalescent) hobnails. Paper label on
base, "Patented June 1, 1886."
Ex coll: George S. McKearin
Comments: This manufacturing
technique was patented by William Leighton and William F.
Russell of Hobbs, Brockunier &
Company and the glass marketed by them as "Opalescent
Dewdrop" although it is now
called "Hobnail" by collectors.
*Parallels: McKearin, American
Glass*, pl. 216, no. 3.

1217B **Bowl**
United States, probably Hobbs,
Brockunier & Co., Wheeling,
West Virginia
ca. 1886-1895
H. 8.3 cm; W. 19.6 cm x 20 cm

63.4.163

Square; amber shading to red
with overall pattern of opalescent hobnails; fluted rim.
Ex coll: Lola Kincaid Ford. Gift
of Fletcher Ford and Sally
Recker in memory of Lola Kincaid Ford.

1218 **Bowl**
Probably Tarentum, Pennsylvania; Challinor, Taylor & Company
ca. 1886-1891
H. 8.4 cm; D. (rim) 20.0 cm

54.4.73

Translucent and opaque white,
pink, and lilac marbleized glass.
Bequest of Ellen D. Sharpe
Comments: This pattern is called
Dart Bar by modern collectors
and is found in light blue,
opaque white, and purple slag
glass.
Parallels: Belknap, p. 320.

1219 **Pair of vases**
Probably Tarentum, Pennsylvania; Challinor, Taylor & Company
ca. 1886-1891
H. 20.2 cm; D. (rim) 11.4 cm

54.4.74 A,B

Opaque white, pink, and lilac
marbleized glass.
Bequest of Ellen D. Sharpe
Comments: David Challinor patented his "Mosaic Glass" in
1886.
Parallels: Belknap, third color
plate; *Innes, Pittsburgh Glass*,
Fig. 460.

1220 Pair of covered bowls
Silver Age pattern
Wheeling, West Virginia, Central Glass Company, of Hobbs, Brockunier & Company
ca. 1891-1892
H. 18.4 cm; D. 15.3

76.4.37 A,B

1221 Tazza
Silver Age pattern

52.4.76

Colorless non-lead glass; cylindrical bowl with eight frosted, pressed images of U.S. coins in relief, dated 1892, around the sides. Matching lid has eight coins around sides and one on knob.
Gift of Eleanor Palmer (bowls)
Comments: This pattern was put out just as the two factories above entered the United States Glass Company merger in 1891. Production of the pattern is said to have been stopped by the United States government under the counterfeiting law before the year was out. It is now called Coin by collectors.
Parallels: Revi, pp. 108, 109; *Lindsey,* Book I, pp. 88 ff.

1222A Medal
United States, maker unknown, possibly Libbey Glass Company
Toledo, Ohio
ca. 1893
D. 2.1 cm; Thickness, 0.5 cm

72.4.173

Blue glass; profile of Columbus on one side with "WORLD'S COLUMBIAN EXPOSITION CHICAGO/1892" around; reverse has a ship and two globes with "WORLD'S COLUMB. EXPOSIT. CHICAGO/1892."

1222B Paperweight
United States
ca. 1892-1893
D. 8.2 cm; H. 3 cm

78.4.74

Colorless weight with impressed portrait of Christopher Columbus and inscription WORLD'S COLUMBIAN/1492/EXPOSITION/1892.

1223　Pitcher
Dunkirk, Indiana, Beatty-Brady
Glass Company
ca. 1898-1900
H. (at lip) 22.2 cm

74.4.103

Colorless non-lead glass;
pressed design with a portrait of
Admiral Dewey flanked by a
marine and a sailor; inscription
"Gridley, you may fire when re-
ady" and a scroll naming the
ships taking part in the battle of
Manila; upright rocket shells
around base of body.
Gift of Charles A. Farr
Comments: There are two variants of this pitcher, one having
balls in place of cannon shells.
The cannon ball version was
patented September 20, 1898.
Parallels: Revi, pp. 56, 61; *Metz,
Book II*, pp. 184, 185.

1224 Covered butter dish
Probably Midwest
ca. 1890-1910
H. (with cover) 10.7 cm;
D. 18.5 cm

74.4.47

Colorless non-lead glass; base
nearly flat with scalloped flange
and star design pressed into the
exterior.
Gift of Ruth I. Roth

1225 Covered butter dish
Probably Midwest
ca. 1890-1910
H. (with cover) 12.8 cm;
D. 19.3 cm

74.4.84

Colorless non-lead glass; cover
with crown around top edge;
plate with star design in center
and row of spherical knobs
around edge of flange.
Gift of Ruth I. Roth

1226 Covered butter dish
Probably Midwest
ca. 1890-1910
H. (with cover) 13.6 cm;
D. 21.1 cm

74.4.85

Colorless non-lead glass.
Gift of Ruth I. Roth
Comments: This is a typical colonial pattern of the turn of the
century; it is so heavy it might
well be hotel or restaurant ware.

1227 Covered butter dish
Virginia pattern
Gasport, Indiana, United States
Glass Company
ca. 1890-1910
H. (with cover) 16.2 cm;
D. 20.6 cm

74.4.58

Colorless non-lead glass.
Gift of Ruth I. Roth
Comments: This pattern was reis-
sued as 15,071 by the United
States Glass Company, and the
name was changed to Mirror in
1907.
Parallels: Kamm, Book II, p. 89;
Revi, pp. 318, 319.

1228 Covered butter dish
Probably Midwest
ca. 1890-1910
H. (with cover) 10.7 cm;
D. 19.6 cm

74.4.91

Colorless non-lead glass; eleven
hexagonal panels around cover
and eight around base.
Gift of Ruth I. Roth
Comments: This is a hotel- or
restaurant-weight pattern.

1229 Covered butter dish
Probably Midwest
ca. 1890-1910
H. (with cover) 15.8 cm;
W. 13.5 cm

74.4.44

Colorless non-lead glass.
Gift of Ruth I. Roth

1230 Butter Dish
Puritan pattern
Newark, Ohio, A. H. Heisey &
Co.
ca. 1901-1910
H. 16.3 cm; D. 21.2 cm

74.4.31

Colorless non-lead glass;
marked with an "H" in a dia-
mond on the base.
Gift of Ruth I. Roth
Parallels: Vogel, Clarence W.
Heisey's First Ten Years; Book I,
Plymouth, Ohio: Heisey Publi-
cations, 1969, p. 37.

1231 Covered butter dish
Pittsburgh pattern
Pittsburgh, Pennsylvania; Bryce
Brothers and United States
Glass Company
ca. 1890-1910
H. (with cover) 16.2 cm;
D. 19.1 cm

74.4.76

Colorless glass; vertically ribbed; tall knob.
Gift of Ruth I. Roth
Comments: Bryce's Pittsburgh
pattern was introduced at an exposition in Pittsburgh, in 1890.
Parallels: Kamm, Book IV, p. 73;
Lee, Victorian Glass, pl. 63; *Revi*,
p. 89.

1232 Covered butter dish
Probably Midwest
ca. 1890-1910
H. (with cover) 13.3 cm;
D. 18.4 cm

74.4.90

Colorless non-lead glass.
Gift of Ruth I. Roth

1233 Covered butter dish
Probably Midwest
ca. 1890-1910
H. (with cover) 13.4 cm;
D. 18.6 cm

74.4.36

Colorless non-lead glass with ten
vertical bands of cable on base
and eight on bowl and cover;
acorn knob.
Gift of Ruth I. Roth
Parallels: Lee, E.A.P.G., pl. 164.

1234 Covered butter dish
Probably Midwest
ca. 1900-1910
H. (with cover) 13.7 cm;
D. 20.5 cm

74.4.55

Colorless non-lead glass with plain cover.
Gift of Ruth I. Roth
Comments: Montgomery Ward illustrates this in a retail catalog dated 1901 (53 cents for a four-piece table set).
Parallels: Kamm, Book V, pl. 35.

1235 Covered butter dish
Midwest, probably United States Glass Company
ca. 1891-1900
H. (with cover) 13.4 cm;
D. 19.3 cm

74.4.89

Colorless non-lead glass; vertical bands of diamonds alternating with plain bands on bowl and cover.
Gift of Ruth I. Roth
Comments: Very heavy glass, typical of the 1890's. Revi (see bibliography) shows this pattern as King, Son & Company No. 204 introduced in the 1870's or 1880's, but this glass is not characteristic of the earlier period; it seems likely that the United States Glass Company reissued the pattern as they did others.
Parallels: Revi, p. 223.

1236 String holder
Midwest, United States Glass Company
ca. 1890-1905
H. 11.7 cm; D. (base) 14.7 cm

72.4.116

Cobalt blue glass; hole ground at top for string.
Gift of Preston R. Bassett
Comments: This string holder appears in a United States Glass Company catalog of 1904.

Alaska pattern
United States, Indiana, Pennsylvania, Northwood Company or Wheeling, West Virginia, Northwood Glass Company
ca. 1897-1905

Opalescent yellow glass; vertically and horizontally ribbed pattern on body.
Gifts of Mr. and Mrs. William Gelabert (1237-1241)
Comments: This color was advertised as "pearl yellow."

Parallels: Heacock, William. *Encyclopedia of Victorian Colored Pattern Glass, 2, Opalescent Glass from A to Z*, Jonesville, Michigan, Antique Publications, 1975, pp. 26, 100.

1237 Water pitcher
Square body with four paw feet
H. 19.2 cm; W. 23.2 cm

79.4.146

1238 Creamer
Alaska pattern

79.4.147

1239 Footed dishes
Alaska pattern

79.4.148 A,B

1240 Pair of Tumblers
Alaska pattern

79.4.149 A,B

1241 Spooner
Alaska pattern

79.4.170

1242 Covered butter dish
Georgia pattern
Midwest, United States Glass
Company
ca. 1895-1910
H. (with cover) 13.5 cm;
D. 18.1 cm

74.4.79

*1243 Hand lamp
Georgia pattern
H. 15 cm; D. (base) 11.3 cm

66.4.111

Colorless non-lead glass with
pattern of eleven peacock feathers; scalloped knob; base with
peacock feathers around side.
Gift of Ruth I. Roth
Parallels: Kamm, Book I, pp. 77,
78; *Revi*, p. 314; *Lee, E.A.P.G.*,
pl. 106.

Bequest of Lavina Stewart

1244 Salver
Georgia pattern
Bequest of Lavina Stewart
(1244-1249)
H. 11.1 cm; D. (rim) 21.6 cm

66.4.113

1245 Syrup pitcher
Georgia pattern

66.4.114

1246 Cruet
Georgia pattern

66.4.115

1247 Covered sugar bowl
Georgia pattern

66.4.116

1248 Mug
Georgia pattern

66.4.117

1249 Tumbler
Georgia pattern

66.4.118

1250 String holder
Probably Midwest
ca. 1890-1900
H. 10.1 cm; D. (at base) 12 cm

72.4.115

Amber glass; pattern of hobnails
all around sides.
Gift of Preston R. Bassett

1251 Whiskey jug
Pittsburgh, Pennsylvania, King,
Son & Company
ca. 1891
H. (with lock) 21.6 cm;
D. (max) 12.7 cm

74.4.114

Colorless non-lead glass; thick
collar with metal rim; body
engraved with "C. M. Finch";
heavy applied handle; pressed,
flat-top stopper which does not
fit well; brass lock top with "pat.
APPD FOR."
Comments: Patented February
1891 by William King, Patent
No. 20, 505, as pattern no. 500.
King, Son & Company was ab-
sorbed into the United States
Glass Company July 1, 1891.
Parallels: Peterson, Arthur, *Glass
Patents and Patterns*, Sanford,
Florida: author, 1973, p. 98;
Revi, p. 214.

1252 Decanter or cologne
Probably Midwest
ca. 1890-1920
H. (with stopper) 19.4 cm;
D. (base) 8.5 cm

69.4.44

Purplish transparent glass;
cylindrical shape; six-sided with
three deep bull's-eyes on each
side; circular base shows mark
characteristic of glass pressed
from the bottom and tooled
shut.
Gift of Mr. and Mrs. William A.
Hampton

1253 Covered butter dish
Wheeling, West Virginia,
Northwood Glass Company
ca. 1910-1919
H. (with cover) 14.5 cm;
D. 19.8 cm

62.4.65

Opalescent glass; a design of
concentric circles around rim;
star in base; draped design
around sides of cover; marked *N*
on bottom of base.
Parallels: Hartung, Marion T.
*Northwood Pattern Glass in Color:
Clear, Colored, Custard, Carnival*, Emporia, Kansas: author,
1969, pp. 41, 64; Hartung, Marion T. *Opalescent Pattern Glass*,
Des Moines, Iowa: Wallace-
Homestead Book Company,
1971, p. 35.

1254 Pitcher
United States, Indiana, Pennsylvania, Northwood Glass
Works, or Wheeling, West Virginia, Northwood Glass Company
ca. 1898-1919
H. 11.8 cm; D (at rim), 9.6 cm

79.4.92

Pink and white marbled or slag
glass; scroll pattern on sides and
four scroll feet.
Gift, in part, of William Hammond
Comments: This pattern is called
Inverted Fan and Feather by
collectors and some pieces are
found with Northwood's
trademark. He is said to have
produced pink slag in both of
the factories listed above.
Parallels: Hartung, Marion T.
*Northwood Pattern Glass in Color:
Clear, Custard, Carnival*, Emporia, Kansas, author, 1969, p. 72.

1255 Syrup pitcher
Probably Pittsburgh, Pennsylvania, United Glass Company
ca. 1891-1910
H. 16 cm; D. (base) 7.5 cm

67.4.121

Colorless non-lead glass; lid
with thumb latch; applied handle on one side.
Gift of Mrs. Neddie O'Moore
Roberts
Comments: This pattern appears
in the United States Glass
Company catalog in the Museum's collection.

1256 Covered butter dish
Indiana, Pennsylvania; The
Northwood Glass Works; or
Wheeling, West Virginia, The
Northwood Glass Company
ca. 1898-1910
H. (with cover) 15.4 cm;
D. 19.4 cm

65.4.38

Opaque yellowish white glass
with gilt trim; scroll pattern on
cover and dish; four gilded scroll
feet.
Gift of Mrs. Herbert Evans
Comments: This pattern, called
Louis XV and introduced in
September 1898, was produced
in both of Northwood's factories.
Parallels: Revi, pp. 265-269.

1257 Oval bowl
Probably Grapeville, Pennsylvania, Westmoreland Glass Company
ca. 1890-1910
H. (at handle) 11.3 cm;
L. 26.8 cm

51.4.651

Translucent white glass; oblong,
with spout at one end and a
handle at the other.

1258 Covered butter dish
Probably Midwest
ca. 1890-1910
H. (with cover) 13.2 cm;
D. 18.5 cm

74.4.65

Colorless non-lead glass.
Gift of Ruth I. Roth
Parallels: Kamm, Book IV, p. 83;
Metz, Book II, pp. 178, 179.

1259 Covered butter dish
Probably Midwest
ca. 1890-1910
H. (with cover) 11.9 cm;
D. 18.2 cm

74.4.26

Colorless non-lead glass.
Gift of Ruth I. Roth
Parallels: Lee, E.A.P.G., pl. 81.

1260   Covered butter dish
Probably Midwest
ca. 1890-1910
H. (with cover) 10.2 cm;
W. 18.3 cm

74.4.35

Colorless non-lead glass.
Gift of Ruth I. Roth

1261   Covered butter dish
Probably Midwest
ca. 1890-1910
H. (with cover) 13.2 cm;
L. 21.5 cm

74.4.32

Colorless non-lead glass.
Gift of Ruth I. Roth

1262   Goblet
United States Glass Company,
probably Pittsburgh factory
ca. 1891-1900
H. 15.7 cm

73.4.61

Slightly greenish non-lead glass.
Gift of Mrs. Robert Brearey
Comments: This pattern was originally marketed as California or
no. 15059 and came in emerald
green and colorless glass. It has
been widely reproduced.
Parallels: Lee, E.A.P.G., pl. 63.

1263   Covered butter dish
Probably Midwest
ca. 1890-1910
H. (with cover) 13.6 cm;
D. 18.1 cm

74.4.59

Colorless non-lead glass.
Gift of Ruth I. Roth
Parallels: Kamm, Book VII, p.
53; *Lee, E.A.P.G.*, pl. 164, no.
16.

1264 Covered butter dish
Probably Midwest
ca. 1890-1910
H. (with cover) 13.8 cm;
D. 19 cm

74.4.39

Colorless non-lead glass with gilt decoration; flower in base; gilding around knob and edge of cover and base.
Gift of Ruth I. Roth
Parallels: Lee, E.A.P.G., pls. 14, 87.

1265 Covered butter dish
No. 271 pattern
Follansbee, West Virginia, Jefferson Glass Company
ca. 1907-1920
H. (with cover) 14.5 cm;
D. 19 cm

74.4.53

Colorless non-lead glass.
Gift of Ruth I. Roth
Parallels: Revi, p. 209

1266 Covered butter dish
Probably Midwest
ca. 1890-1910
H. (with cover) 14.8 cm;
D. 19.7 cm

74.4.42

Colorless non-lead glass.
Gift of Ruth I. Roth

1267 Compote
Greentown, Indiana, Indiana Tumbler and Goblet Company
1903
H. 11.4 cm; L. 19.1 cm

62.4.48

Colorless non-lead glass; oval shape; holly leaf design around sides, in base, and on flaring hollow stem.
Comments: Colorless objects in this pattern are said to have been trials of the molds later used to make Golden Agate glass.
Parallels: Herrick, Ruth. *Greentown Glass*, Grand Rapids, Michigan, published by the author, 1959, p. 29; *Kamm, Vol. I*, p. 322.

1268 Covered butter dish
Golden Agate pattern
Greentown, Indiana; Indiana
Tumbler and Goblet Company
January-June, 1903
H. (with cover) 15.2 cm

62.4.4

Opalescent and clear amber glass; domed cover with alternating opalescent raised ribs and panels of amber glass with a meandering holly pattern.
Comments: This pattern was marketed as Golden Agate glass but is now called Holly Amber by collectors. A fire destroyed the plant in June 1903.
Parallels: Herrick, Ruth. *Greentown Glass*, Grand Rapids, Mich: author, 1959, pp. 28-30.

1269 Bowl
Golden Agate
H. 7 cm; D. 19.1 cm

63.4.127

Ex coll: Lola Kincaid Ford; gift of Fletcher Ford and Sally Recker in memory of Lola Kincaid Ford

1270 Dish
Greentown, Indiana; Indiana
Tumbler and Goblet Company
1900-June 1903
H. 5 cm; D. (rim) 13 cm

63.4.148

Opalescent brown glass; three oval medallions alternating with leaf sprays around sides.
Ex coll: Lola Kincaid Ford; gift of Fletcher Ford and Sally Recker in memory of Lola Kincaid Ford
Comments: This was sold as Dewey pattern. It is a butter dish with the cover missing.
Parallels: Herrick, Ruth. Greentown Greentown Glass, Grand Rapids, Michigan: author, 1959, pp. 15-16.

1271 Sauce dish
Greentown, Indiana, Indiana
Tumbler and Goblet Company
1901-June 1903
H. 4.7 cm; D. (rim) 10.4 cm

62.4.84

Brown glass with milky white opalescence; sides divided into eight panels, each with a stylized cactus plant; scalloped foot rim; opalescence shows mainly on interior.
Comments: This color was marketed as "chocolate" glass and the color was introduced by this company for the Pan American Exposition in Buffalo in 1901; the factory burned in June of 1903.
Parallels: Herrick, Ruth. *Greentown Glass*, Grand Rapids, Michigan: author, 1959, pp. 23-24.

*1272 Bowl
In the same pattern
H. 10 cm; D. (rim) 23.9 cm
63.4.136

Ex Coll: Lola Kincaid Ford; gift of Fletcher Ford and Sally Recker in memory of Lola Kincaid Ford.

1273 Punchbowl set
Grape pattern
Wheeling, West Virginia,
Northwood Glass Company
ca. 1910-1919
(Bowl) H. 35.5 cm; D. 20.4 cm;
(Cups) H. 6.7 cm; D. 8.5 cm
(dimensions vary from cup to
cup)

76.4.13A-S

Amethyst glass with an iridescent finish; circular shape with
grape design; separate base and
twelve cups; bowl and cups
marked Ⓝ in base.
Gift of Mr. and Mrs. Harold
Ludeman
Comments: This set was illustrated in a catalog of Butler

Brothers, Fall, 1910, and priced
at $4.25.
Parallels: Hartung, Marion T.
Fourth Book of Carnival Glass,
Emporia, Kansas: author, 1963,
pp. 116-142; *Glassware, 1910*;
reprint of Butler Brothers
catalog, Antiques Research Publications, 1910.

1274 Three-footed bowl
As above
D. 23.6 cm

75.4.9

Gift of Mr. and Mrs. Carlton
Schleede

1275 Flat bowl
As above
H. 6.7 cm; D. (rim) 22.3 cm

62.4.63

1276 Footed bowl
Wheeling, West Virginia,
Northwood Glass Company
ca. 1905-1919
H. 11.3 cm; D. (rim) 19.5 cm

63.4.157

Iridescent reddish glass with a
blackberry or raspberry pattern
inside bowl; stylized floral pattern outside; three splayed feet.
Ex coll: Lola Kincaid Ford; gift
of Fletcher Ford and Sally
Recker in memory of Lola Kincaid Ford
Comments: This pattern is supposed to be Northwood's
Blackberry although it is not
marked.
Parallels: Hartung, Marion T.
Third Book of Carnival Glass,
Emporia, Kansas: author, 1962,
p. 87.

1277 Window pane
Addison, New York, Addison
Glass Factory
ca. 1894-1908
12.7 cm x 10.2 cm

51.4.652

Transparent blue glass.
Gift of Thurston Thacher, nos.
1277-1308

1278 Another
Lily of the Valley design

51.4.674

*1279 Another

51.4.675

*1280 Another

51.4.676

*1281 Another

51.4.677

Amber.

Aqua.

Purple.

Blue.

1282 **Another**
Vine design
10 cm x 10 cm

51.4.667

*1283 **Another**

51.4.671

Turquoise.

Amber.

1284 **Another**
Circular Vine design

51.4.662

*1285 **Another**

51.4.664

*1286 **Another**

51.4.669

Pink.

Blue.

Amber.

1287 **Another**
Swan design

51.4.673

Colorless.

1288   **Another**   Blue.
        Leaf design

        51.4.665

*1289   **Another**   Turquoise.

        51.4.666

*1290   **Another**   Amber.

        51.4.668

*1291   **Another**   Purple.

        51.4.672

*1292   **Another**   Blue.
        12.7 cm x 12.7 cm

        51.4.678

*1293   **Another**   Amber.

        51.4.685

*1294   **Another**   Colorless.

        51.4.686

*1295   **Another**   Aqua.

        51.4.687

1296   **Another**   Blue.
        Diamond pattern

        51.4.679

*1297   **Another**   Purple.

        51.4.681

*1298   **Another**   Amber.

        51.4.684

1299 **Another**
Grape pattern
26 cm x 12.7 cm

51.4.690

Colorless.

*1300 **Another**

51.4.692

Aqua.

1301 **Another**
Net and Vine pattern

51.4.691

Aqua.

*1302 **Another**

51.4.696

Purple.

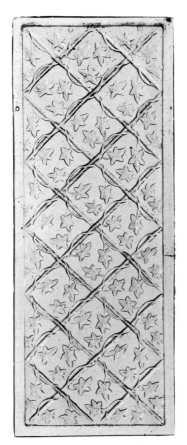

1303   **Another**
Vine pattern

51.4.695

*1304   **Another**

51.4.694

*1305   **Another**
Dogwood pattern

51.4.697

*1306   **Another**
Quatrefoil pattern
20.2 cm x 12.7 cm

51.4.698

Blue.

Aqua.

Blue.

Blue.

1307   **Wooden frame with eleven colored panes**
Frame overall, H. 56.3 cm;
W. 55.2 cm

51.4.699

*1308   **Wooden frame with nine colored panes**
Frame overall, H. 51.2 cm;
W. 50.4 cm

51.4.700

1309 Covered butter dish
Tarentum, Pennsylvania, Tarentum Glass Company
ca. 1898-1899
H. (with cover) 14.8 cm;
D. 19.9 cm

74.4.51

Colorless non-lead glass.
Gift of Ruth I. Roth
Parallels: Kamm, Book II, p. 102;
Lee, Victorian Glass, pl. 23; *Metz, Book I*, p. 215; *Revi*, p. 286.

1310 Covered butter dish
No. 15018 pattern
Midwest, United States Glass Company
ca. 1891-1910
H. (with cover) 15.4 cm;
D. 17.3 cm

74.4.92

Colorless non-lead glass.
Gift of Ruth I. Roth
Comments: See also No. 1330, a similar pattern.
Parallels: Kamm, Book 2, p. 73.

1311 Covered butter dish
Midwest
ca. 1890-1910
H. (with cover) 9.9 cm;
D. 17.4 cm

74.4.93

Colorless lead glass.
Gift of Ruth I. Roth
Comments: This pattern is still being produced and sold in stores like Woolworth's.

1312 Pickle castor
No. 26
New Bedford, Massachusetts, Pairpoint Manufacturing Company
ca. 1890-1900
H. 10.5 cm; D. (at base) 7.7 cm

65.4.31 A,B,C

Amber glass; conical silver-plated lid and holder with round base and carrying handle above with hook for fork (missing); marked on base of holder "PAIRPOINT MANUFACTURING COMPANY QUADRUPLE PLATE 606P."
Gift of Gladys Doherty
Comments: Although both jar and holder are Pairpoint, the jar is too small for the metal holder and belongs in pickle castor No. 616, shown in a catalog in The Corning Museum of Glass Library.

1313 **Covered butter dish**
Probably Midwest
ca. 1890-1910
H. (with cover) 12.1 cm;
D. 18.4 cm

74.4.82

Colorless non-lead glass.
Gift of Ruth I. Roth.

1314 **Covered butter dish**
Oregon pattern
Midwest, United States Glass
Company
ca. 1900-1910
H. (with cover) 12.9 cm;
D. 18.9 cm

74.4.30

Colorless non-lead glass.
Gift of Ruth I. Roth
Comments: This is United States
Glass Company pattern no.
15,073, originally issued as Oregon. The United States Glass
Company was a consortium of
factories, and it is not known in
which one this piece was made.
Parallels: Kamm, Book III, p. 8;
Book VIII, p. 18; *Lee, E.A.P.G.*,
pl. 76; *Metz, Book 2*, pp. 156,
157; *Revi*, p. 317.

1315 **Plate**
United States
ca. 1900
D. 7.5 cm

65.4.78

Colorless glass.
Gift of Mrs. Leon S. Bard
Comments: This may also be a
lens or light cover of some kind.
Parallels: Lee and Rose, p. 401,
no. 894, where it is listed as a
butter chip.

1316 **Covered dish**
Plutec pattern
Jeannette, Pennsylvania,
McKee Glass Company
ca. 1904-1920
H. (with cover) 12.7 cm;
D. 19.2 cm

74.4.67

Slightly grayish lead glass.
Gift of Ruth I. Roth
Comments: This is McKee's Prescut line. Pattern introduced in
1904.
Parallels: Kamm, Book III, p. 87,
Book VI, pl. 22; *Revi*, p. 240;
Stout, Sandra, *Complete Book of
McKee Glass*, North Kansas City:
Trojan Press, 1972, p. 24.

1317 Covered butter dish
Probably Midwest
ca. 1890-1910
H. (with cover) 13.9 cm;
D. 21.3 cm

74.4.68

Colorless non-lead glass.
Gift of Ruth I. Roth
Parallels: Kamm, Book II, p. 76.

1318 Covered butter dish
Probably Midwest
ca. 1890-1910
H. (with cover) 12.5 cm;
D. 18.6 cm

74.4.40

Colorless non-lead glass with
greenish tinge.
Gift of Ruth I. Roth
Comments: This has been called
Fine Cut and Feather, Indiana
Feather, Indiana Swirl, and
other names by collectors.
Parallels: Kamm, Book I, pp. 72,
73; *Lee, Victorian Glass*, pl. 57;
Metz, Book I, pp. 140, 141.

1319 Covered butter dish
Probably Midwest
ca. 1890-1910
H. (with cover) 14.7 cm;
D. 19 cm

74.4.52

Colorless non-lead glass.
Gift of Ruth I. Roth
Parallels: Kamm, Book IV, p. 75.

1320 Covered butter dish
Bellaire, Ohio, Imperial Glass
Company
ca. 1902-1910
H. (with cover) 15.8 cm;
D. 20.4 cm

74.4.56

Colorless non-lead glass.
Gift of Ruth I. Roth
Parallels: Kamm, Book IV, p. 74;
Book VII, pl. 80.

1321 Covered butter dish
Probably Midwest
ca. 1900-1920
H. (with cover) 9.5 cm;
D. 13.9 cm

74.4.97

Colorless non-lead glass.
Gift of Ruth I. Roth

1322 Covered butter dish
Probably Midwest
ca. 1890-1910
H. (with cover) 14.3 cm;
D. 20.3 cm

74.4.69

Colorless non-lead glass.
Gift of Ruth I. Roth
Parallels: Kamm, Book III,
p. 135.

1323 Covered butter dish
Doric pattern
Jeannette, Pennsylvania,
McKee Glass Company
1896 - ca. 1900
H. (with cover) 13.3 cm;
D. 18.1 cm

74.4.41

Colorless non-lead glass.
Gift of Ruth I. Roth
Comments: This pattern was first
introduced in 1896.
Parallels: Kamm, Book I, p. 73;
Lee, Victorian Glass, pl. 57; *Metz,
Book I*, pp. 140, 141.

1324 Covered butter dish
States or No. 15093
Unitee States Glass Company
ca. 1910
H. (with cover) 13.1 cm;
D. 21 cm

74.4.28

Colorless non-lead glass.
Gift of Ruth I. Roth
Comments: The United States
Glass Company was a combine
of a number of midwestern factories, and there is nothing to
indicate in which one this pattern was made. The pattern appears in a United States Glass
Company catalog of 1910.
Parallels: Metz, Book I, p. 215.
Heacock, William, *Encyclopedia
of Victorian Colored Pattern Glass*,
Book 5, Marietta, Ohio, 1978,
p. 145.

1325 Covered butter dish
Bridgeville, Pennsylvania, J.B.
Higbee & Company
ca. 1905-1915
H. (with cover) 12.9 cm;
D. 19.8 cm

74.4.74

Colorless non-lead glass.
Gift of Ruth I. Roth
Parallels: Revi, p. 92.

1326 Butter dish lid
Pattern No. 16,041
Pittsburgh, Pennsylvania,
United States Glass Company
ca. 1891-1910
H. (with cover) 12.5 cm;
D. 18.4 cm

74.4.61

Colorless non-lead glass; high
domed shape; pattern of blocks
and fans.
Gift of Ruth I. Roth
Parallels: Lee, Victorian Glass,
pl. 44; *Revi* p. 312.

1327 Covered butter dish
Probably Midwest
ca. 1900-1920
H. (with cover) 13.5 cm;
D. 20.6 cm

74.4.78

Colorless non-lead glass with
slight greenish tint.
Gift of Ruth I. Roth
Parallels: Kamm, Book V, p. 146.

1328 Covered butter dish
Washington, Pennsylvania,
Duncan & Miller Glass
Company
ca. 1894-1910
H. (with cover) 14 cm;
D. 20.4 cm

74.4.48

Colorless non-lead glass; edge of
plate and cover gilded.
Gift of Ruth I. Roth
Comments: Revi calls this pattern
Button Arches.
Parallels: Revi, p. 148.

1329 Punch bowl on stand and cups
United States, probably
Midwest
ca. 1900
H. (bowl and stand) 32.5 cm;
Bowl: D. (rim) 37.1 cm;
Cups: H. 6 cm, D. (rim) 8 cm

80.4.57 A-D

Colorless non-lead glass pressed
in a pattern of hobstars and
splits; half-spherical bowl with
serrated rim; capstan-shaped
stand with depression for bowl;
three cups with matching pattern.
Gift of John Gillespie

1330 Fruit stand
Majestic pattern
Jeannette, Pennsylvania,
McKee & Brothers
ca. 1900
H. 24 cm, L. 26.2 cm

79.4.119

Colorless non-lead glass pressed
in a geometric pattern; bowl up-
curved to hold fruit; hollow stem
and base.
Gift of Mary Allyene Roland
Comments: McKee advertised
this as Majestic in 1893 and as
Puritan in 1899.
Parallels: Kamm, Book 2, p. 71,
Book 6, pl. 70. See also No.
1310, a similar pattern.

1331 Plate
Dithridge & Company
Fort Pitt Glass Works,
Pittsburgh, Pennsylvania
ca. 1900
D. 16.4 cm

79.4.159

Opaque white glass; with pattern of rooster, hen and chicken, and inscription "NO EASTER WITHOUT US"; and "72" on base.
Gift of Mr. and Mrs. William Gelabert
Parallels: Belknap, Fig. 3e; Ferson, Regis and Mary. *Yesterday's Milk Glass Today*. Pittsburgh, Pa.: authors, 1981, pp. 15, 134.

1332 Small plate
United States, probably
Westmoreland Specialty Company, Grapeville, Pennsylvania
ca. 1908
D. 18.8 cm

79.4.160

Opaque white glass; with a decoration of eagles, stars and flags.
Gift of Mr. and Mrs. William Gelabert
Comments: Similar plates with William Jennings Bryan and William Howard Taft in the center are also known, so this must be the same period as their presidential campaigns in 1908.
Parallels: Belknap, pls. 6c, 6d, 9c, 9d.

1333 Plate
United States, Grapeville,
Pennsylvania, Westmoreland
Glass Company
ca. 1900-1950
D. 18.8 cm

79.4.162

Opaque white glass; edged with an anchor and chain and showing a sailboat with triangular sail in center.
Gift of Mr. and Mrs. William Gelabert
Comments: Westmoreland was still making this plate when Belknap was doing his research in the 1940's.
Parallels: Belknap, fig. 13a, fig. 271, p. 271.

1334 Bowl
United States
ca. 1913
H. 8.5 cm; D. (rim) 12.2 cm

70.4.9

Colorless non-lead glass; "Owen & Co. 1913" stamped on base.
Comments: The identification of Owen & Co. has not been discovered, but it does not seem to have been a glass firm.

1335   Bust of Michael J. Owens
Toledo, Ohio, Libbey Glass
Company
1923
H. 12.5 cm; L. 13.2 cm

71.4.17

Grayish translucent glass in the
form of a bust of Michael J.
Owens.
Gift of Mrs. Donovan Farrell
Comments: Michael J. Owens
was the inventor of the Owens
bottle machine and other notable improvements in the manufacture of glass. This bust was
produced by the Libbey company as a commemorative item
shortly after his death.

1336   Bowl
United States
ca. 1920's or later
H. 8.6 cm, D. 21.1 cm

63.4.9

Colorless non-lead glass; with
impressed hobstar; poor quality
glass with many inclusions.
Comments: This a blank for cutting which came from T. G.
Hawkes & Company, a Corning
cutting firm.

1337   Covered butter dish
Moundsville, West Virginia;
Fostoria Glass Company
ca. 1915-1970
H. (with cover) 14.4 cm;
D. 18.7 cm

74.4.60

Colorless non-lead glass in a
pattern of concave and convex
diamonds.
Gift of Ruth I. Roth
Parallels: Weatherman, Hazel
Marie. *Fostoria, Its First Fifty
Years.* Springfield, Mo.: The
Weathermans, 1972, pp. 85, 86.

1338   Casserole
Corning, New York, Corning
Glass Works
ca. 1936
H. 7.5 cm; D. (rim) 21.4 cm

71.4.39

Colorless Pyrex® glass. Pressed
in circular shape with a lattice
work design on the exterior and
a leaf spray design on each side.
Gift of Joseph G. Stenger
Comments: The blueprint for this
design is stamped "Approved
May 6, 1936." It was made ex-
clusively for Russakov, Chicago,
Illinois, as a premium. Approx-
imately 10,000 were made.

1339 Measuring cup
Dundee, New York, H. P.
Sinclaire & Co.
ca. 1926-1927
H. 8.1 cm; W. 11.5 cm

76.4.39

Pressed of yellowish heat-resistant glass; square shape; markings embossed on front indicate measurements; on base, "RADNT."
Gift of Mrs. Frederick Farrar
Comments: This was a heat-resistant kitchenware developed by the Sinclaire company as an adjunct to their artistic glassware. The plant at Dundee was built to produce this "Radnt" ware in continuous tanks but had scarcely gone into production before H. P. Sinclaire died and the company closed.

1340 Bowl
Rochester, Pennsylvania, H. C.
Fry Glass Company
ca. 1920-1934
H. 3.3 cm; D. 23.2 cm

60.4.783

Colorless heat-resistant glass with a slightly opalescent tinge; circular; marked on base "FRY OVEN GLASS, 1939-9. Pat 5-8-17. Pat 5-27-19."
Gift of Miss Bernadine Forgett

*1341 Plate
As above
D. 14.2 cm

60.4.782

1342 Cereal bowl
Dogwood pattern
United States, Charleroi, Pennsylvania, Macbeth-Evans Glass Company
1929-1932
H. 3.5 cm; D. 14.3. cm

80.4.26

Pink glass with leaf and stem pattern around body.
Gift of Donald S. Hall
Comments: This pattern was also made in green, crystal (colorless), Monax (translucent white), Cremax (translucent cream-colored) and yellow.
Parallels: Klamkin, p. 22, p. 38, pp. 58-59.

1343 Bread and butter plate
Dogwood pattern
D. 15.3 cm

80.4.27

Gift of Donald S. Hall

1344   Cup and saucer
Dogwood pattern
D. (saucer) 15.1 cm;
H. (cup) 6.3 cm

80.4.28

Gift of Donald S. Hall

1345   Grill plate
(partitioned plate)
Dogwood pattern
D. 26.6 cm

80.4.29

Gift of Donald S. Hall

1346   Plate
American Sweetheart pattern
Macbeth-Evans Glass Company,
Charleroi, Pennsylvania
ca. 1934-1936
D. 15.2 cm

71.4.153

Machine-pressed of deep red
glass with a pattern of festoons,
ribbons and scrolls around rim.
Gift of Corning Glass Works
Parallels: Weatherman, Hazel
Marie. *Colored Glassware of the
Depression Era*, 1970, pp. 39-40.

1347   Plate
Ivex glass, Oxford pattern
Macbeth-Evans Division, Corn-
ing Glass Works, Charleroi,
Pennsylvania
ca. 1939-1942
D. 20.2 cm

71.4.160

Machine-pressed of opaque
white glass with a dark
reddish-brown fluted edge.
Gift of Corning Glass Works
Parallels: Weatherman, Hazel
Marie. *Colored Glassware of the
Depression Era 2*, Springfield,
Mo.: Glassbooks, 1974, pp.
259-261.

1348 Plates
Petalware glass
Macbeth-Evans Division, Corn-
ing Glass Works,
Charleroi, Pennsylvania
ca. 1937-1940
D. 20.2 cm

71.4.161A, C

Machine-pressed of opaque
white glass with fluted edge; C
has enameled decoration in the
Regency pattern of three knots
of ribbon.
Gift of Corning Glass Works
Parallels: Weatherman, Hazel
Marie. *Colored Glassware of the
Depression Era 2*, Springfield,
Mo.: Glassbooks, 1974, p. 252.

1349 Baking dish
Pyrex®
Corning Glass Works, Corning,
New York
ca. 1921-1940
H. 7.9 cm; D. 23.6 cm

69.4.18

Machine-pressed of amber glass
in a cylindrical shape; decorated
with stone cutting of leaves and
flowers.
Comments: According to Otto
Hilbert of Corning Glass Works
Archives, this type of cutting on
Pyrex was done by Corning
Glass Works in 1921-1925 and
1931-1940 only.

1350 Bowl
Lorraine pattern
United States, Dunkirk, Indi-
ana, Indiana Glass Company
1929-1932
H. 4.6 cm; L. 24.9 cm,
W. 16.7 cm

80.4.13

Green glass; rectangular shape
with basket-of-flowers design in
corner.
Gift of Donald S. Hall
Parallels: Klamkin, p. 37, pp.
105-106.

1351 Bowl
Princess pattern
United States, Lancaster, Ohio,
Hocking Glass Company
1931-1935
H. 10 cm; D (rim) 23.5 cm

80.4.14

Green with stylized floral
design.
Gift of Donald S. Hall
Parallels: Klamkin, p. 28, pp.
98-99.

1352   Goblet
Miss America pattern
United States, Lancaster, Ohio,
Hocking Glass Company
1935-1937
H. 13.9 cm; D (rim) 8.3 cm

80.4.16

Colorless glass with diamond
pattern on body; square foot.
Gift of Donald S. Hall
Parallels: Klamkin, p. 31.

1353   Dish
Oyster and Pearls pattern
United States, Lancaster, Ohio,
Anchor-Hocking Glass Company
ca. 1939-1940
H. 4.4 cm; W. 15.4 cm

80.4.22

Ruby red glass with panel and
bead pattern on body; one handle.
Gift of Donald S. Hall
Comments: "Royal Ruby" color.
Parallels: Klamkin, p. 13.

1354   Sherbet
Cherry Blossom pattern
United States, Jeannette, Pennsylvania, Jeannette Glass Company
ca. 1930-1939
H. 7 cm; D. (rim) 9.8 cm

80.4.18

Lavender opalescent glass; scal-
loped rim.
Gift of Donald S. Hall
Comments: This color was mar-
keted as "Delphite".
Parallels: Klamkin, pp. 68-69.

1355   Salt and Pepper shakers
Cubist pattern
United States, Jeannette,
Pennsylvania, Jeannette Glass
Company
1929-1933
H. (both) 8.0 cm; D. (base)
5.2 cm

80.4.15 A,B

Green glass with overall cube
pattern and metal top.
Gift of Donald S. Hall
Parallels: Klamkin, p. 69.

1356 Vase
Swirl pattern
United States, Jeannette, Pennsylvania, Jeannette Glass Company
ca. 1937-1938
H. 21.5 cm; D (rim) 12.6 cm

80.4.17

Bright aquamarine glass with swirled ribs around body; round foot.
Gift of Donald S. Hall
Comments: "Ultramarine" color.
Parallels: Klamkin, pl. 19, pp. 76-77.

1357 Bowl
United States, possibly Jeannette Glass Company, Jeannette, Pennsylvania
ca. 1928-1932
H. 3.8 cm; D. 11.3 cm

70.4.99

Pink glass molded into a honeycomb pattern; two handles.
Gift of Otto W. Hilbert
Parallels: Klamkin, pp. 114-115.

1358 Bowl
Mt. Pleasant pattern
United States, Mt. Pleasant, Pennsylvania, L. E. Smith Company
ca. 1920-1934
H. 8.4 cm; W. 14.1 cm

80.4.19

Cobalt blue glass; triangular shape with three feet.
Gift of Donald S. Hall
Parallels: Gene Florence. *The Collectors Encyclopedia of Depression Glass*, 4th Ed., Paducah, Kentucky, Collector Books, 1979, pp. 120-121.

1359 Sugar bowl and creamer
Cloverleaf pattern
United States, Clarksville, Virginia, Hazel-Atlas Glass Company
1930-1936
H. (A) 9.2 cm; (B) 9.7 cm;
W. (A) 11.2 cm; (B) 10.6 cm

80.4.20 A, B

Dark green glass appearing black; floral design on body.
Gift of Donald S. Hall
Parallels: Klamkin, p. 81.

1360 Pitcher
Florentine No. 2 pattern
United States, Clarksville, West
Virginia, Hazel-Atlas Glass
Company
1934-1937
H. 19.1 cm; W. 17.5 cm

80.4.23

Yellow glass with floral design
around body.
Gift of Donald S. Hall
Comments: "Topaz" glass.
Parallels: Klamkin, pp. 82-83.

1361 Soup bowl
Patrician pattern
United States, Columbus, Ohio,
Federal Glass Company
ca. 1933-1937
H. 6.2 cm; D. 14.8 cm

80.4.24

Light amber glass; geometric
pattern around body; two handles.
Gift of Donald S. Hall
Comments: This was sold as a
4¾" cream soup bowl in amber.
Parallels: Klamkin, pp. 15, 36, 50.

1362 Covered jar
Sharon pattern
United States, Columbus, Ohio,
Federal Glass Company
ca. 1935-1939
H. 19.5 cm; D. 15 cm

80.4.25

Light amber glass with panels of
a floral design around body.
Gift of Donald S. Hall
Comments: Sold as "Candy Jar
and cover, amber."
Parallels: Klamkin, p. 53.

1363 Washboard
United States
ca. 1920-1927
(Glass) L. 21.6 cm; W. 18 cm
(Frame) L. 46 cm; W. 22 cm

70.4.86

Wooden frame with an inserted rectangle of greenish corrugated glass; painted on frame is advertisement below.
"IDEAL FOR SILKS, HOSIERY AND LINGERIE OR HANDKER-CHIEFS.
JUST THE RIGHT SIZE TO FIT A BUCKET, PAIL OR LAVATORY.
PACKS EASILY INTO SUITCASE OR TRAVELING BAG."
Gift of Kenneth M. Wilson
Comments: This item was made by the Columbus Washboard Company of Columbus, Ohio. The company appeared in Columbus city directories only between 1920 and 1927. The address was 1309-1311 Cleveland Avenue.

1364 Washboard
United States, made for National Washboard Company.
ca. 1940's
L. 60.5 cm; W. 31.7 cm

80.4.37

Wooden frame with colorless glass scrub section. Frame is inscribed "NATIONAL WASHBOARD CO./No NATIONAL 512/TRADE-MARKS REG. U.S. PAT. OFF. MADE IN U.S.A./SAGINAW, CHICAGO, MEMPHIS" on one side and on reverse VICTORY/GLASS/ USE THIS WASHBOARD MADE OF MATERIALS NOT NEEDED IN THE WAR EFFORT AND HELP WIN THE WAR"; glass is embossed "NATIONAL."
Gift of Olive Allen

1365 Orange reamer
United States, Elmira, New York, Thatcher Glass Company
ca. 1930's
H. 8.1 cm; W. 21.3 cm

80.4.21

Opaque white glass with "Sunkist" molded into each side and "Thatcher Glass Co. Elmira NY/Licensed Sunkist Mfg" on base.
Gift of Donald S. Hall
Comments: Sold by mail and in stores with Sunkist fruit; 50¢ in United States of America, 65¢ in Canada.
Parallels: Klamkin, pp. 136-138.

1366   18 Glass coins
Corning, New York, Corning
Glass Works
ca. 1942, 1943
Size range from nickel
to quarter

70.4.178

Seven plain glass blanks, five
"coins" bearing view and legend
"Blue Ridge Glass Corp"; one
five-cent coin, silvered on one
side and bearing view of Mon-
ticello; two plain blanks silvered
on both sides; three rough
"black" glass "coins."
Gift of Otto W. Hilbert
Comments: The demand for
metal was so great during World
War II that the government considered replacing pennies and
nickels with non-metal coins.
Replacement coins had to be
near the same size and weight in
order to use them in vending
machines. These coins were
submitted by Corning Glass
Works to the government for
consideration, but glass was not
adopted for coinage.

1367   Glass bullet
Corning, New York, Corning
Glass Works
ca. 1942
L. 9 cm

70.4.176 A,B

Glass bullet in metal casing.
Gift of Otto W. Hilbert
Comments: Bullets were developed by Corning Glass Works
during World War II for possible
use in practice shooting. They
were never produced commercially and were not used.

*1368   Two smaller bullets
As above
L. 3.4 cm

70.4 177B, C

Gift of Otto W. Hilbert

**1369   Cartridge with glass
buckshot**
Corning, New York, Corning
Glass Works
ca. 1942-1943
L. 6.7 cm

70.4.175 A,B

Gift of Otto W. Hilbert
Comments: These cartridges are
for clay pigeon shooting. The
glass pellets were considered instead of lead because of the
scarcity of metal. They were not
used because the glass shot
would not break the clay pi-
geons.

1370 Flatiron
Corning, New York, Corning
Glass Works
ca. 1933-1935
L. 21 cm

65.4.3

Colorless Pyrex® heat-resistant
glass with blue insert.
Gift of Otto W. Hilbert
Comments: This piece is a pro-
totype developed by Corning
Glass Works because of metal
shortages but never manufactured commercially.

1371 Glass buttons
Corning, New York, Corning
Glass Works
ca. 1942-1945
D. 1.4 cm

67.4.90

White glass, two-hole, 24 corset
buttons, 16 shirt buttons.
Gift of Otto W. Hilbert
Comments: Experimental ware
produced because of wartime
shortage of mother-of-pearl from
the West Coast.

1372 Ashtray
Corning, New York, Corning
Glass Works
ca. 1928
H. 5.4 cm; D. (top) 6.6 cm

70.4.37

Ruby glass in the form of a
miniature Fresnel lens.
Gift of Otto W. Hilbert
Comments: A souvenir item given
to Corning Glass Works employ-
ees attending the first annual
service dinner in 1928 held in
the Masonic Temple, Corning.
This size of ashtray was never
manufactured commercially.

1373 Thimble
Corning, New York, Corning
Glass Works
ca. 1945
H. 2.3 cm; D. 2 cm

69.4.176

Comments: This is an experimental item made because of
war shortages of metal but never
marketed.

1374 **Cup plate**
United States
ca. 1920's
D. 8.8 cm

61.4.34

Colorless glass.
Parallels: Lee and Rose, p. 414,
pl. 128.

1375 **Cup plate**
United States
ca. 1930's
D. 8.8 cm

61.4.35

Colorless glass.
Parallels: Lee and Rose, p. 416,
pl. 129; reproduction of no. 698.

1376 **Cup plate**
United States
ca. 1930's
D. 8.8 cm

61.4.36

Colorless glass.
Parallels: Lee and Rose, p. 415,
pl. 129; reproduction of no. 643.

1377 **Cup plate**
United States
ca. 1930's
D. 8.8 cm

61.4.37

Colorless glass.
Parallels: Lee and Rose, p. 408,
pl. 127; reproduction of no. 564.

1378 Cup plate
United States
ca. 1930
D. 9.2 cm

63.4.50

*1379 Cup plate
United States
ca. 1930
D. 8.6 cm

63.4.52

Colorless glass.
Gift of Helen R. Wormser
Parallels: Lee and Rose, p. 415;
reproduction of nos. 643 and
644.

Colorless glass.
Parallels: Lee and Rose, p. 416;
reproduction of no. 697.

1380 Pair of candlesticks
United States
ca. 1930
H. 23.4 cm; D. (base) 9.8 cm

60.4.781 A, B

Cobalt blue glass; pressed in one
piece with mold seam running
through "wafer" in center of
shaft.
Gift of Louise S. Esterly

1381 Picture hook
Probably United States
ca. 1920-1935
L. 5.8 cm; D. (rim) 6.8 cm

60.4.819

*1382 Another

60.4.820

Light blue glass and steel;
flower form with imbedded
screw shank.
Gift of Louise S. Esterly

Yellow.
Gift of Louise S. Esterly

1383 **Pair of plates**
Probably Europe
ca. 1930-1950
H. 1.8 cm; D. 21.8 cm

70.3.2 A,B

Pressed of colorless glass with
purple staining in center; beehive pattern.
Gift of Mrs. Alfred B. O'Neil
Comments: See nos. 100-102 in
this catalog.

1384 **Pair of curtain tiebacks**
United States or possibly
Europe
ca. 1910-1930
D. 11.1 cm

51.4.739 A,B

*1385 **Another**
D. 8.5 cm

68.4.644

Blue glass; six-petaled rosette
with pewter shank.
Comments: see nos. 1058-1062.

Light amethyst.
Gift of Louise S. Esterly

1386 **Goblet**
United States
ca. 1920-1940
H. 16.5 cm; D. (rim) 8.1 cm

63.4.43

Colorless glass in the Pioneer or
Westward Ho pattern.
Gift of Abraham & May
Comments: See nos. 1102-1103 in
this catalog for 19th-century
pieces in this pattern.

1387 Toothpick holder
United States, Elwood, Indiana,
St. Clair Glass Works
1965
H. 6.1 cm; D. 2.7 cm

65.4.5

*1388 Another

65.4.6

Pressed of caramel and opalescent glass in the Holly pattern.
See nos. 1267, 1268 for early pieces in this pattern.
Gift of Wes Barker (from Joseph St. Clair)

Caramel.
Gift of Wes Barker (from Joseph St. Clair)

1389 Sugar bowl
England, probably made to the order of Mrs. Graydon-Stannus
ca. 1920-1930
H. 14.3 cm; D. (rim) 11.7 cm

60.2.35

1390 Creamer
As above

60.2.36

Nearly colorless lead glass with a slight grayish cast; blown and pattern-molded with applied chain decoration; knopped stem and hand-pressed square base with rosette underneath.
Comments: Bowl early 18th century in style but pressed foot of late 18th- or early 19th-century type.
Parallels: Anon. *Old Irish Glass*, London, 1925 (illustrates many related forgeries).

1391   Flower pot
Bellaire, Ohio, Imperial Glass
Company
1970
(Pot) H. 9.4 cm; D. (at rim) 12.3
cm; (Saucer) H. 2.8 cm;
D. 13 cm

70.4.154

Pressed of opaque light blue
glass in a truncated conical
shape.
Comments: Reproduction of a design attributed to the Boston &
Sandwich Glass Company,
Sandwich, Massachusetts, ca.
1830. The only known existing
example of this flower pot is in
the collection of The Metropolitan Museum of Art; this reproduction was made to their order.

**1392   Covered sugar and covered
creamer**
United States, Grapeville,
Pennsylvania, Westmoreland
Glass Company
ca. 1963
(Sugar) H. 12.6 cm; L. 15 cm;
(Creamer) H. 12 cm;
L. 13.5 cm

63.4.31 A,B

Pressed of opaque white "milk"
glass in an oval shape with a de-
sign of cattails around sides; im-
pressed on base with a mark of a
"W" superimposed on a "G."
Both pieces have a paper label
bearing the words "AUTHEN-
TIC/MILK GLASS/WESTMORE-
LAND/HAND/MADE/GLASS."
Gift of Westmoreland Glass
Company
Parallels: Belknap, p. 280.

1393   Pair of candlesticks
United States, Grapeville,
Pennsylvania, Westmoreland
Glass Company
ca. 1963
H. 23.5 cm; D. (base) 9.5 cm

63.4.32 A,B

Pressed of opaque white glass.
W impressed on base and paper
sticker as above on each stick.
Gift of Westmoreland Glass
Company
Comments: See nos. 874-878 for
19th-century dolphin candle-
sticks.

1394 **Dolphin candlestick**
United States
ca. 1930
H. 26.5 cm; D. (base) 9.5 cm

61.4.40

Pressed of opaque white glass.
Ex coll: George S. McKearin
Comments: See nos. 874-878 for
19th-century dolphin candlesticks.

1395 **Duck covered dish**
Grapeville, Pennsylvania,
Westmoreland Glass Company
ca. 1963
H. 12.5 cm; L. 20 cm

63.4.34

Opaque white glass; head of
duck has glued-in amber eyes;
both pieces marked **W** for
Westmoreland Glass.
Gift of Westmoreland Glass
Company

1396 **Swan covered dish**
Grapeville, Pennsylvania,
Westmoreland Glass Company
ca. 1963
H. 14 cm; L. 24.7 cm

63.4.33

Pressed of opaque white glass;
marked on base **W**.
Gift of Westmoreland Glass
Company

1397 **Plate**
Grapeville, Pennsylvania,
Westmoreland Glass Company
ca. 1963
D. 22 cm; H. 2.5 cm

63.4.41

Pressed of black glass;
enameled in opaque white.
Gift of Westmoreland Glass
Company

1398 Oval bowl
Grapeville, Pennsylvania,
Westmoreland Glass Company
ca. 1950
L. 42.25 cm; H. 14 cm

51.4.556

Opaque white glass.
Gift of Westmoreland Glass
Company

1399 Oval bowl
Grapeville, Pennsylvania,
Westmoreland Glass Company
1963
H. 11 cm; L. 26.5 cm

63.4.35

Pressed of opaque white glass.
Comments: This is a reproduction
of No. 1257 in this catalog.
Gift of Westmoreland Glass
Company

1400 Plate
Grapeville, Pennsylvania,
Westmoreland Glass Company
ca. 1950
H. 2.2 cm; D. 33.5 cm

51.4.555

Colorless glass.
Comments: This is an adaption of
early 19th-century lacy pressed
glass designs, rather than an
exact reproduction.
Gift of Westmoreland Glass
Company

Pressed Glass outside the United States

Mechanical pressing must have begun in England by the early 1830's, probably in the Stourbridge area, if the following quotation is accurate: "The manufacture of pressed glass by means of metallic moulds, in imitation of cut glass—an American invention was this year [1834] introduced into England by Messrs. Richardson of Strowbridge [sic]"[1] We know that Apsley Pellatt was applying for a patent on a method of assembling the molds for a press in 1831 (see Introduction), so he actually may have started earlier. Val Saint-Lambert in Belgium and Baccarat in France probably were the earliest continental firms to press glass, and Val Saint-Lambert, at least, showed pressed glass in a catalog by 1829. The firm of Johann Meyr in Adolf, Bohemia, displayed pressed glass at an exhibition in Prague in 1836 in response to the flood of American and French pressed glass in its markets.[2]

The earliest English pieces seem to be a group marked "W," "WR" or "D" in the 1830's, perhaps in the Stourbridge area (Nos. 1401-1405, 1408): Several of these pieces commemorate Victoria's coronation and her marriage, which helps to date them. One of the marked English designs is nearly identical to a design found on marked Baccarat pieces, so it is clear that designs were copied in Europe as well as in the United States; at this point it is impossible to know who copied whom. Since metalworking was a British specialty at this period, some molds may have been made in Sheffield or Birmingham for Continental factories.

By 1842, the English had begun a system of registering design patents and stamping registry marks which included dates on many pressed glass pieces. Therefore, after 1842, it is somewhat easier to date English pressed glass. Few lacy-style pieces have survived, but some stippling was used into the 1880's. Judging from the scarcity of early stippled wares, English pressing did not really get underway until the 1840's and 1850's when heavy paneled and fluted patterns imitating cut glass were popular. At this time English cut glass was considered to be the best in the world, and pressed glass remained imitative of it until the 1880's and 1890's when pressed designs included marbled and opalescent glasses as well as novelty items fairly similar to the wares being produced in America at the same time.

Continental manufacturers, in contrast, provided a much greater variety of lacy or stippled ware. This seems to have been popular from the 1830's until the 1850's. Much of the French stippled glassware may have been blown into a mold using the newly invented Robinet steam-powered piston rather than pressed with a plunger. Close examination of some pieces of holloware indicates that they were mold-blown rather than pressed, as the design can be felt on the inside, something that is not possible in glass pressed with a plunger. Several of these mold-blown pieces have been included in this catalog. Their designs are so similar to pressed ones that a collector might be confused. Flat pieces such as plates were doubtless pressed; it may be that the utilization of this power-blowing process explains why the French were able to make "lacy" tumblers and goblets before the Americans did.

Trade catalogs are the best source of information on European designs. The catalogs of Paris glass seller Launay, Hautin et Cie, printed in the 1840's (two different copies are in The Corning Museum of Glass Library), are helpful in the study of French pressed glass. Launay, Hautin et Cie was a retailer for glass made by the Baccarat, Saint-Louis, Choisy, and Bercy factories. One 1829 catalog of the Val Saint-Lambert glass company was discussed in *Antiques* in 1939,[3] and photocopies of two more, dated 1832 and 1843, are also in The Corning Museum of Glass Library. One Bohemian catalog from the 1840's which shows a few pieces of pressed glass is in the library of the Victoria and Albert Museum in London, and a few Scandinavian catalogs, showing pressed glass production of the 1850's and after, are available in Scandinavian museums. It was then that Scandinavian countries began producing lacy glass, much of it clearly copied from earlier French and American designs. Since Northern Europen factories were later in manufacturing pressed glass, it may be that they had purchased outdated American and French molds. In any case, they apparently imported their molds, whether new or used, probably from England, the United States, or France.

Even Japan was not averse to entering the pressed glass market. The Corning Museum of Glass Library has one catalog from a Japanese firm, Shimada Glass Factory, which illustrates a few pieces of lacy pressed glass. This catalog is undated but seems to be about 1890-1910, and since it was printed in English, the ware must have been intended for export.

Considerably more research needs to be done in this field before pressed glass other than American can be identified with confidence. The pieces shown here are but the tip of a very large iceberg.

1. Bishop, J. Leander. *A History of American Manufactures from 1608 to 1860*. Philadelphia: Edward Young & Co., 1864, Vol II, pp. 389-390.
2. Pazaurek, Gustav E. *Gläser der Empire und Biedermeierzeit*. Leipzig: Klinkhardt & Biermann, 1923, pp. 36-37.
3. Pike, Mildred "A Question in Cup Plates." *Antiques* 35, no. 1, January 1939, pp. 16-18.

†1401 **Plate**
England
ca. 1829-1836
H. 2.3 cm; D. 19.7 cm

76.2.13

Colorless lead glass; "WR" in rim.
Gift of Kenneth Moyer
Comments: "WR" may be the mark of the mold-maker, possibly William Reading of Birmingham. The rim decoration on this piece is very similar to that on a number of pieces made by Cristalleries de Baccarat in France in the 1840's, but several pieces marked "WR" are known with different designs, all of which seem to be English.
Parallels: Launay, Hautin, 1840, pl. 17; *Launay, Hautin, 1842,* No. 1941; *Morris,* p. 191, Fig. 123.

1402 **Cup plate**
England
ca. 1830-1840
D. 10.6 cm

65.2.22

Colorless lead glass.
Gift of Mrs. Leon S. Bard
Comments: This plate is identical, except for size, to the marked plate above, but the center design appears in the Launay, Hautin catalog.
Parallels: Lee and Rose, p. 399, no. 859; *Launay, Hautin, 1842,* No. 1941 (St. Louis).

1403 **Toddy plate**
England
ca. 1837-1840
H. 1.8 cm; D. 12.9 cm

63.2.11

Colorless lead glass; crown and "VR" in the center.
Gift of Louise S. Esterly
Comments: This plate is nearly identical to one illustrated by Ruth Webb Lee and marked "WR" in the rim. It is similar to one in the 1840 catalog of Launay, Hautin et Cie., attributed to Cristalleries de Baccarat.
Parallels: Launay, Hautin, 1840, pl. 17; *Lee, Sandwich Glass,* pl. 86.

1404 Toddy plate
England, possibly Thomas
Webb
ca. 1840
H. 1.8 cm; D. 13 cm

60.2.73

Medium blue glass with profiles
of Victoria and Albert in the center and inscription in script capi-
tals, "VICTORIA & ALBERT,"
around busts.
Gift of Louise S. Esterly
Comments: Two private collectors
have plates which may be from
the same mold but have a "W"
just below Victoria's bust, where
this plate has a scar. This might
be the mark of a mold-maker.
Presumably, this plate commemorates the royal marriage in
1840.
Parallels: Lee and Rose toddy
plate no. 825 is similar.

1405 Cup plate
England
ca. 1837-1840
D. 9.8 cm

60.2.72

Colorless lead glass with Queen
Victoria in the center below
"VICTORIA" and a crown in the
rim.
Gift of Louise S. Esterly
Comments: A private collector
has an identical plate with "W"
in the rim, probably the mark of
the mold-maker. See preceding
plate.
Parallels: Lee and Rose, p. 316,
no. 572.

1406 Sauce dish
England
ca. 1842
H. 1.6 cm; D. 11.3 cm

61.2.12

Bright blue glass with the three
ostrich plumes of the Prince of
Wales in the center.
Gift of Louise S. Esterly
Comments: Probably pressed in
1842 to commemorate the birth
of the Prince of Wales to Queen
Victoria and Prince Albert.
Parallels: Lee and Rose, no. 828.

1407 **Toddy plate**
Probably English
ca. 1842-1850
D. 12.1 cm

60.2.76

Colorless lead glass.
Gift of Louise S. Esterly
Comments: The plate was probably made to commemorate the
birth of the Prince of Wales in
1842.
Parallels: Lee and Rose, p. 389,
no. 828.

1408 **Toddy plate**
Probably English
ca. 1837-1850
D. 11.6 cm

60.2.75

Colorless lead glass.
Gift of Louise S. Esterly
Comments: The significance of
the "D" on the rim of this plate
is unknown, but it probably indicates the moldmaker.
Parallels: Lee and Rose, p. 388,
no. 818.

1409 **Cup plate**
Probably English, possibly
Scandinavian
ca. 1850-1870
D. 9.3 cm

65.2.16

Colorless lead glass.
Gift of Mrs. Leon S. Bard
Comments: This design was also
made in Sweden by both Kosta
and Eda Glasbruks.
Parallels: Lee and Rose, p. 400,
no. 882.

1410 **Toddy plate**
England, probably George
Davidson & Co., Gateshead-
on-Tyne
ca. 1870-1890
D. 11.4 cm

58.2.10

Greenish bubbly non-lead glass.
Gift of J. E. Pfeiffer
Comments: This design was also
made in Denmark and in
Bohemia.
Parallels: Lee and Rose, p. 388,
no. 820.

1411 Toddy plate
England, probably George
Davidson & Co., Gateshead-
on-Tyne
ca. 1870-1890
D. (rim) 14.2 cm

61.2.13

Colorless non-lead glass.
Comments: This design was also
made in Denmark and in
Bohemia.
Parallels: Lee and rose, p. 388,
no. 820

1412 Shallow bowl
England
ca. 1830-1850
D. 10.3 cm

65.2.15

Colorless glass.
Gift of Mrs. Leon S. Bard
Parallels: Lee and Rose, p. 400,
no. 876.

1413 Goblet
England
ca. 1850-1860
H. 13.7 cm; D. (rim) 9 cm

80.2.32

Colorless lead glass, pressed in a
pattern of rows of circles; plain
stem and foot; polished pontil
mark.
Comments: This is similar in design to American pieces of the
same period but much heavier
and of a slightly different shape.
Parallels: Lattimore, p. 33.

1414 **Covered sugar bowl**
England
ca. 1840-1860
H. 19 cm; D. 12.4 cm

66.2.3

Light yellowish-green vaseline glass.
Gift of Mrs. Allan Cornwell
Parallels: Wakefield, pls. 88A, 88B.

1415 **Plate**
England, or possibly United States
ca. 1870
H. 1.7 cm; D. 14.7 cm

60.2.77

Colorless non-lead glass; peacock with spread tail filling entire plate.
Gift of Louise S. Esterly
Comments: Dr. Green (see bibliography) says fragments of this design were found at Sandwich, and the few known examples have turned up in New England. However, the plate is extremely rare and uncharacteristic of any designs in American glass, and very late in design and type of glass.
Parallels: Green, Charles W. "Little Known Sandwich," *Antiques*, 38, no. 2, Aug. 1940, p. 70, Fig. 6.

1416 **Footed bowl**
Probably England, possibly United States
ca. 1850
H. 9.5 cm; D. 14.2 cm

59.2.25

Dark blue glass; egg and dart molding on rim.
Gift of Louise S. Esterly
Comments: This piece is comparatively rare and appears only in this color and green. Authorities have differed as to its origin.
Parallels: Rose, no. 336.

1417 **Bust of a man**
England
ca. 1850
H. 15.9 cm; W. 10.3 cm

63.2.4

Colorless glass pressed in the form of a man with 17th century wig and dress.
Comments: There seems to be some doubt as to whom this figure is meant to represent. It has been published as both John Milton and John Wesley.
Parallels: Catalog, Sotheby & Co., London, June 3, 1974, no. 73, lists this piece as Milton.

1418 **Cup**
England, Sunderland, Henry Greener, Wear Flint Glass Works
ca. 1869
H. 6.5 cm; D. (rim) 6.5 cm

72.2.13

Colorless non-lead glass; stippled background with inscription "GEORGE PEABODY" between two rows of stars; handle pressed as part of body; concentric circles and illegible registry mark on base.
Gift of Mr. and Mrs. Harry A. Snyder
Comments: Commemorates the American philanthropist, George Peabody. Design registered Dec. 7, 1869.
Parallels: Lee and Rose, pl. 117, no. 836; *Wakefield*, pls. 92, 93A; *Morris*, pl. 131.

1419 **Plate**
England, Sunderland, Wear Flint Glass Works of Henry Greener
ca. 1869
D. 12.6 cm

80.2.9

Colorless plate with "GLAD-STONE" around rim and "FOR THE/MILLION" in center around a thistle, shamrock and rose.
Comments: Design registered July 31, 1869, commemorating Gladstone's appointment as Prime Minister.
Parallels: Lattimore, p. 77, pl. 46.

1420 Bust of Sir Robert Peel
England, Birmingham, F. & C.
Osler
ca. 1845-1851
H. 17.4 cm; W. 9.6. cm

79.2.15

Colorless glass; head and shoulders in classical drape on eight-sided cut plinth; marked on back of shoulder "F. & C. OSLER/44 Oxford St., LONDON"; ground and polished pontil mark on base.
Parallels: Morris, p. 45, Fig. 48.

1421 Salt
England, Sunderland, Wear
Flint Glass Works of Angus and
Greener
ca. 1868-1880
H. 3.2 cm; L. 8.1 cm; W. 6.4 cm

78.2.12

Colorless lead glass, pressed; rectangular shape with a "Drape" pattern on all four sides. Registry mark on bottom for "April 1, 1868."
Ex coll: Mr. and Mrs. George Lookup

1422 Vase
England, Gateshead-on-Tyne,
Sowerby's Ellison Glass Co.,
Ltd.
ca. 1877-1890
H. 15 cm

71.2.1

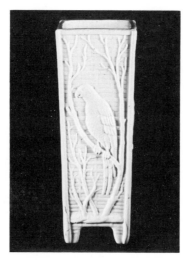

Opaque white (vitro porcelain) glass with a bird in a tree on each side. English registry mark dated 1877 on interior as well as crowned bird trademark.
Comments: This design was registered by Sowerby's Ellison Glass Co., Ltd. and the trademark is that of the Gateshead-on-Tyne factory.
Parallels: Wakefield, pl. 94A.

1423 Loving cup
England
ca. 1860-1900
H. 26 cm; W. 22.1 cm

74.2.19

Colorless lead glass; pressed in a cylindrical shape, applied handles; engraved with the inscription "A PRESENT/FROM/ GLOSSOP" between scrolls; two fern leaves on opposite sides.
Comments: Glossop is a town between Manchester and Sheffield in England.

1424 "Penny Lick" or "Joey"
England
ca. 1870-1900
H. 9.2 cm; D (rim) 5.1 cm

79.2.23

Colorless glass; trumpet shaped bowl which is solid glass except for a shallow depression in top; circular foot.
Comments: Supposed to have been used by street vendors to serve ices before the invention of ice cream cones.

1425 Pair of bowls
Probably Manchester, England
ca. 1865-1875
H. 2.7 cm; D. (rim) 10.5 cm

78.2.16 A,B

Colorless glass; outer surface roughened by grinding; multi-pointed star on base.
Gift of Mrs. Grace Milnor
Comments: The contrast between clear colorless glass and an acid-roughened or ground opaque surface was popular with glassmakers in Manchester in the 1860's and 1870's.
Parallels: Morris, p. 195.

†1426 **Cream jug**
England, probably Gateshead,
either Sowerby's Ellison Glass
Co., Ltd. or George Davidson &
Co.
ca. 1880-1890
H. 8.7 cm; D. 6.3 cm

80.2.30

Turquoise and white marbled
glass; with a fern pattern around
sides; rustic handle and three
feet.

†1427 **Cream jug**
Northern England, probably
Gateshead, either Sowerby's El-
lison Glass Co., Ltd. or George
Davidson & Co.
ca. 1880-1890
H. 12.7 cm; D. 7.3 cm

80.2.29

Blue and white marbled glass
with a pattern of torches and
chains around sides; scalloped
foot.

†1428 **Small vase**
England, probably Gateshead,
Sowerby's Ellison Glass Co.,
Ltd. or George Davidson & Co.
ca. 1880-1890
H. 7.6 cm; D. (rim) 6.6 cm

80.2.31

Blue and white marbled glass.
Cylindrical with three handles
around sides and row of dots
near top and bottom; scrolled
base.

1429 **Flower holder**
England, Newcastle, Sowerby's
Ellison Glass Co., Ltd.
ca. 1878
H. 8.3 cm; L. 12.8 cm;
W. 4.1 cm

80.2.12

Opaque black glass pressed in a
rectangular shape with pattern
on sides showing Old King Cole
and his three fiddlers in high
relief; peacock head on base.
Parallels: Lattimore, pp. 52-54.

1430 **Flower holder**
England, Gateshead, Sowerby's
Ellison Glass Co., Ltd.
ca. 1886-1890
L. 36.8 cm; W. 9.2 cm;
H. 6.6 cm

79.2.17

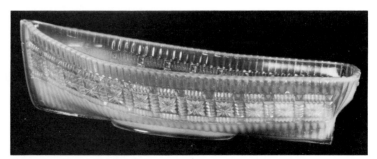

Yellowish-green opalescent
glass; pressed in the shape of a
boat with one pointed and one
square end; marked "Rd 42927"
on inside.

Comments: This design was registered in 1886. It has a stand
which is missing.
Parallels: Lattimore, Fig. 20.

1431 Salt
England, Gateshead-on-Tyne,
Sowerby's Ellison Glass Co.,
Ltd.
ca. 1887
H. 4.6 cm; W. 6.9 cm

79.2.25

Colorless non-lead glass; hexagonal with vertically ribbed sides, marked on inside base "Rd 87777"; peacock's head trademark on interior and exterior base.
Gift of Colin Lattimore
Comments: This design was registered in 1887.
Parallels: Lattimore, Fig. 3.

1432 Pair of candlesticks
England
ca. 1880-1890
H. 26.6 cm; W. (base) 11.5 cm

73.2.27 A,B

Colorless lead glass; square base with cherubs' heads on two faces and classical urns on the other two; foot rim ground.
Comments: These candlesticks are similar to some made by Sowerby's Ellison Glass Co., Ltd. at Gateshead and also John Derbyshire & Company, Manchester.

1433 Wall vase or match safe
England, Gateshead-on-Tyne,
Sowerby's Ellison Glass Co.,
Ltd.
ca. 1877-1890
H. 19.1 cm; D. (at top) 7.1 cm

74.2.18

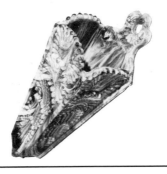

Gray, green, and white marbled slag glass with a hole for hanging at top of back; crowned peacock trademark on one side of base; British registry mark for February 1877 on other.
Ex coll: Mrs. Ogden Ray Smith
Comments: The trademark is that of Sowerby's Ellison Glassworks.

1434 Plate
England
ca. 1888-1890
H. 4.5 cm; D. 23.7 cm

73.2.5

Pressed of colorless non-lead glass; "PEACE AND PLENTY" and "RdNo115743" near rim.
Gift of Mrs. Irving C. Doe
Comments: This design was registered in 1888.
Parallels: Wakefield, pls. 92, 93A.

1435 **Compote**
England
ca. 1888-1895
H. 18.1 cm; D. (rim) 23.4 cm

79.2.24

Colorless non-lead glass; diamond-filled panels alternating with pairs of ribs around bowl; ribbed stem; circular base. "Rd 96945" on exterior of one rib.
Comments: This design was registered in 1888.

1436 **Salt**
England, Gateshead-on-Tyne, George Davidson & Co.
ca. 1880-1890
H. 4.9 cm; D. 10.5 cm

79.2.22

Colorless glass; circular with vertically ribbed sides; lion trademark on base.
Gift of Colin Lattimore
Parallels: Lattimore, Fig. 3.

1437 **Plate**
England, probably Gateshead-on-Tyne, George Davidson & Co.
ca. 1887
D. 24 cm

66.2.22

Colorless, non-lead glass; laurel wreath and crown with "1837" above and "1888" below in center of plate; "THE QUEEN'S/ JUBILEE" around rim.
Comments: One of a number of souvenir pieces in honor of Queen Victoria's Golden Jubilee.
Parallels: Morris, p. 205, Fig. 131.

1438 **Plate**
England
ca. 1900
H. 2.8 cm; D. 25.6 cm

65.2.11

Colorless non-lead glass; inscription, "ROBERTS PRETORIA/ ENTERED JUNE 5 1900."
Parallels: Wakefield, pls. 92, 93A.

1439 Bowl
England, Staines, Middlesex,
United Glass Bottle Manufac-
turers Ltd.
ca. 1936-1940
D. 21.1 cm, H. 12.1 cm

73.2.4

Amber glass; hexagonal form
with an acid-etched design of a
hummingbird in flight on three
sides and hummingbird sitting
on a branch on the other three
sides; near base "Rd NO
810280."
Gift of Mrs. Berenice Kent
Comments: This number was registered on Feb. 26, 1936.
Parallels: C.C. Manley, "English Glass: My Latest Finds,"
The Antiques Journal, 36, No. 6,
June 1981, pp. 15, 17.

1440 Base for "Fairy" lamp
England, made for Samuel
Clarke of London
ca. 1886-1892
H. 3.8 cm; D. 7.4 cm

79.2.21

Colorless non-lead glass; circular
with overall pattern of diamonds
around sides; marked inside
"CLARKE/FAIRY PYRAMID."
Gift of Colin Lattimore
Comments: "Fairy" lamps were
patented candle holders with a
variety of different types of
shades.
Parallels: Lattimore, pp. 125-126.

1441 Buttons
England
ca. 1880-1900
D. (A) 2.6 cm, (B) 1.8 cm, (C)
2.1 cm, (D & E) 1.7 cm

79.2.20 A-E

Opaque black glass; circular
disks; (A) arches around rim; (B)
shell design; (C) star design,
iridescent surface; (D & E)
stylized anchor design.
Gift of Colin Lattimore

1442 Tumbler
England
ca. 1910-1920
H. 11.5 cm; D. 7.6 cm

79.2.19

Orange glass; trumpet-shaped
bowl with cobweb design on exterior.
Gift of Mrs. Barbara Richards
Comments: Some "Carnival"
glass was also made in England.

1443 Plate
England
1902
D. 25.3 cm

64.2.12

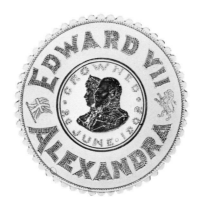

Colorless glass; with portraits of
Edward VII and Queen
Alexandra and inscription
"CROWNED 26 JUNE 1902."

1444 Bowl
England
1937
D. 14.4 cm

73.2.7

Colorless glass with a crown in
the center and a scalloped rim;
inscription "GOD SAVE THE
KING/CORONATION OF KING
GEORGE VI, MAY 12, 1937."
Gift of Mrs. Robert Brearey

1445 Bowl
England
1937
D. 14.6 cm

73.2.8

Colorless glass; circular shape
with a crown in the center and a
scalloped rim; inscribed,
"CORONATION/GEORGE THE
SIXTH/ELIZABETH/1937."
Gift of Mrs. Robert Brearey

1446 Plate
France, probably Cristalleries de
Baccarat
ca. 1835-1845
H. 2.5 cm; D. 11.4 cm

60.3.91

Colorless heavy glass with
upcurving walls and sawtooth
pattern rim.
Parallels: Launay, Hautin 1842,
pl. 14, no. 1106 (Baccarat) is in
the same pattern.

1447 Plate
France, probably Cristalleries de
Baccarat
ca. 1835-1845
D. 22.7 cm; H. 2.1 cm

63.3.114

Colorless glass; sulphide, head
of a man in classical dress in center.
Comments: This plate, without
the sulphide, appears in the
catalog listed below.
Parallels: Launay, Hautin 1842,
pl. no. 1962 (Baccarat).

1448 Desk set
France, probably Cristalleries de
Baccarat
ca. 1835-1845
H. 6.4 cm; L. 20.8 cm

61.3.225

Brilliant green glass with brass
fittings; tray and compartment
pressed in one section with separate lid; three interior wells for
ink, sand, etc.
Gift of Louise S. Esterly.
Comments: Very rare in this country; one in green is in the Metropolitan Museum and one in
blue is in the Duckworth Collection in The Toledo Museum
of Art but is missing its lid. This
design is shown in the French
catalog listed below.
Parallels: Green, Charles. "Little Known Sandwich," *Antiques*,
38, no. 2, August, 1940, Fig. 3,
p. 69; *Launay, Hautin 1840*, Part
II, pl. 37, no. 1583 (Baccarat).

1449 Covered box
France, Cristalleries de Baccarat
ca. 1840
H. 12.3 cm; L. 14.4 cm;
W. 9 cm

79.3.7

Colorless lead glass, ormolu mounts; a pattern of raised diamonds within arches around sides and four paw feet.
Parallels: Launay, Hautin, 1840, Part II, pl. 37. no. 1583.

1450 Vase
France, probably Cristalleries de Baccarat
ca. 1835-1850
H. 24.5 cm; D. (rim) 16 cm

58.3.219

Colorless lead glass with urn-shaped top; top rim cut.
Gift of Louise S. Esterly
Comments: Vases of this type are shown in the French catalog listed below; the base is related to several American pieces.
Parallels: Launay, Hautin, 1840, Part II, pl. 27, no. 1406B.

1451 Pair of toilet bottles
France, probably Cristalleries de Baccarat
ca. 1840-1850
H. (with stopper) 16.8 cm;
D. (body) 9 cm

50.3.17 A, B

Amber glass; mold-blown in a hexagonal design; an arch on each of the six sides and gilded floral decoration around the arches; ground and polished pontil mark on base; tall pressed hexagonal lily stopper.
Comments: Although this type of toilet bottle is usually attributed to Bohemia, this shape is nearly identical to one in the Launay, Hautin catalog, see below.
Parallels: Launay, Hautin, 1842, Part II, pl. 78, no. 2399B.

1452 Pair of toilet bottles
France, probably Cristalleries de
Baccarat
ca. 1840-1850
H. (with stopper) 16.2 cm;
D. (body) 10 cm

54.3.52 A,B

Transparent amber glass mold-
blown in a hexagonal shape;
horizontal ovals on each of the
six sides; ground and polished
pontil mark on base; conical
pressed stopper with mush-
room-like finial enclosing a tear.
Bequest of Ellen D. Sharpe
Comments: This type of perfume
bottle is usually attributed to
Bohemia, but it occurs in the
Launay, Hautin catalog cited
below.
Parallels: Launay, Hautin 1842,
pl. 79, no. 2460.

1453 Footed tumbler
France, probably Cristalleries de
Baccarat
ca. 1840-1850
H. 11.7 cm; D. (at rim) 8.7 cm

54.3.107

Transparent amber glass.
Bequest of Ellen D. Sharpe
Comments: This type is usually
attributed to Bohemia, but it
appears in the Launay, Hautin
catalog listed below.
Parallels: Launay, Hautin, 1842,
pl. 79, no. 2431B.

1454 Compote
France, Cristalleries de Baccarat
ca. 1916
H. 15.5 cm; D. (top) 20.2 cm

66.3.33

Colorless glass with pink stain
covering parts of the top;
marked inside center base
"BACCARAT DEPOSE."
Parallels: Revi, Albert C.
*Nineteenth Century Glass, Its
Genesis and Development,* rev. ed.,
New York: Thomas Nelson and
Sons, 1967, p. 25.

1455 Plate
France, Cristalleries de Baccarat
ca. 1900-1920
H. 1.9 cm; D. 13.9 cm

66.3.34

Bright blue glass; marked inside center "BACCARAT
DEPOSE"; ground and polished
base rim.

1456 Bowl
France, Cristalleries de Baccarat
ca. 1900-1920
H. 4.6 cm; L. 17.3 cm

66.3.35

Dark reddish glass; marked
"BACCARAT" in base; ground
and polished base rim.

1457 Dish
France, Cristalleries de Baccarat
ca. 1900-1920
H. 4.9 cm; D.(top) 8.5 cm

66.3.36

Medium green glass; marked in
center of bowl "BACCARAT."

1458 Compote
France, Cristalleries de Baccarat
ca. 1900-1920
H. 4.5 cm; D. (at rim) 14.7 cm

70.3.17

Yellowish-green glass; marked in
center of bowl "BACCARAT DE-
POSE."
Gift of Henry Faul

†1459   **Footed tumbler**
France, Vosges, Verrerie de
Portieux
Probably ca. 1840-1850
H. 11.3 cm; D. (at rim) 8.4 cm

54.3.142

Translucent white glass; gilt de-
coration on the sides, rim, and
rim of foot; impressed on base
"PORTIEUX."
Ex coll: Jerome Strauss
Comments: The glass factory in
Portieux was founded in 1757
and merged with that of
Vallerysthal in 1872.

1460   **Breakfast set**
France, probably Lorraine,
Verrerie de Vallerysthal
ca. 1850-1870
D. (tray) 27 cm; H.(cups) 5.1
cm; H.(container) 6.8 cm

61.3.199

Pressed of opaque grayish white
glass with traces of gilding
around rims; circular plate with
six depressions, each holding a
separate footed egg cup with a
leaf design on the outside; center depression holds a divided
container possibly for condi-
ments or seasonings.
Gift of Mrs. Minni L. Schuelein
Parallels: Belknap, pl. 205.

†1461   **Covered bowl**
France, Lorraine, Verrerie de
Vallerysthal
ca. 1870
H.(with cover) 14.0 cm; D.(rim)
12.8 cm

55.3.56

Translucent white glass; bowl
resting on three dolphin feet
with a rosette at center bottom
and a frieze of shells around the
sides of bowl and around cover;
shell finial on cover.
Gift of Mrs. David B. Ouellet
Comments: This area was an-
nexed by Germany in 1870. The
design appears in a Vallerysthal
catalog in the collections of the
Henry Ford Museum under
"Butterdosen."

†*1462   **Another**
H. 16.5 cm

68.3.26

Colorless.

†1463 **Goblet**
France, probably Vosges,
Verrerie de Portieux
ca. 1840-1860
H. 9.1 cm; D. (at rim) 7 cm

74.3.127

Transparent amber glass.
Bequest of Mrs. Jason Westerfield
Comments This goblet is similar
to those listed below which are
marked "PORTIEUX."

†1464 **Large and small goblets**
France, Vosges, Verrerie de
Portieux
ca. 1840-1860
(A) H. 12.9 cm; D. max. (rim)
9.0 cm; (B) H. 7.8 cm; D. max.
(rim) 5.6 cm

77.3.46 A,B

Colorless non-lead glass;
enameled in green, black, and
purple with grapes, grape leaves,
and vines. (B) is marked on
underside of base, "PORTIEUX."
Comments: The owner originally
had a set of sixteen of these,
eight in each size; only the
smaller ones were marked. See
preceding goblet which is a
nearly identical shape.

1465 **Inkstand**
France, probably Cristalleries de
Saint-Louis
ca. 1835-1845
H. 7.4 cm; L. 15.2 cm

52.3.22

Opaque brick-red glass; ground
and polished top surface having
two holes; chain design below
rim and elaborate scrolled feet
with shells and leaves; inkwell
and sand shaker are separate,
both with ground and polished
tops.
Comments: A similar inkwell and
a plate with the identical chain
design appear in the 1842 catalog
of Launay, Hautin & Cie., see
below, both made by Saint-
Louis; See also nos. 1475, 1477.
Parallels: Launay, Hautin, 1842,
no. 1963 and no. 1221.

1466 Covered bowl
France, Cristalleries de Saint-
Louis
ca. 1900
H. (with cover) 13 cm;
D. (rim) 11.5 cm

55.3.2

Colorless glass; pattern of leaves
and blossoms which are silver-
stained amber; marked inside
base "SAINT LOUIS."
Ex coll: Jerome Strauss

1467 Mug
France, Cristalleries de Saint-
Louis
ca. 1830-1850
H. 9.1 cm; D. (with handle)
10.5 cm

73.3.33

Colorless glass; scroll designs
stained amber.
Anonymous gift
Parallels: Launay, Hautin, 1842,
p. 12, no. 1046.

†1468 Plate
France, probably Cristalleries de
Saint-Louis
ca. 1835-1855
D. 19.5 cm; H. 2.1 cm

73.3.450

Colorless glass; underside of the
base is cased with blue glass and
then cut in a checked pattern.
Comments: The rim of this plate
is very similar to that of plate no.
1401 in the English section of
this catalog.

1469 **Plate**
Probably France, perhaps
Cristalleries de Saint-Louis
ca. 1835-1850
D. 20.2 cm; H. 3.4 cm

60.3.98

Colorless glass, diamond-filled
sunburst in center.
Gift of Louise S. Esterly
Comments: The Museum has
five more pieces in this pattern
and variations, and there has
been a great deal of discussion
about whether the pieces are
American or French. Fragments
of this pattern are said to have
been found at Sandwich in the
excavations mentioned in the Introduction. However, the pattern definitely appears on Plate
17 of the Launay, Hautin
catalog, attributed to Saint-
Louis. It may, of course, have
been made in both places.
Parallels: Lee, Sandwich Glass,
pl. 130; *McKearin, American
Glass,* pl. 136, no. 5; *Rose,* nos.
157, 197; *Launay, Hautin, 1840,*
pl. 17, no. 1218.

1470 **Another**
D. 12.8 cm

60.3.93

Pale green.

*1471 **Another**
D. 16 cm

60.3.99

Colorless.

*1472 **Another**
D. 18.6 cm

51.3.337

Ex coll: George S. McKearin

1473 **Another**
D. 10.5 cm

51.3.338

Ex coll: George S. McKearin

*1474 **Compote**
In the same pattern
H. 11.5 cm; D. 18.2 cm

68.3.77

Ex coll: Louise S. Esterly

†1475 **Footed tumbler**
France, Cristalleries de Saint-
Louis
ca. 1830-1850
H. 10.3 cm; D. 9.7 cm

75.3.9

Pressed of opaque brick-red
glass.
Gift of Lillian Nassau, Ltd.
Comments: See nos. 1465 and
1477 for pieces in similar glass.
Parallels: Launay, Hautin, 1842,
pl. 7, no. 2283.

1476 **Bottle**
Belgium, Liège, Val Saint-
Lambert
ca. 1830-1845
H. (with stopper) 10.8 cm;
D. (rim) 4.1 cm

53.3.12

Dark blue glass; probably
mold-blown; concentric circles
on top; cut star on polished
base; mushroom-shaped
stopper.
*Parallels: Val Saint-Lambert,
1832,* pl. 17, no. 471.

†1477 **Plate**
France or Belgium
ca. 1830-1845
H. 2.8 cm; D. 18.1 cm

60.3.32

Opaque brick-red glass, slightly
marbleized.
Ex coll: George S. McKearin
Comments: This plate appears in
both of the catalogs listed below,
and is meant as a saucer for a
large tea cup.
Parallels: Launay, Hautin, 1840,
pl. 31, no. 1676 (Saint- Louis);
Val Saint-Lambert, 1832, pl. 14,
no. 406.

1478 Plate
Belgium, Liège, Val Saint-
Lambert
ca. 1830-1850
H. 2.2 cm; D. 17.7 cm

60.3.95

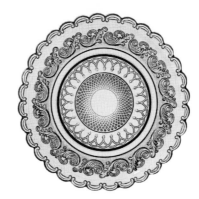

Colorless non-lead glass.
Comments: This plate appears in
the catalog listed below.
*Parallels: Val Saint-Lambert,
1832,* pl. 16, no. 437.

1479 Compote
France or Belgium
ca. 1830-1850
H. 17.9 cm; D. (rim) 24.5 cm

70.3.28

Colorless lead glass; square
base, waffled underneath.
Comments: This compote appears in both of the catalogs
listed below.
Parallels: Launay, Hautin, 1840,
Part II, pl. 30, no. 1604 (Baccarat); *Val Saint-Lambert, 1832,*
pl. 17, no. 483.

1480 Wineglass
France or Belgium
ca. 1830-1850
H. 9.6 cm; D. (rim) 4.8 cm

71.3.142

Colorless glass; polished pontil
mark and waffle pattern on
underside of foot.
Comments: This piece appears in
both of the catalogs listed below.
Parallels: Launay, Hautin, 1840,
no. 1085 (Saint-Louis); *Val
Saint-Lambert, 1832,* pl. 15, no.
427.

1481 Cup plate
Probably Val Saint-Lambert,
Belgium
ca. 1830-1850
D. 9.4 cm

57.3.175

Colorless glass.
Gift of James H. Rose
Parallels: Lee and Rose, p. 394,
no. 852.

1482 Cup plate
Probably Val Saint-Lambert,
Belgium
ca. 1830-1850
D. 11.4 cm

65.3.66

Colorless glass.
Gift of Mrs. Leon S. Bard
Parallels: Lee and Rose, p. 394,
no. 855.

1483 Cup plate
Probably Val Saint-Lambert,
Belgium
ca. 1830-1850
D. 10.2 cm

65.3.62

Colorless glass.
Gift of Mrs. Leon S. Bard
Parallels: Lee and Rose, p. 394,
no. 856.

1484 Cup plate
Probably France or Belgium
ca. 1830-1850
D. 9.6 cm

57.3.176

Colorless glass.
Gift of James H. Rose
Parallels: Lee and Rose, p. 399,
no. 865.

1485 **Cup plate**
France or Belgium
ca. 1830-1850
D. 10.3 cm

57.3.174

Colorless glass.
Gift of James H. Rose
Parallels: Lee and Rose, p. 399,
no. 866.

1486 **Cup plate**
Probably Val Saint-Lambert,
Belgium
ca. 1830-1850
D. 10.2 cm

65.3.64

Colorless glass.
Gift of Mrs. Leon S. Bard
Parallels: Lee and Rose, p. 394,
no. 851; *McKearin, American
Glass*, pl. 137-4.

1487 **Cup plate**
France, Belgium, or possibly
England
ca. 1830-1850
D. 9.8 cm

57.3.178

Colorless glass.
Gift of James H. Rose
Comments: This possibly may be
English as its center pattern ap-
pears in a piece marked "WR"
in a private collection.
Parallels: Lee and Rose, pp. 394 ff.

1488 **Cup plate**
France or Belgium
ca. 1830-1850
D. 10.2 cm

57.3.177

Colorless glass.
Gift of James H. Rose
Parallels: Lee and Rose, pp. 394 ff.

1489   **Plate**
Belgium, Val Saint-Lambert
ca. 1900
D. 18.3 cm

80.3.19

Colorless, with star in center and
C-scrolls around edge.
Gift of Peter Kaellgren
Comments: See plates, below.

1490   **Bowl**
Belgium, Val Saint-Lambert
ca. 1900
D. 9.6 cm

80.3.20

Colorless with star in center and
C-scrolls on rim.
Gift of Peter Kaellgren
Comments: See above.

1491   **Cup plate**
Belgium, Val Saint-Lambert
ca. 1900
D. 10.2 cm

80.3.21

Colorless glass.
Gift of Peter Kaellgren
Comments: See above.

1492   **Cup plate**
France or Belgium
ca. 1830-1850
D. 10.2 cm

65.3.65

Colorless glass.
Gift of Mrs. Leon S. Bard
Parallels: Lee and Rose, p. 400,
no. 880; *McKearin, American
Glass*, pl. 137-5.

1493   **Medallion**
        Europe, probably France
        ca. 1830-1840
        H. 1.8 cm; D. 8.5 cm

        71.3.128

Pressed of colorless lead glass in
a waffled pattern with sulphide
head of a man (probably Napoleon) in center.
*Parallels: McKearin, American
Glass,* pl. 135.

1494   **Salt dish**
        France, probably Baccarat or
        Saint-Louis
        ca. 1835-1850
        H. 5.7 cm; D. 7.1 cm

        59.3.85

*1495   **Another**

        63.3.113

Colorless glass; top rim and bottom of feet ground and
polished.
Gift of Louise S. Esterly
Parallels: Launay, Hautin, 1840,
pl. 16, no. 1182; *Neal,* HN 18a,
p. 115.

Opalescent.
Gift of Louise S. Esterly

1496   **Salt dish**
        France or Belgium
        ca. 1830-1850
        H. 3.8 cm; D. 7.4 cm

        78.3.34

Colorless glass; hexagonal waf-
fled base.
Ex coll: Mr. and Mrs. George
Lookup
Comments: Not previously listed
in colorless glass.
Parallels: Neal, HN11, p. 105.

1497   **Salt dish**
        Probably France
        ca. 1835-1850
        H. 4 cm; D. 8.4 cm

        60.3.94

Grayish glass; diamond and
swirl design underneath ground
and polished base.
Parallels: Neal, RD34, p. 345.

1498 Salt dish
Europe or possibly United
States
ca. 1840-1860
H. 5.5 cm; L. 10.5 cm

61.3.339

Colorless glass; ovoid shape with
flaring ends and scrolls on sides.
Gift of Louise S. Esterly
Parallels: Lee, Sandwich Glass,
pl. 74, lower left; *Neal*, OP20,
p. 270.

1499 Salt dish
Europe, or possibly United
States
ca. 1840-1860
H. 4.5 cm; L. 8.5 cm

68.3.80

Colorless lead glass; rectangular;
design resembling a stag's head
on sides and ends.
Gift of Mr. and Mrs. Harry A.
Snyder.
Comments: A variation of *Neal*,
SN3, p. 434.
Parallels: Launay, Hautin, 1840,
pl. 16, no. 1184.

1500 Salt dish
France
ca. 1835-1850
H. 4.3 cm; L. 8 cm

68.3.74

Amber glass with a star on each
end, a shell on each side, and a
checkered base with a flower in
each square.
Ex colls: Louise S. Esterly; Edward McGowan
Parallels: Launay, Hautin, 1840,
pl. 16, no. 1177; *Neal*, SL15,
p. 421.

1501 Salt dish
Probably France or Belgium
ca. 1840-1850

68.3.76

Colorless lead glass.
Ex coll: Louise S. Esterly
Parallels: Neal, RP31, p. 381.

1502 Salt dish
Probably France or Belgium
ca. 1840-1850
H. 7 cm; D. 8.1 cm

68.3.75

Colorless lead glass.
Ex coll: Louise S. Esterly
Parallels: Neal, RP32, p. 382;
Launay, Hautin, 1840, pl. 17, no.
1210 (Baccarat and Saint-Louis);
Val Saint-Lambert, 1832, pl. 12,
no. 350.

1503 Candlestick
Probably France
ca. 1850
H. 8.2 cm; D. (base) 5.2 cm

55.3.52

Opaque turquoise blue glass.
Comments: See no. 617 for a related piece.

1504 Pair of goblets
France, probably Baccarat or
Saint-Louis
ca. 1840-1850
H. 14.1 cm; D. (rim) 8.2 cm

58.3.193 A,B

Pressed of opaque black glass
and cinnamon red glass in iden-
tical patterns; waffle pattern
underneath foot.
Ex coll: Jerome Strauss
Comments: According to
Pazaurek, these goblets appear
in a catalog of Launay, Hautin &
Cie. but they do not appear in
either of the two Launay
catalogs in the collection of The
Corning Museum of Glass.
Parallels: Pazaurek, Gustav. E.
*Gläser der Empire und Bieder-
meierzeit.* Leipzig: Klinkhardt &
Biermann, 1923, Fig. 317, p.364.

1505   Egg cup
Probably Europe
ca. 1830-1850
H. 8.2 cm; D. (rim) 7 cm

58.3.220

Pressed of colorless glass.
Gift of Louise S. Esterly
Comments: While this has been
published as American glass, it
seems much more similar to
European glass in design.
Parallels: Lee, Sandwich Glass,
pl. 141, lower; *Rose*, no. 171.

1506   Tumbler
France or Belgium
ca. 1830-1850
H. 9.8 cm; D. (rim) 8.1 cm

59.3.51

Colorless heavy glass.

†1507   Tumbler
France or Belgium
ca. 1830-1850
H. 6.2 cm; D. (rim) 4.9 cm

60.3.33

Transparent dark blue glass.
Ex coll: George S. McKearin

1508 Plate
France or Belgium
ca. 1830-1850
H. 3.6 cm; D.(rim) 20.2 cm

60.3.90

Colorless heavy glass.
Gift of Louise S. Esterly
Parallels: Lee, Sandwich Glass,
pl. 88, lower.

1509 Plate
France, Belgium or possibly
England
ca. 1830-1850
H. 2.4 cm; D.(rim) 12.0 cm

60.3.92

Colorless glass.
Gift of Louise S. Esterly
Parallels: Lee, Sandwich Glass,
pl. 88, lower, is related.

1510 Plate
France or Belgium
ca. 1830-1850
H. 1.5 cm; D. 10.6 cm

60.3.97

Colorless glass.
Gift of Louise S. Esterly

1511 Bowl
France or Belgium
ca. 1830-1850
H. 2.5 cm; D. 13 cm

60.3.100

Colorless glass.
Gift of Louise S. Esterly
Comments: This has been published as American but is very
similar to Continental pieces.
Parallels: Lee, Sandwich Glass,
pl. 86, center right; *Rose,* no. 151.

† **1512   Covered bowl**
France or Belgium
ca. 1830-1850
H. 19 cm; L. 25.4 cm

63.3.23

Colorless glass.
Comments: Although this must
be a French or Belgian piece,
nothing at all like it was found in
the catalogs of Launay, Hautin
or Val Saint-Lambert.

1513   Candlestick
Probably France or Belgium;
possibly Bohemia
ca. 1830-1850
H. 18.5 cm

66.3.83

Colorless glass with a mold-
blown urn-shaped socket;
mold-blown swirled stem;
pressed round foot with a waffle
pattern underneath.
Gift of Mrs. Henry Bickelhaupt

1514   Miniature bowl
Probably France or Belgium
ca. 1830-1850
H. 2.5 cm; D.(rim) 2.6 cm

67.3.70

* **1515   Another**
H. 3.5 cm

69.3.104

Colorless glass; ground and
polished base.
Gift of Mr. and Mrs. Harry A.
Snyder
Comments: "Jouets" or toys appear in both the Launay, Hautin
and Val Saint-Lambert catalogs.

Gift of Mr. and Mrs. Harry A.
Snyder

1516 Vase
France or Belgium
ca. 1830-1850
H. 11.9 cm; W. 11.7 cm

78.3.26

Colorless glass, pressed or
mold-blown in an oval shape;
oval base waffled underneath.
Comments: These vases are also
found with a plain base.

1517 Miniature tumbler
France or Belgium
ca. 1830-1850
H. 3.3 cm; D.(rim) 2.8 cm

68.3.78

Colorless glass with a plain rim
and a scroll design on a stippled
background around most of
body.
Gift of Mr. and Mrs. Harry A.
Snyder
Comments: See above.

1518 Miniature tumbler
Probably France or Belgium
ca. 1830-1850
H. 3.5 cm; D. (rim) 2.7 cm

68.3.79

Colorless glass; a design of
Gothic arches around the sides.
Gift of Mr. and Mrs. Harry A.
Snyder

1519 **Goblet**
France or Belgium
ca. 1830-1850
H. 14.9 cm; D. (top) 9 cm

70.3.26

Colorless glass; waffle pattern underneath base.

1520 **Lamp**
Probably France or Belgium
ca. 1890-1920
H. 27.5 cm; D. (base) 11.8 cm

72.3.183

Colorless non-lead glass with a pewter screw-in double whale oil burner attached to a spherical blown font with a band of cut facets around midpoint; wide flaring collar below font, attached by a wafer to hollow pressed or mold-blown stem. Marked "FRANCE" beneath base.
Gift of Preston R. Bassett
Comments: Candlesticks similar to this lamp appear in both the Val Saint-Lambert and Launay, Hautin catalogs. However, due to the base marking, this lamp was probably made after 1891.

1521 **Tumbler**
Probably France or Belgium
ca. 1830-1850
H. 5.9 cm; D. 5 cm

74.3.128

Colorless glass.
Bequest of Mrs. Jason Westerfield

1522 Tumbler
France
ca. 1852-1870
H. 8.75 cm; D. (rim) 6.75 cm

50.3.104

Colorless non-lead glass; circular medallion with bust profile of Napoleon III and, on reverse, scroll with "VIVE L'EMPEREUR"; rayed design on base.

1523 Plate
France or possibly Bohemia
ca. 1840-1860
D. 14.8 cm

80.3.29

Colorless glass with stippled background and floral design.

1524 Plate
France or possibly Bohemia
1840-1860
D. 13.3 cm

80.3.30

Colorless glass with portions amber-stained; stippled background with geometric design.

1525 Salt
France, or possibly Bohemia
ca. 1840-1860
H. 5.7 cm; D. 7.0 cm

80.3.51

Colorless glass; pressed in a pattern of dots and arches.
Bequest of Donald F. Clark
Comments: These salts are found mold-blown in the same pattern.
Parallels: McKearin, American Glass, pl. 99.

1526   Covered Compote
Probably Bohemia, possibly
France
ca. 1840-1850
H. 23.8 cm; D. 14.3 cm

72.3.186

Colorless non-lead glass; blown
bowl and cover, both with cut
diamond design; applied to a
pressed stem and foot, ending in
a circle of rosettes.
Gift of Preston R. Bassett
Comments: For lamps with related bases, see the Lighting
Devices section.
Parallels: Jarmila Brožová, *České
Sklo 1800-1860*, Uměleckop-
růmyslové Muzeum, Prague,
1978, no. 18D.

1527   Plate
Bohemia
ca. 1880-1890
D. 13.5 cm

80.3.28

Blue glass with inscription
"SVATY JAN NEPOMUCKY"
around portrait of patron saint of
Prague.

1528   Wineglass
Continent
ca. 1890-1900
H. 10.2 cm; D. (rim) 5.5 cm

61.3.158

Colorless non-lead glass with
vertical flutes around bowl and
stem.
Gift of J. H. Schuelein-Steel

1529   Goblet
Europe, probably Bohemia
ca. 1850-1870
H. 16.2 cm; D. (at rim) 9.0 cm

56.3.70

Colorless glass; diamond pattern with amber stain on the diamonds.

†**1530   Plate**
Probably Germany, possibly
Wear Flint Glass Works, Sunderland England
ca. 1890-1900
H. 2.5 cm; L. 25.6 cm

57.3.49

Transparent bright blue glass; inscription around rim sides says "LEIDE KEINE NOTH, DOCH VERSCHWENDE NICHT" (Do not suffer, do not waste either). Gift of Rudolf Vollgraf
Comments: The Wear Flint Glass Works made a nearly identical plate in amber with the inscription WASTE NOT, WANT NOT. This may be an export item rather than a German product.

1531   Cordial glass
Finland, Karhula Glass Works
ca. 1870
H. 9.8 cm; D.(rim) 4.1 cm

72.3.51

Colorless glass with nine vertical panels around bowl; plain stem, round foot, marked "KARHULA" on base.
Gift of Jacob Seela

1532 Cordial glass
Finland
ca. 1825-1865
H. 6.9 cm; D.(at rim) 3.7 cm

73.3.432

Colorless glass; eight vertical
panels around bowl; rough pontil mark; round foot.
Gift of Jacob Seela

1533 Box
Probably Russian
Late 19th century
H. 10.2 cm; L. 10.8 cm

65.3.91

Pressed of light blue opaque
glass with white metal fittings;
cover hinged to box; waffle pattern around sides; Russian imperial eagle and inscription in
Cyrillic on base. "Vassily Perlov
Co., firm in existence since
1787."

† **1534 Bread plate**
Russia
ca. 1850
H. 4.3 cm; L. 35.3 cm

77.3.32

Pressed of colorless glass in a
rectangular shape with the Russian inscription in Cyrillic
around sides: "I welcome you
with bread and salt." and checkered pattern in center.
Gift of Mrs. Rafi Mottahedeh

†1535 **Tumbler**
Portugal, Real Fabrica de Por-
celana Vidro y Processes
Chimicas (Fabrica Vista Alegré)
or possibly France
Probably ca. 1837-1840
H. 10 cm; D.(rim) 7.5 cm

66.3.9

Pressed of colorless glass in a
cylindrical shape; diamond pattern around sides and sulphide
portrait head of Dona Maria the
Second, Queen of Portugal
(1834-1853).
Parallels: Pinto, Augusto Car-
doso. "Portuguese Glass
Cameos," *Connoisseur*, 138, no
551, March 1956, pp. 32-34,
Fig.3.

1536 **Goblet**
Japan
ca. 1900-1925
H. 10.8 cm; D.(rim) 7.5 cm

73.6.3

Pressed of greenish opalescent
glass with a vertically ribbed
pattern around the bowl.
Ex coll: Dorothy Blair

Index

F3